Turkey at the Crossroads

Ottoman Legacies and
A Greater Middle East

DIETRICH JUNG

WITH

WOLFANGO PICCOLI

D0003704

Zed Books
LONDON & NEW YORK

Turkey at the Crossroads was first published in 2001 by
Zed Books Ltd, 7 Cynthia Street, London N1 9JF, UK and
Room 400, 175 Fifth Avenue, New York, NY 10010, USA

Distributed in the USA exclusively by Palgrave, a division of
St Martin's Press, LLC, 175 Fifth Avenue, New York, NY 10010, USA.

Copyright © Dietrich Jung and Wolfango Piccoli, 2001

Cover designed by Andrew Corbett
Set in 10/12 pt Joanna
by Long House, Cumbria, UK
Printed and bound in Malaysia

A catalogue record for this book
is available from the British Library

US CIP has been applied for

ISBN   Hb 1 85649 866 2
        Pb 1 85649 867 0

Contents

Acknowledgements   vii

1   Introduction: The Turkish Puzzle   1

**PART I THE CONTINUITIES OF OTTOMAN–TURKISH
MODERNISATION**   9

2   Modernisation as a Theoretical Concept   11
Turkey and modernity   11
Social reproduction, power and domination   12
Traditional and modern societies as ideal types   17
Monopolisation and feudalisation   20
Social actors, hegemonic blocs and the social habitus   23

3   Reform and Decline: Modernisation in the Ottoman Empire   28
Incentives and character of the early Ottoman reforms   28
The historical and structural conditions behind the reform process   31
Destruction of the traditional order and feudalisation of the state   35
The Tanzimat and the 'Eastern question'   38
Hamidian absolutism and the end of the Ottomans   47
Conclusions: demise and survival of the Ottoman Empire   54

4   National Resurrection: The Early Turkish Republic   59
The Republican state and its cultural revolution   59
Security predicaments behind the foundation of the Turkish Republic   62
The man and his principles   72
Conclusions: revolution and continuity   78

5   Western Integration: The Multi-Party Period   83
'The Return of the Janissaries': Turkish military in politics   83
The guardians in action: socio-political developments and military intervention   86
The army, multi-party politics and the Turkish elite: modern diversification,
*   patronage and traditional elitism*   94
Conclusions: Ottoman–Turkish continuities and the Greater Middle East   103

v

PART II   TURKEY IN THE GREATER MIDDLE EAST   109

6   **Kemalism Challenged: Susurluk, Political Islam
    and Kurdish Nationalism**   111
    Economic liberalisation and counter-insurgency: Susurluk and its socio-historical
       background   111
    Domestic problems in the prism of Sèvres: social conflicts and Kemalist perceptions   115
    Political Islam: the rise of the Welfare Party and the postmodern coup   118
    Kurdish nationalism: identity construction and militarised conflict   122
    Conclusions: Kemalist political engineering at its limits   127

7   **Encircled by Enemies? Turkey's Foreign Policy and its
    Middle Eastern Neighbours**   132
    Islamist initiatives and Kemalist constraints   132
    Four phases of Turkish foreign policy: from neutrality to activism   134
    Principles and realities: Turkey's foreign policy towards its Arab neighbours and Iran 143
    Conclusions: Turkish politics of securitisation   148

8   **The Uneasy Alignment: Turkey and Israel**   153
    Political activism and Ottoman–Jewish legacies   153
    Historical legacies: the Ottoman and early Kemalist experiences   155
    Hesitation and ambivalence: Turkish–Israeli relations in the Cold War era   157
    The new Turkish–Israeli axis   161
    Factors and goals behind the Turkish–Israeli axis   166
    Conclusions: 'pragmatic escapism'   171

9   **The Revival of Pan-Turkism: Turkish Policies in Central
    Asia and the Transcaucasus**   175
    Enver Pasha's return   175
    Islamic modernism, pan-Turkism and Turkish nationalism: historical ideas and
       their political legacies   176
    Euphoria and disappointments: a Turkish century?   179
    Building co-operation: economic and cultural ties between the Turkish Republic and
       the Turkic states   184
    Cultural avenues: language, history, television and education   188
    Conclusions: facing Ottoman and Kemalist legacies in the Transcaucasus and
       Central Asia   192

10 **Conclusions: The Impasse of Kemalist Modernisation** 198
    State monopolies, social habiti and Ottoman–Turkish continuities   199
    New opportunities and new constraints: Turkish politics after the Cold War   205

Bibliography   211
Index   225

Acknowledgements

The idea for this book developed while I was teaching as visiting assistant professor at the International Relations Department of Bilkent University in Ankara (1997–98). During this time, I had the opportunity to observe Turkish politics directly and to discuss the problems of the country with many of my colleagues and students at Bilkent. Coupled with this was the experience of living as a welcome foreigner and enjoying the experience of Turkey's outstanding hospitality. Puzzled by the contradictions of Turkish society, I began to immerse myself in the fascinating history of the country, finding traces of Ottoman–Turkish continuities and wondering how the current problems of the country might be linked to this submerged legacy.

Yet ideas rarely develop into books on their own, and the help of a number of people was needed to write a study such as this. First of all, I would like to thank my co-author, Wolfango Piccoli, for his indispensable contributions. He not only provided the two draft chapters on the Turkish–Israeli alignment and on Turkey's relations to the Turkic republics in Central Asia and Transcaucasus, he also read the whole manuscript carefully, and we frequently discussed the book's arguments. In addition, he has been keeping me up to date on important events in Turkey. Equally important, though different in kind, was the help of Professor Ahmet Evin and Michael Wech. It was they who brought me to Bilkent University, thus laying the foundation of my interest in Turkish affairs.

While writing the book, I was grateful to have the support of Catherine Schwerin, who saved me by her careful English language editing from the linguistic imponderabilities the non-native speaker has to face. I was also lucky to have the opportunity to discuss various parts of the manuscript with colleagues and friends. For their suggestions and encouragement I would particularly like to thank Professor Gülshan Dietl, Dr David Jacobsen, Lasse Dahlberg, Tor Nonnegaard-Pedersen, Marianne Holm Pedersen and Jesper Sigurdson. Finally, the completion of any book depends on the supportive co-operation of the publisher. In this regard, I am indebted to Robert Molteno and Zed Books, who supported this project from the beginning.

1 Introduction
The Turkish Puzzle

Turkey is often noted for its uniqueness, either in its geographic dimension as the gateway from Europe to Asia, or in the way the country combines 'being Western oriented though Turkish and Muslim at the same time' (Eralp 1996: 93). Turkey's political identity and its future role in world politics have been widely discussed both inside and outside the country. Despite a widespread opinion that Turkey needs to redefine its strategic role in the post-Cold War era, strong differences occur in the judgements made about the political institutions and the future direction of the country.

Some authors consider Turkey to be a 'successful democracy' (Göle 1997: 47)* and a country that has developed a robust multi-party system and a lively civil society with a free press (White 1997:30). According to these positive judgements, Turkey is a real regional power, which will play a central role not only in the Middle East, but also in world politics (Fuller and Lesser 1993: 163). Other commentators evaluate Turkey's achievements less favourably and conclude that 'the Turkish political system is far from being democratic' (Türsan 1996: 216), and that 'the military is able to intervene at will in politics' (Candar 1999: 140). In the view of this more pessimistic camp, Turkey represents not a rising power but rather an 'unwelcome outsider on the margins of both Europe and the Middle East' (Robins 1991: 16).

Indeed, Turkey offers the analyst a broad and intricate fabric of cultural, social and historical threads, which can provide justification for either

---

* As this book is not addressed primarily to experts on Turkey, we have decided against using full Turkish orthography in the transliteration of names and terms. With the exception of the use of two umlauts (ö and ü) which are familiar to a wide spread of language communities, we have replaced accented Turkish characters with their closest English equivalents.

1

assessment of its republican history. On the one hand, Turkey has a whole set of democratic institutions, it is a member of the Council of Europe and of the North Atlantic Treaty Organisation (NATO), and since 1996 has been in a customs union with the European Union (EU). On the other hand, the Turks have had to go through a painful and disappointing process to acquire the desired candidacy status for full membership of the EU. Eventually granted consideration at the Helsinki summit in 1999, Turkey's candidacy looks none too promising owing to major economic obstacles and undeniable deficiencies in its democratic institutions and its human rights record. From a 'political and economic model for its neighbours' (cf. Mango 1993), through a 'bridge between Europe and the Middle East', to an 'awkward and uneasy actor in both European and Middle Eastern politics' (Robins 1991: 115), Turkey has been labelled with a vast spectrum of both positive and negative judgements. This contradictory picture of Turkish foreign and domestic politics can hardly be accidental, but what is the substance behind Turkey's ambiguous image? What is the origin of this Turkish puzzle?

This book is intended to explain Turkey's puzzling image by basing its analysis on two distinct frames of reference. In geopolitical terms, the study puts Turkey into the new geopolitical framework of an emerging 'Greater Middle East'. With the demise of the Soviet Union and the subsequent independence of Transcaucasian and Central Asian states, the Middle East entered into a new evolutionary stage. The Greater Middle East can be defined by variables such as a common history, ethnic links, Islamic civilisation, European-dominated state-formation and overlapping regional conflicts, as well as regional economic competition (cf. Dietl 1999). Partly by accident and partly by design, Turkey has found an eminent role in this emerging geopolitical space. The end of the Cold War changed Turkey's comfortable geo-strategic position and seemed to diminish the country's strategic and military appeal for the West. In an emerging Greater Middle East, Turkey is confronted with new threats and new opportunities. The formation of a Turkish–Israeli axis, the revival of Pan-Turkism, the Turkish military operations in northern Iraq and the threat of using military force against Syria in October 1998 are clear examples that Turkey has already become a more active player in the new political environment of the Greater Middle East.

While grappling with these international and regional developments of the post-Cold War era, Turkey has simultaneously been affected by severe domestic problems. The Kurdish insurgency in south-east Anatolia, the political confrontation between secularist and Islamist forces, the embroilment of its political elite in corruption scandals, the accusation of widespread nepotism, the high budget deficit and years of galloping inflation are just a few instances that, during the 1990s, marred the 'success story' of Turkey's republican history. Both domestic conflicts and international change demand a reorientation of Turkish policies. More than 75 years after the foundation of the Turkish Republic, the 'Kemalist project' has been challenged from within and from without, bringing the country to a crossroads of decisions about its future direction in a changing world.[1] Where is this future direction to be sought?

In answering this question, the geopolitical framework of the Greater Middle East will be overlaid by some theoretical devices grounded in social theory that allow us to analyse the political and social structures of modern-day Turkey. A sound understanding of Turkey's current situation demands an integration of the external and the internal dimensions of the puzzle. Therefore, our analysis of the Turkish puzzle will be related to the particular modernisation process the country has undergone. In order to shed light on Turkey's social structures, some concepts of historical sociology will serve us as the second frame of reference for this book. The coming chapters examine Turkey's domestic conflicts and questions of Turkish foreign policy in the light of Turkey's modernisation from above, which started with the Ottoman reforms in the early nineteenth century. It will be argued that an adequate understanding of modern-day Turkey has to take into account the *'longue durée'* (Braudel) that characterises processes of social change. With regard to this temporal aspect of modernisation, this book claims that Turkey cannot adequately face its challenges as long as its Kemalist state elite denies the striking continuities that connect the Ottoman and the Kemalist phases of Turkish state formation. The modernisation of Turkish society has reached a point where the country must reflect on the impact that the authoritarian legacy of Ottoman habits and statehood has had on the Turkish Republic.

In emphasising the country's past heritage, the book's argument is related to the ongoing debate in Turkey itself. The writings of Kurdish nationalists, Islamists, members of the Alevi community and so-called neo-Ottomanists are attempting to counter the official Kemalist history of Turkey from their own perspectives.[2] Contrary to these often extremely biased or rather romantic approaches to Ottoman–Turkish history, our survey intends to stress the problematic consequences of the Ottoman legacy. In particular, we attempt to show that many of the structural constraints that hamper a real democratisation of Turkish society are linked to the Ottoman past and to the historical and social context in which the Turkish Republic was established. This continuity thesis will be presented in the first part of the book. Then, taking these Ottoman-Turkish continuities as historical and analytical background, the second part discusses both Turkey's current domestic problems and new challenges to Turkish foreign policy. Thereby it becomes apparent that internal and external areas of conflict are interrelated and closely tied to the strains which result from the unique combination of Turkey's Western orientation and its Middle Eastern location.

The first chapter of Part One focuses on political aspects of modernity, and briefly presents the sociological concepts relevant for this study. These concepts are derived from the works of authors such as Pierre Bourdieu, Norbert Elias, Anthony Giddens and Max Weber, and they provide us with the basic theoretical framework necessary to explain Turkish state formation. Modernisation is presented as a heuristic concept to analyse the particular trajectories modern state formation has taken in historically different societies. It is the purpose of this theoretical chapter to lay down the conceptual framework of the authors and to acquaint the reader with both the general theoretical assumptions and the more precise technical terms that are later an explicit or implicit part of the historical analysis. Regarding the application of these theoretical tools, we should stress that they are most explicit in our analysis of Ottoman history and then gradually become more implicit the further the book proceeds.

In order to discern the nature of Ottoman–Turkish continuities, the first part of the book presents the Ottoman reforms, the foundation of the Turkish Republic and Turkey's post-Second World War experiences in chronological order. Beginning with the early Ottoman reform attempts of Sultan Selim III (1789–1807), these chapters concentrate on the development of social structures, state institutions and political ideas, combining descriptive with explicative parts. Throughout, we frequently shift in our observations between two perspectives. On the one hand, Turkish state formation will be presented from the external perspective of an emerging international system that has heavily constrained the outcomes of Ottoman and Turkish modernisation. The explanation of the dismantling of the Ottoman Empire and the resurrection of a Turkish polity as a nation-state, as well as the political, economic and institutional westernisation of Turkey, are inseparably linked to the unfolding of different stages of international relations. Thus, Turkey's polity will be seen to have been shaped within the co-ordinates of different world orders, that is, within the subsequent international structures of imperialism, bipolarity and post-Cold War US hegemony.

It would, on the other hand, be one-sided to portray Turkish state formation only from this external point of view. It is true that, spurred on by the increasingly disadvantageous position of the Ottoman Empire in the European power game, the Ottoman reforms were aiming at safeguarding the territorial integrity and political sovereignty of the Ottoman State in an international environment of competitive nation-states. Yet, irrespective of the fact that the reforms failed to reach this primary goal, they triggered a major process of internal social change that provided the social, institutional and intellectual ground for the evolution of a Turkish national movement. Furthermore, most aspects of the reforms undertaken by Mustafa Kemal Atatürk and his associates were already visible during the period of Ottoman reforms. With regard to this internal modernisation of Ottoman and Turkish society, in the course of the last 150 years a clear continuity in social, political and ideological terms can be discerned. These continuities contradict the myth of the Kemalist revolution and therefore the official reading of Turkish history. The purpose of the first part of the book is to disclose these inherent contradictions and to discern specific characteristics of Turkish modernisation, particularly concerning the political structures of the Turkish Republic and the habits and worldview of its Kemalist state elite.

In the second part of the book we shift the focus to Turkey's most significant domestic and regional problems of the 1990s. These four chapters will address the rise of Kurdish nationalism and political Islam, as well as the challenges and opportunities concerning Turkey's regional foreign policies that result from geopolitical changes after the Cold War. While these chapters are in a topical order, the general historical perspective will be maintained. In dealing with the various aspects of Turkey's domestic crisis, the first of these chapters argues that phenomena such as Kurdish nationalism, the politicisation of Islam and the growing frustration of the public with Turkey's political institutions, although giving rise recently to conflict, are nevertheless deeply rooted in the history of the Turkish Republic. Moreover, each of them is inseparably related to distinct patterns of Kemalist modernisation and has been aggravated by Turkey's armed forces' subsequent attempts to reconstruct Turkish society according to an idealistic Kemalist model.

As with issues of internal stability, it is the particular Kemalist worldview that conditions and limits the ability of Turkey's state elite to find adequate answers to the new foreign policy questions that have arisen since the collapse of the Soviet Union. After a brief tour d'histoire through four phases of republican foreign policy, two major dimensions of Turkey's political role in the Greater Middle East will be examined. First, we discuss the evolution of the new Turkish–Israeli axis, which at first glance seems to signal an end to Turkey's traditionally rather cautious and hands-off Middle Eastern policies. In scrutinising the historical context in which this bold alignment has evolved, the chapter comes to the surprising conclusion that the Turkish–Israeli agreements have a Western rather than a Middle Eastern 'target'.

Furthermore, this foreign policy initiative ran parallel to the severe domestic crisis previously analysed and therefore had strong internal implications, partly serving to confirm the determination of Turkey's establishment to continue on the paths of secularism and Western orientation.

In the last chapter of Part Two, Turkey's relations with the newly independent Turkic states in Central Asia and the Transcaucasus are discussed. Turkey's initiatives in these regions were pointing at the pan-Turkist background of Kemalist nation-building, which lay dormant during the Cold War era because of the ever-present risk of confrontation with the Soviet Union. Yet the initial euphoric reaction in Turkey to the political independence of the 'outside Turks' was quickly replaced by a more pragmatic and cautious strategy of establishing Turkish influence in Central Asia and Transcaucasus. In this regard, relations with the former Soviet republics are an interesting example of the Turkish Republic's options and limitations in the new geopolitical environment of a Greater Middle East.

Against the background of our two general frames of reference, the Turkish modernisation process and the emergence of a Greater Middle East, the concluding chapter will sum up our arguments and float some speculative ideas concerning Turkey's future political role. It is important to stress that these ideas are based, along with the rest of this book, on a specific interpretation of Turkish history. Organised around our thesis of Ottoman–Turkish continuities, this book does not claim to be an 'objective history' of Turkey, nor is it just another historical account of Turkish politics. Rather, it presents selective parts of the historical experience of Ottoman–Turkish modernisation in general and the formation of the Turkish State in particular. With this selective historical approach, we aim to give evidence for our underlying thesis that the explanation of the Turkish puzzle has to take into account the social contradictions that have resulted from the general trajectory Turkish modernisation has taken.

Although arguing from an historical perspective, this book cannot substitute for detailed historical accounts of Ottoman–Turkish history, such as the works of Feroz Ahmad, Bernard Lewis, Serif Mardin or Jan Erik Zürcher. On the contrary, these works provided an indispensable basis for our investigation into Ottoman–Turkish continuities. Our historical approach to Turkish state formation is almost entirely based on secondary sources, interpreting the course of events according to the specific question of this book. Therefore, the first part of our study does not claim to present new historical data, but to reorganise the available material in our sociological framework in order to provide a new, theoretically informed narrative about Turkish state formation.

In line with this approach, the sociologically guided, selective interpretation of secondary sources clearly dominates the account of Ottoman–Turkish continuities. The four chapters of the second part, however, do present new data derived from different primary sources.[3] In particular, the two chapters on the Turkish–Israeli alignment and on Turkey's relations with Central Asia and the Transcaucasus are much more descriptive than the previous chapters. This is due not only to their explanatory purpose, but also to their claim to document some of the facts behind Turkey's newest foreign policy initiatives in the Greater Middle East.

In general, the book is built of both historical description and analytical explanation. In this way we try to offer a comprehensive account of Turkey's domestic problems and its Middle Eastern relations in a historical perspective. Comprehensiveness does not mean giving a detailed historical account of these themes; instead, we have combined a narrative of historical events with analysis of political and social structures, and of agency, in a study that is based on a cogent line of theoretically guided argument. Accordingly, our primary reader is not seen to be the Turkey expert; rather, we have tried to suit the expectations of both an academically interested audience and the general reader who seeks a better understanding of Turkish affairs. We hope that experts on Turkey might also find the one or the other of our arguments interesting and that the book will thus contribute to the general efforts to solve the Turkish puzzle.

Notes

1 The political ideology named Kemalism has its origin in the radical reform measures implemented by Mustafa Kemal Atatürk, the first president of the Turkish Republic (1923–38). In 1931, Kemalism entered the programme of the Republican People's Party and was defined by six principles: nationalism, populism, statism, republicanism, revolutionism and secularism. Since then, Kemalism has developed into the leading state doctrine of Turkey's political and military–bureaucratic establishment.

2 These different, community-oriented approaches to Ottoman–Turkish history are discussed in the following articles: Bruinessen (1989, 1998), Cizre-Sakallioglu (1998b), Engin (1996), Göle (1996, 1997), Kilic (1998), Kushner (1997), Mango (1994b), Meeker (1991), Seufert (1997, 1999), Vorhoff (1998), Yavuz (1998), Yegen (1996).

3 These primary sources comprise newspaper articles, statistical and other official publications, and oral information from interviews and private talks conducted by the authors while studying and working in Turkey.

PART ONE

The Continuities
of Ottoman–Turkish
Modernisation

2 Modernisation as Theoretical Concept

Turkey and modernity

A brief glance at scholarly work on Turkey reveals that the history of Turkey has often been examined under the rubric of modernisation. Bernard Lewis' *The Emergence of Modern Turkey*, Feroz Ahmad's *The Making of Modern Turkey*, Erik Jan Zürcher's *Turkey: A Modern History*, Serif Mardin's *Religion, Society and Modernity in Turkey*, and many other titles of leading studies indicate that there is a strong tendency to establish a link between Turkey and modernity. Apparently, the country's history provides us with an 'ideal example' of the modernisation process itself, and one can assume that the ideas of Kemalism and its political programme of a radical modernisation instigated from above have been partly reflected in these studies. Meanwhile, however, modernity has become a contested category whose validity is challenged by the rise of post-modern theories; the once unproblematic association of historical processes with modernisation is put in question.

In older studies, such as Weiker (1981) and Trimberger (1978), we frequently find only implicit definitions of modernity. Neither author sketches out his or her understanding of modernisation. The direction and the features of this social transformation were obviously self-evident to them. The classic comparison, *Political Modernization in Japan and Turkey*, edited by Robert Ward and Dankwart Rustow in 1964, gives a descriptive rather than an analytical theoretical framework. In their introduction, the editors present a list of general characteristics of a modern polity and they indicate that modernising societies offer a mixture of both modern and traditional elements.[1] Nevertheless, a tendency to a linear notion of modernisation is common to all three of them. Bernard Lewis' classic work on the late Ottoman Empire and the foundation of the Turkish Republic is also guided by this linear concept of modernisation. Furthermore, it conveys to some extent the

11

Kemalist reading of Turkish history and a rather idealistic notion of modernity. According to Lewis, 'qualities of Western civilisation', such as the ideas of process, development, and organic structure, have 'become more and more effective in Turkish public life' (Lewis 1961: 16–17). He views these cognitive qualities as prerequisites shaping individuals and institutions as well as political, economic and cultural aspects of modern society. With his equation of modernisation and westernisation Lewis represents a tradition of scholars sympathetic to the Kemalist dogmas. They interpret Turkish history with the antithesis of old and new, and while the Ottoman Empire was 'traditional', the Turkish Republic is perceived as modern.[2]

Erik Jan Zürcher claims that more recent books, such as Feroz Ahmad's *The Making of Modern Turkey* (1993), are still characterised by this unhistorical and ideological paradigm of modernisation (Zürcher 1999: 11). Against this positivist and simplistic notion of modernity, Zürcher proposes that we should avoid putting history into a rigid theoretical straitjacket at all. He calls his theoretical approach 'eclectic', and attempts to present different aspects of the modern history of Turkey over the last two hundred years. Turkey's integration into the capitalist world market, its involvement in the power struggle of European states, and the impact of ideas such as nationalism, liberalism, secularism and positivism serve him as points of reference for Turkey's modern history (Zürcher 1993: 1–7). Zürcher's approach reminds us of both the general reluctance of historians to apply precise theoretical concepts and the current impact of post-modern ambiguity on them.

However, as Peter Burke showed in his watershed essay about the Renaissance, neither the demarcation of historical epochs nor the differentiation between theoretical antitheses fit the complex reality of historical processes (Burke 1987). Moreover, both approaches to categorising history are mutually dependent. Anyone who draws a line between epochs, whether as a historian or as a social scientist, must always apply theoretical concepts either implicitly or explicitly. This study, therefore, will first lay down the theoretical terms and conceptual devices encompassed by the category of modernisation that will be applied in its interpretation of Turkish history. In the theoretical framework that now follows we will try to sustain the attempt to explain the history of Turkey in the light of a social theory of modernity without repeating the mistakes of earlier linear, normative and simplistic approaches.

Social reproduction, power and domination

In his critique of realism in international relations theory, Justin Rosenberg points out that 'whenever we use the term "modernity" we reiterate the claim that there is a huge gulf – a structural discontinuity – which separates the way the world used to be from the way it is now' (Rosenberg 1994: 1). Modernisation, the 'Great Transformation' of traditional societies (Polanyi 1957), means the successive spread of elements of modern capitalist society in a global dimension. This transformation is a non-linear process in which traditional modes of production, forms of social organisation and political domination, as well as traditional ideas and values, are gradually superseded by patterns of modern society. From its outset, modernisation has been a global process more or less affecting all existing societies, although uneven in degree, time, and space.

In its macro-sociological dimension, modernisation leads to global structures of world society, represented by the world market, the international system of states and international law, while its micro-sociological dimension is visible in the societal, cultural and economic changes of everyday life. However, this social transformation has nothing to do with determination or the unfolding of a plan. In turn, modernisation has to be seen as an unplanned, long-term social process in which social structures are shaped and sustained by the unintended outcomes of the intended acts of social actors (Elias 1997). But what theoretical devices can grasp this complex process and its historical variations?

First of all we need some general concepts of social reproduction, which comprehend both traditional and modern societies. According to Norbert Elias, social reproduction is generally based on three elementary functions all societies have to fulfil: the control of physical force, the guarantee of material means of life, and the production and preservation of symbolic means of orientation (Elias 1983: 32). The particular ways in which these functions are organised lead to historically and culturally different forms of societal structure. At the centre of Elias' theory of modernisation as a civilising process stands the aspect of the control of violence. On the one hand, violence has a ubiquitous character. As the most direct form of power, physical force is at everybody's disposal. Although they do not have to, human beings are all able, individually or collectively, to act violently. On the other hand, physical force can be used in an almost universal way, and is of an absolute character in threatening the very physical existence of human beings. Due to its ubiquity and absoluteness, Elias calls the use of physical force the 'ultima ratio' in social relations, and for him the control of violence builds the organisational core of social life. Consequently, he defined historical societal forms such as tribes or states, which are basically constituted by their claim to control the means of violence, as 'survival units' (Elias 1986: 152).

In Max Weber's terminology, these survival units are organisations whose political character is defined in terms of the means peculiar to them, the use of physical force (Weber 1968a: 55). The state is only a late result of the development of 'political communities', which are all characterised by the tendency to monopolise the means of violence:

> Violent social action is obviously something absolutely primordial. Every group, from the household to the political party, has always resorted to physical violence when it had to protect the interests of its members and was capable of doing so. However, the monopolization of legitimate violence by the political–territorial association and its rational consociation into an institutional order is nothing primordial, but a product of evolution. (Weber 1968b: 904–5)

Both physical force and power are relational concepts. They acquire meaning only when we apply them to social interactions among individuals or groups. In talking about power we always think of it in terms of power relations. However, while its ubiquitous, direct, and absolute character defines physical force, power, as a general concept in the social sciences, is of an amorphous and vague character. This becomes clear in Weber's definition: 'Power (Macht) is the probability that one actor within a social relationship will be in a position to carry out his own will despite resistance, regardless of the basis on which this probability rests' (Weber 1968a: 52).

With reference to this general definition, power is an asymmetric structural feature of all social relations. As a sociological concept, power stands for the 'transformative capacity' between interdependent actors with power resources at their disposal. Power is the capability of social actors 'to intervene in a given set of events so as in some way to alter them' (Giddens 1985: 7). All three of Elias' elementary functions, the means of physical force, of material and of symbolic reproduction, are sources of power. Against this general background we can speak about political, economic and ideological sources of power (cf. Hall 1985: 250), which are polymorphic and subject to variable levels of social differentiation. However, the control of physical force and the establishment of a political order within a society are prerequisites for the unfolding and differentiation of power resources beyond mere physical force.

If power relations rest on the probability of imposing one's own will despite resistance, this probability alone is not able to transform power relations into stable social structures. This applies especially to societal associations like political communities. While the direct and arbitrary character of violence endangers rather than guarantees the establishment and maintenance of social orders, the stability of these orders can not be sufficiently explained by underlying power structures which are not based on the means of violence. Only institutionalised power relations create a social order. According to Weber's definition, these institutionalised power relations form a system of domination, a stable set of rules that are considered legitimate for both rulers and ruled. In his definition, Weber specifies a kind of domination which rests upon the alleged absolute duty to obey, regardless of personal motives or interests:

> the situation in which the manifested will (*command*) of the *ruler* or rulers is meant to influence the conduct of one or more others (*the ruled*) and actually does influence it in such a way that their conduct to a socially relevant degree occurs as if the ruled had made the content of the command the maxim of their conduct for its very own sake. (Weber 1968c: 946)

Weber does not deny the importance of material interests in relationships of domination. Therefore he distinguishes between two types of domination: domination by virtue of authority and domination by virtue of a constellation of interests. In empirical systems of domination the two types are always combined. The borderline between compliance owing to material benefits or to obeyed authority is therefore fluid (Weber 1968c: 943). Nevertheless, whereas 'power' means to carry out one's will despite resistance, both forms of domination require a certain acceptance of these asymmetric relations on the part of the subordinate. Thus, domination cannot be interpreted as a mere power relation. In a system of domination the social actions of the rulers and the ruled are oriented to a common order that allows them to consider a particular way of conduct as legitimate or not.

This concept of domination as power relations stabilised by a legitimate order combines the material and normative structures of society with the concrete action of social forces. In a system of domination, social structures are maintained and changed by social action, which is itself based on the social structures of a given society. The explanation of historical forms of domination requires therefore the analysis of interests and ideas of social actors. In this respect, Elias' theoretically distinct elementary functions are in reality interdependent. The monopolisation of physical force within a political community, as well as the distribution of its material means, has to be justified by a legitimate order. Yet legitimacy is linked to the third elementary function of societies, the production and preservation of symbolic means of orientation.

Legitimacy is a central category in Weber's sociology of domination. While power resources are the external means of a system of domination, legitimacy refers to their inner justification, to the question of when and why people obey (Weber 1991: 78). According to Weber's typology there are three basic legitimations of domination: charismatic authority, traditional authority, and legal authority.

• *Charismatic* authority rests on 'devotion to the exceptional sanctity, heroism or exemplary character of an individual person, and of the normative patterns or order revealed or ordained by him'.

• Traditional authority rests on 'an established belief in the sanctity of immemorial traditions and the legitimacy of those exercising authority under them'.

• Legal ('Rational') authority rests on 'a belief in the legality of enacted rules and the right of those elevated to authority under such rules to issue commands'. (Weber 1968a: 215)

In differentiating these three pure types[3] of legitimate domination, Weber provides us with a conceptual framework for analysing historical forms of domination: 'All ruling powers, profane and religious, political and apolitical, may be considered as variations of, or approximations to, certain pure types. These types are constructed by searching for the basis of legitimacy, which the ruling power claims' (Weber 1991: 294). The decisive difference between charismatic authority on the one hand and traditional or legal authority on the other is the fact that charismatic domination is not based on a set of rules. Charismatic authority is not a stabilising but a revolutionary force. While systems of traditional or legal domination represent stable social orders, phenomena of charismatic domination are mainly related to times of social crisis. Due to its extraordinary character, charismatic authority is sharply opposed to rational and traditional forms of domination (Weber 1968a: 244). However, as an extraordinary system of domination based on the personal qualities of a charismatic leader, charismatic domination has to change its character radically if it is not to remain a transitory phenomenon. Charismatic authority, therefore, has a tendency to become either traditional-ised or rationalised in order to take on the character of a permanent relation-ship (Weber 1968a: 246).

Starting with Elias' elementary functions, the concepts presented so far – survival units, political communities, power, domination, and legitimacy – are heuristic tools for the comparative analysis of historically different social phenomena. They are all applicable to both traditional and modern societies, and necessarily abstract. Moreover, as they are not specified by the distinction between tradition and modernity, they provide us with the conceptual framework for examining modernisation in its empirically variable forms as a process transforming traditionally organised societies into modern ones. Building on these universal concepts, we now have to define the fundamental differences between traditional and modern forms of social associations. In Rosenberg's terms: How can we theoretically grasp the 'structural dis-continuity', this 'huge gulf', separating traditional from modern societies?

Traditional and modern societies as ideal types

In order to answer this question we must return to Weber's typology of domination. The distinction between traditional and modern appears there in the types of traditional and legal/rational authority. Although the two types are stable forms of social order, they are clearly distinguishable in terms of inner justification. Legal forms of domination rest on impersonal purpose and obedience to abstract norms, whilst traditional forms of domination rest on a strictly personal loyalty and norms that are sanctified by tradition. Although personal in its character, traditional authority must not be confused with charismatic authority. Contrary to the extraordinary character of personal leadership in systems of charismatic domination, traditional domination rests on personal loyalty which results from common upbringing. The legitimacy of a traditional ruler is claimed for and believed in 'by virtue of the sanctity of age-old rules and powers' (Weber 1968a: 226–7). While traditional social relationships may be characterised as direct, personal and invariable, modern social relationships are impersonal, formal and subject to change. If we elaborate further on this distinction, we can define two ideal types of modern and traditional societies. With reference to Elias' elementary functions, the political, economic and symbolic forms of these ideal types are as follows.

In the form of capitalistic production of commodities, the material reproduction of modern society is profit-oriented, competitive, and completely commercialised and monetised. Modern capitalist production rests on a specific form of the division of labour: the manufactural division of labour that culminates in factory-style large-scale industry. Here, the principal division is not between different goods manufactured by different producers, but between workers producing different parts of a single product. In the modern economy, all economic factors – goods, labour, land and money, with their prices: goods-price, wage, ground rent and interest – are organised according to market structures. Economic transactions establish social relationships based on formal rationality that can be defined as the instrumental and quantitative calculation of means appropriate to their ends.

As in the economic field, other sectors of society follow the principle of formal rationality. Political authority is organised in the modern state with its regularised administration of territory and populace. According to Weber, the modern state is a political community 'that (successfully) claims the monopoly of the legitimate use of physical force within a given territory' (Weber 1991: 78). It is a compulsory organisation based on legal authority with a formal order subject to change by legislation (Weber 1968a: 56). Both modern economy and modern politics are organised as 'associative types' of social relationships.

In a modern society social action is oriented towards an abstract symbolic order whose values and ends are deliberately produced artefacts. The norms of the social order 'are established rationally, appeal to the sense of abstract legality, and presuppose technical training' (Weber 1968c: 1006). The modern world-view is of an abstract, general and open character and social action is based not on the sanctity of traditional regulations, but on a set of formal rules and laws.

In traditional societies, the economy is not separated from society, but is a function of the whole system of social organisation (cf. Heinemann 1976). Material reproduction is submerged in the social relationships of the community. 'Neither the process of production nor that of distribution is linked to specific economic interests attached to the possession of goods; but every single step in that process is geared to a number of social interests which eventually ensure that the required step be taken' (Polanyi 1957: 46). Economic action is therefore related to motivations unspecific to pure economic interests; it rests in social relationships established by blood and family ties, religious or feudal duties, marriage, mystical or magic com-munities. Labour and land are socially bound, and the material reproduction of traditional communities is neither competitive nor profit-oriented. Market structures do not exist within communities but between them. Instead of market structures, the material reproduction of traditional societies is shaped by the structure of patriarchal households. 'The production and distribution of goods is organized in the main through collection, storage, and redistribu-tion, the pattern being focused on the chief, the temple, the despot, or the lord' (Polanyi 1957: 52).

Contrary to the situation in the modern state, the control of the means of physical force in traditional states is fragmented. Traditional states are made up of different political communities and are, thus, segmental in character. Neither the territory nor the populace of a traditional state is entirely under the control of the state administration, and whereas the modern state has clear marked borders, traditional states have frontiers, peripheral areas 'in which the authority of the centre is diffuse or thinly spread' (Giddens 1985: 50). The political authority of the rulers rests on traditional legitimacy, which is rooted in the patriarchal domination of the master over his household (Weber 1968c: 1006–8). The symbolic order is of a religious, mythological or magic nature, while its norms and values are sanctified by age-old rules and not subject to change. Traditional world-views have a closed character, and social action is guided not by formal rules, but by concrete and self-evident regulations.

These two pure types of society, the traditional and the modern, whose political, economic and symbolic dimensions have been sketched out above, are necessarily of a static and ideal character. They are ideal not in an evaluative sense, but as logically precise constructions for analytical and explanatory purposes. As heuristic tools, we use them to understand empirical instances, yet the pure concepts never correspond exactly to the instances. In other words, neither was the Ottoman Empire in its political organisation a pure traditional society, nor was the Turkish Republic the historical blueprint of a modern state. In both of them we can find patterns of tradition and modernity, both are social organisations resembling a patchwork of societal elements which can be discerned in comparison with the abstract conceptual framework presented here. Against the background of these two ideal types, modernising societies can be located somewhere in this continuum between the traditional and the modern.

In a theoretical sense the two ideal types represent a clear structural discontinuity. Modernisation as a historical process, however, has to be understood as the continuous change of societal structures from the traditional towards the modern type. In this historical transformation, structural change is characterised by two tendencies. First, there is an increasing differentiation on the one hand between and on the other within the three elementary functions: there is a tendency towards the severance between the functions of the control of violence, economic reproduction and symbolic reproduction; they become separate systems of political, economic and cultural interaction; functional differentiation also occurs within these three basic realms, establishing a variety of subsystems such as law, administration, education, production, and services. Second, in the modernisation process, associative types of social relationships gradually supersede community types, group-determined social action by individual strategies. While social action in the communal type 'is based on a subjective feeling of the parties, whether affectual or traditional, that they belong together', associative relationships 'rest on a rationally motivated adjustment of interests' which are based on 'values or reasons of expediency' (Weber 1968a: 40–41). This tendency to move from emotionally and traditionally based communal relationships to rationally and interest-oriented associative relationships is paralleled by the dissociation of social units from interaction groups. Whereas the social relationship in a traditional market place, for instance, is congruent with the direct interaction between buyer and seller, the so-called world market is of a completely different nature. In linking the material reproduction of individuals on a global level, the structures of the world market are social relations, but established in an abstract manner far removed from direct interaction. In the modernising process more and more social relations acquire an abstract character, transcending the face-to-face character of direct interaction.

These tendencies are just two examples of the importance of what Elias calls a process-sociological approach to modernisation. The formation of modern nation-states, the establishment of a global economy, the creation of rational sciences and of abstract bodies of law, as well as the formation of individualised social personality structures are important and interdependent aspects of this long-term process that Elias calls the 'civilising process'.

However, without setting economic and societal aspects completely aside, this study of Turkey's modernisation and its political role in an emerging Greater Middle East focuses on the formation of the modern Turkish state. Hence we have to conceptualise further some aspects of modernisation more directly linked to state formation. The sociological core of state formation, as previously mentioned, is what Weber called a long process of political expropriation, lasting centuries: 'the monopolisation of the legitimate use of physical force as a means of domination within a territory' by the state. In this process all autonomous functionaries who formerly controlled the legitimate use of physical force as a means of domination have been expropriated by the modern state. 'The state has taken their position and now stands in the top place' (Weber 1991: 83).'

Monopolisation and feudalisation

Norbert Elias provides us with two process-sociological concepts to explain processes of state formation: *monopolisation* and *feudalisation*. Both concepts refer to structural problems and lines of development that occur during state formation and which will help us later to examine the Ottoman–Turkish example. With regard to the Ottoman reforms, one can observe both processes at the same time: the attempt to centralise and therefore to monopolise state power in order to counter the feudalisation of the Ottoman state by the growing independence of regional power-holders. In his chapter 'On the Monopoly Mechanism', Elias traces the origin of the state monopoly of physical force back to its opposite, the unrestricted and violent contest in which any individual or small group struggles among many for sources not yet monopolised (Elias 1994: 351). Two phases of the monopoly mechanism can be distinguished:

> First, the phase of free competition or elimination contests, with a tendency for resources to be accumulated in fewer and fewer and finally in one pair of hands, the phase of monopoly formation; secondly, the phase in which control over the centralized and monopolized resources tends to pass from the hands of an individual to those of ever greater numbers, and finally to become a function of the interdependent human web as a whole, the phase in which a relatively 'private' monopoly becomes public. (Elias 1994: 354)

In the historical example of European state formation, the first phase can be observed in the formation of the Absolutist State, the second in the 'socialisation' of the state in the course of bourgeois revolutions. However, it would be short-sighted to limit the phenomenon of monopoly formation to the power resource of physical force. The monopolisation of physical force is always accompanied by the formation of a monopoly of taxation: 'The financial means thus flowing into this central authority maintain its monopoly of military force, while this in turn maintains the monopoly of taxation' (Elias 1994: 346). The gradual pacification of social relations by the emerging state is paralleled by the monetisation of economic exchange. Both developments are interdependent in the creation of stable organs of central authority. 'Money payment keeps all recipients permanently dependent on the central authority. Only now can the centrifugal tendencies be finally broken' (Elias 1994: 437). This explains how the transition from tributary, collective contributions to direct and individual taxation could take place.

The monopolisation of physical violence, and therefore the differentiation between two distinct realms of politics and economy, opens space for the development of new power sources within these realms. New functional social classes monopolise these resources, leading to a change of the internal power balances of a state. More and more new functional classes, such as professional armed forces, entrepreneurs, bureaucrats and jurists, acquire dominant positions in modernising societies. The replacement of the European aristocracy by a class of economic specialists gives an example of this development (Elias 1983: 32 ff.); the rise of a powerful class of Western-educated Ottoman bureaucrats during the nineteenth century is another. However, the establishment of the monopolies of physical force and of taxation are not mere political and economic processes. They also need to be grounded in the symbolic order of society.

The integration of segmented societies into pre-state confederations or patrimonial empires took place in close relation with the spread of universal religious systems (Giddens 1985: 71). The European example shows the conflict-prone nature of the symbolic foundation of patrimonial states on religious orders. For centuries, European state formation was characterised by the power struggle between and among political and religious functionaries. This conflict came to an end in the process of confessionalisation, as the territorial principalities succeeded in establishing political domination over religious life. It was this third key monopoly of the early modern state, symbolised by the territorially and confessionally bounded church, which was sealed with the Treaty of Westphalia in 1648 (Schilling 1992: 216, 230). We will discuss this attempt at a state-controlled symbolic order further under the heading of republican Turkish 'secularism', the strict adherence of the state elite in Turkey to the Kemalist principle of laicism.

The processes of monopolisation, in which modern states in Europe were able to establish at least tentative control over the power resources of all three elementary functions, were accompanied by other developments closely associated with state formation. First, there is the field of public knowledge. Formalisation, textualisation and centralisation of knowledge were conditions for the establishment and monopolisation of a body of abstract knowledge with which to administer and therefore to rule. 'Surveillance as the mobilizing of administrative power – through storage and control of information' rests on the standardisation, formalisation and implementation of a written language by the state (Giddens 1985: 181). Furthermore, the capacity of the modern state to monitor its populace depends on the development of the means of communication. Modern lines of transportation like roads and railways as well as the establishment of systems of telegraphy and of electric power supply therefore not only serve economic ends, but also enhance the surveillance and policing capacities of the modern state.[4] Second, there is the social disciplining of the individual. Oestreich describes this change in the moral, mental and psychological fabric of people as a fundamental process which runs parallel to the centralisation of political power in the era of European Absolutism (Oestreich 1980: 187 ff). Norbert Elias refers to the linkage between the monopolisation and centralisation of power and the formation of the 'sociogenic apparatus of individual self-control' under the heading of a transformation from outer-control to self-restraint (Elias 1994: 447).

It has to be reiterated that the processes sketched out here under the concept of monopolisation do not take on the form of linear state formation. They are subject to integrative and disintegrative historical developments in which state-like political formations can also vanish. Elias categorised those disintegrative developments with the help of another process-sociological concept: *feudalisation*. This concept he based on the historical experience of the decentralisation of western France in the tenth and eleventh centuries. 'This gradual decentralization of government and territory, this transition of the land from the control of the conquering central ruler to that of the warrior caste as a whole is nothing other than the process known as "feudalization"' (Elias 1994: 286). However, using Elias' concept of feudalisation for an explanation of Turkish state formation does not imply that the epoch of European feudalism is seen as a necessary stage in the formation of a modern state. The concept is used to comprehend under what conditions systems of domination are prone to disintegrate in state-building processes. European feudalism as a 'constitutional system', whose three phases – military, princely–

corporate, and manorial–aristocratic – reached from the eleventh to the nineteenth centuries, is a particularity of European history (Hintze 1970: 23).

In Max Weber's terminology, the structural problems linked to feudalisation are addressed as the 'appropriation of administrative resources'. In its political sense, domination refers mainly to a ruling organisation based on an established order (Weber 1968a: 53). The maintenance of domination is therefore subject to means of administration, and every kind of domination both expresses itself and functions as administration (Weber 1968c: 948). The continuation of all systems of domination rests on the existence of an administrative staff that externally represents the system of domination and guarantees the execution of the political order. It is important for the administrative structure of political domination how the necessary delegation of administrative power is organised. In other words, it is decisive whether the staff own the administrative means themselves or whether they are separated from them. This distinction runs principally through all administrative organisations, and the appropriation of administrative means is what Elias calls feudalisation.

The link between domination as administration and the disintegration of systems of domination becomes clearer in Weber's concept of the *patrimonial state*. Patrimonialism is a result of the formation of systems of traditional authority which transcend the territorial and societal dimensions of pre-bureaucratic types of patriarchal organisations, such as family, household or clan. 'Patrimonial domination is thus a special case of patriarchal domination – domestic authority decentralized through assignment of land and some times of equipment to sons of the house or other dependants' (Weber 1968c: 1011). In some forms of patrimonial domination, of which the estate system of the European Middle Ages is an example, the administrative staff of the patrimonial ruler is able to appropriate the means of administration and thus political and economic power resources. If this appropriation continues and vassals, provincial governors, local chiefs or tax farmers establish their own independent political authority, the patrimonial state disintegrates and a process of feudalisation can be observed. Feudalisation becomes particularly precarious if it affects the control of the means of physical force. The appropriation of physical violence by the administrative staff of a system of domination can lead to the complete disintegration of state structures. In short, the formation of modern states is historically characterised by interrelated processes of monopoly formation and feudalisation.[5]

Social actors, hegemonic blocs and the social habitus

The conceptual framework presented so far helps us to understand structural developments that take place in processes of modernisation. However, social structures do not exist without actors who establish, reinforce and change them. Modernisation, as a specific change of the modes of social reproduction, means also a transformation of the shape and constitution of social actors. The rise and fall of social groups accompany the differentiation of power resources in all three elementary functions. The commodification of land and labour and the monetisation of economic exchange undermine the traditional relationships of the manorial system. The asymmetric but reciprocal relation between landed gentry and peasants, in which political and economic functions are combined, gives way to the contractual association of private property owners and rural workers. The separation of political and economic functions creates a whole set of new social formations. Traditional societies, which consist of a variety of semi-independent communities based on social relationships with a segmental, tribal, or estate character, are gradually superseded by modern associative organisations in which the individual participates not holistically but according to specific roles and interests.

The formation of the modern bureaucratic state leads to a number of new social groups, associated with different power resources, which result from the internal differentiation of the state apparatus. These modern actors resemble the functional division of the modern state with its organs of physical force – the police and the military – its bureaucratic system of administration, its division of executive, legal and juridical powers, and its educational system. As a heterogeneous middle class, these clerks, functionaries, lawyers, army officers, teachers, and members of the intelligentsia play a major role in the political struggle for the establishment and consolidation of the legal authority of a modern nation-state. Both the specific distribution of power resources among traditional and modern social actors and the ideas guiding their social actions shape the historically different paths modernisation takes. The Ottoman reforms provide a good insight into these dynamics between state formation, the emergence of modern social actors, and the transformation of the symbolic order.

Furthermore, traditional and modern social forces not only compete for power positions, they also form alliances to defend themselves from other competitors. In the historical formation of a modern state we can observe the constitution of *hegemonic blocs*, 'the configuration of social forces upon which state power ultimately rests' (Cox 1987: 105). Hegemonic blocs can consist of a particular co-operation among traditional and modern social actors who shape not only the institutional setting of the emerging nation-state, but also the world-view of its political establishment. Taking the German example, Norbert Elias examined the link between the formation of a hegemonic bloc and a specific German national character. In nineteenth-century German state formation, parts of the middle class and the modern bourgeois stratum of society joined forces with the traditional German aristocracy. The compromise of interests led to a merger of attitudes and values of bourgeois and aristocratic forces. The so-called national character of the Germans, the prominent role played by military values, such as discipline and strict obedience, is thus a derivative of the particular *social habitus* of the hegemonic bloc that formed Germany's early state elite (Elias 1990).

According to Pierre Bourdieu and Norbert Elias, the social habitus comprises a system of historically and socially constructed generative principles granting a frame in which individuality unfolds. For Elias the social habitus marks the connection between the individual and society (Elias 1991: 244). He points out 'that each individual person, different as he or she may be from all others, has a specific make-up that he or she shares with other members of his or her society. This make-up, the social habitus of individuals, forms, as it were, the soil from which grow the personal characteristics through which an individual differs from other members of his society' (Elias 1991: 182). The world-view, which is rooted in the social habitus, provides a general reservoir of cognitive and normative resources to which individual strategies of action correspond. As a 'generative grammar' of patterns of action, the habitus forms the intersection between society and the individual, between structure and action (Bourdieu 1992: 33). These generative principles are the means for social groups to shape their particular ways of action in pursuing their interests. Rationally calculated interests are, therefore, transformed into action in the light of this set of ideas.

The concept of the social habitus seems to be an appropriate heuristic tool to show, first, how cognitive and ideological patterns, which are historically rooted social constructions, influence the action of concrete actors. Second, the concept of the social habitus can explain how social structures find their way into the mind-set of a specific group of actors, not in the sense of determination, as in a crude application of Marxism's basis and superstructure model, but as an awareness of the fact that material and ideational structures of society have an interdependent relation. Although the political and economic structures of a society are interdependent with the social habitus of collective actors, it is an important point for this study that structural change and the change of the social habitus do not necessarily happen in parallel. Whereas the historical and social constructions of the social habitus stress its liability to change, the social habitus also remains a relatively stable disposition of groups and individuals, acquired by socialisation. Thus, in times of accelerated modernisation the social habitus might become anachronistic to the structures of a changing social and political environment (Müller 1986: 164).

The persistence of the cognitive patterns of the symbolic world, linked to the relatively stable character of the social habitus of elite groups and the general populace alike, can best be illustrated by giving an example. In his article on centre–periphery relations in Turkish politics, Serif Mardin examines the huge gulf between the Ottoman state and its mainly rural populace. The latter considered the court, officials, and politics 'as grim things from which they kept apart'. This scary power relation between state and people survived for centuries in the meaning of the word 'siyaset' (politics) as used by Turkey's peasantry. According to a study carried out in the late 1960s, 'the modern Turkish word siyaset still retained the grim connotation of its earlier meaning under Ottoman rule, where it was in official parlance also a synonym for a death sentence imposed for reasons of state' (Mardin 1973: 173).

Let us finally reiterate that in the analysis of the formation of modern Turkey, the conceptual framework will serve us in a purely systematic sense. Its application has neither normative claims, nor does it imply any historical determinism. Moreover, it is a fundamental presupposition of our approach that political, economic, cultural or societal aspects of modernity have no theoretically determining quality on the modernising process as a whole. On the contrary, as a pluralistic theory of modernity this conceptual framework serves us as an abstract and general standard of comparison and enables us to discern the particularities of the various concrete trajectories modernisation acquires in different historical cases. The general concepts introduced in this chapter will help us analytically to understand the segmental and unequal nature of modernising societies whose different faces are a result of what Ernst Bloch once called 'the contemporaneity of the non-contemporaneous' (cf. Bloch 1985). The fact is that although societies represent a whole of social reproduction, modernisation structures them as uneven and non-contemporaneous societal patchworks in which modern and traditional elements coexist. To provide a basis for understanding the historical construction of one of these patchworks – the example of Turkey – is now the task that our conceptualisation of modernity has to fulfil.

Notes

1   See the introduction to Ward and Rustow (1964: 7).
2   A good example for this dichotomy of traditional and modern in interpreting Turkish history gives the following quotation: 'In Turkey, the early phases of change were in a manner defensive, since they were effected to preserve the authority of the traditional ruling elite; the changes after 1919 were effected in a genuinely progressive spirit' (Chambers 1964: 301–2)'.

3   I use the terms 'pure type' and 'ideal type' as synonyms which both refer to Weber's methodology of theoretically constructing sociological concepts. They are pure or ideal only in the sense of their logical construction.

4   For two intriguing studies on the relation between communicational infrastructure, policing, and state formation, see Schivelbusch (1986; 1989).

5   About state formation as interrelated processes of the monopolisation of physical force and of the accumulation of capital, see Tilly (1990).

3 Reform and Decline
Modernisation in the Ottoman Empire

Incentives and character of the early Ottoman reforms

On the night of June 15–16 1826, only two weeks after Sultan Mahmud II (1808–39) announced the establishment of a new army, the traditional military backbone of the Empire, the Janissaries, went out in open rebellion against him. The intended reform of the Ottoman army to European standards of training and equipment, and the forced integration of parts of the Janissaries into the newly formed corps were perceived as a direct threat against their traditional privileges. Five battalions of the Janissaries, followed by a violent mob, assembled in the Hippodrome of Istanbul, where their barracks were located, and where the new troops had already started to exercise.

In contrast to his predecessor, Sultan Selim III (1789–1807), who was deposed after a similar uprising, Mahmud II expected the rebellion and was prepared to meet the mutineers. Furthermore, the Janissaries failed this time to rally the support of the religious establishment, the *ulema*, and even within their own ranks the mutiny was not wholeheartedly supported. Whereas in May 1807 Selim III failed to establish his *nizam-i cedid* corps and was deposed on the basis of a legal statement issued by the chief *mufti*, the highest religious dignity, Mahmud II and his new troops were able to crush the rebellion. On 17 June 1826, a proclamation by the Sultan announced the abolition of the Janissary regiments.[1]

The Janissaries, once the elite troops of the Ottoman Empire, loyal exclusively to the Sultan and the Ottoman state, had developed into a 'state within the state'. During the weakening of central power in the late seventeenth and eighteenth centuries, the instrument of domination gradually acquired means of power and control over the institutions of the state. In 1628, for the first time, a former commander of the Janissaries was appointed

grand vezir,[2] with the support of the *ulema* (Inalcik 1964: 46). From that time
onwards, tentative coalitions of traditional social forces, formed by the
Janissaries, local notables and low-ranking *ulema*, were able to provoke social
upheavals against unpopular sultans in order to stop reform attempts by the
political leadership.[3] At the end of the eighteenth century, the Janissaries had
degenerated into an idle military caste carefully protecting their traditions and
privileges. By that time, the former military power core of the Empire was
unable to defend the Ottoman state against its foreign enemies, but was still
strong enough to prevent internal reforms. With the massacre and abolition of
the Janissaries in 1826, these coalitions of traditional interests were deprived
of their physical force, which marked the advent of an era of military,
administrative and legal reforms aiming at strengthening central state control.

As indicated before, the reform attempts of Selim III can be seen as a
prelude to the Ottoman reforms of the nineteenth century. His acceptance of
European practice and French advisers marked a clear deviation from the
classical approach of Ottoman sultans, who had always been oriented towards
the restoration of traditional institutions of a glorified past.[4] Furthermore, it
was Selim III himself who was committed to the reforms and tried to
safeguard their implementation.[5] Although his reforms did not achieve their
ends – owing to inner resistance, financial mismanagement, chronic favouritism and corruption, and a tendency of the traditional bureaucracy to subvert
the goals of reform 'from service of the state to self-service' (Findley 1972:
395) – Selim's reign opened new channels of communication with the West.
The appointment of foreign instructors at the newly opened military schools,
the posting of administrative staff to Europe, and the establishment of the first
permanent Ottoman embassies in London, Vienna, Berlin, and Paris provided
an institutional foundation for the dissemination of Western ideas and
practices into the Ottoman Empire (Zürcher 1993: 23–6).

Under Mahmud II, military matters were the major stimulus for reform,
just as they had been the motivation behind the tentative approach of Selim
III. After effectively crushing the last serious rebellion of the Janissaries, Sultan
Mahmud's reforms emphasised the building-up of a modern army called 'the
Trained Victorious Muslim Troops' (Levy 1971: 21). Yet the establishment of
a modern army was not possible without sufficient financial resources from
the state. The military reforms therefore necessarily entailed the creation of
centralised structures for tax administration. One of the major problems
Mahmud's reform attempts had to face was the lack of educated staff for both
the army and the administration. Although in 1836 a small number of
Prussian and British officers arrived in Istanbul, their influence on officer
training and the evolution of a new military leadership remained practically

insignificant. The general level of education was very low, with even the majority of Ottoman officers being illiterate, and the study programmes of the military schools established under Mahmud II were limited to basic subjects such as reading, writing, arithmetic, Arabic and military tactics (Levy 1971: 24–34).

The formation of the 'Translation Office of the Sublime Porte' and its growth in size and importance from 1833 onwards can be seen as the embryonic stage of what later became the institutional framework for the emergence of a new modern class of Ottoman bureaucrats.[6] For Ali and Fuad Pasha, two of the three leading bureaucratic statesmen of the nineteenth century, the Translation Office was the springboard for their political careers (Findley 1972: 404). Around this nucleus of a modern bureaucracy, the functional organisation of government in ministries and administrative subdivisions developed. New bureaucratic bodies like the 'Council for Public Affairs' and the 'Fiscal Council' were set up, indicating the incorporation of new fields of state function into the Ottoman administration (Chambers 1964: 319–20). Nevertheless, the administration during Mahmud's reign was far from being an effective apparatus and far from resembling a bureaucratic structure able to maintain the system of domination required by a modern state. What made this phase of early reforms under Selim III and Mahmud II important was not their actual achievements, but the fact that they laid the foundations for the specific way of Turkish modernisation: a top-down modernisation centred around a military–bureaucratic elite.

The accelerated transformation of the traditional structures of the Ottoman Empire thereafter was a result of the so-called Tanzimat period, which started with the first Tanzimat edict, the Hatt-i Sherif of Gülhane in 1839, and ended with the dissolution of the first Ottoman parliament by Sultan Abdülhamid II in 1878.[7] During this period of the Tanzimat i-Hayriye, 'the beneficial reforms', the Ottoman Empire saw the spread of modern elements among its judicial, administrative and educational structures, and the formation of modern social forces whose power resources were directly linked to the reform process.[8] The initiatives of Selim III and Mahmud II to create a modern administrative staff for the state apparatus thus gathered momentum and 'the centre of power now shifted from the palace to the Porte, the bureaucracy' (Zürcher 1993: 52). Only during the absolutist reign of Abdülhamid II (1876–1908) could the dominance of the military-bureaucratic element within the hegemonic block of the Ottoman Empire be pushed back. With the Young Turk revolution in 1908, however, the military wing of the new elite resumed its dominant position and paved the way for the establishment of the Turkish Republic.

In order to understand the structural constraints behind the Ottoman reforms, we will first take a look at the traditional order of the Ottoman Empire. Then, in applying the category of feudalisation, the general impact of the modernisation process on this traditional order will be examined. The third section discusses the political–administrative reforms of the Tanzimat against the historical and structural background of the so-called 'Eastern Question'.[9] Furthermore, we will analyse the interrelation between the reforms and the rise of an internal opposition of modern social forces. The fourth section of this chapter deals with the 'Hamidian period', the despotic reign of Sultan Abdülhamid II, which ended with the seizure of power by the 'Young Turk Movement'. We will base our analysis of the absolutist and pan-Islamic posture of Abdülhamid II and of the simultaneous birth of Turkish nationalism on a retrospective look at the economic and political developments of the nineteenth century, which culminated in the Hamidian period. The chapter ends with some concluding remarks about general patterns and features of Turkish modernisation as they were established during the decay of the Ottoman Empire.

The historical and structural conditions behind the reform process

Before examining the Tanzimat in a more detailed way, it is necessary to have a look at the social forces and the structural constraints behind the Ottoman reform process. The modernisation of the Ottoman Empire was not triggered by the aspirations of an economically self-confident bourgeoisie claiming a formal legal framework for their property rights and demanding political participation. The Ottoman reforms started and continued to be a classic example of modernisation from above oriented towards the protection of the political interests of its dominant court elite and of the upper echelons of both the administration and the army (Davison 1963: 6–8). Guided neither by the interests of a rising bourgeoisie nor by the spirit of an 'enlightened absolutism',[10] they were an attempt to safeguard the integrity of the Empire in a world that was becoming increasingly dominated by European powers and Western civilisation (Davison 1963: 6). The instrumental adoption of modern scientific knowledge and organisational devices of Western states seemed to be the right means to this end. Hence, the new hegemonic bloc which formed the Ottoman state elite after the destruction of the Janissaries represented a coalition of traditional forces, whose power resources were linked to the sultanate, and modern social forces associated with the modernisation of the state apparatus. The common denominator of this heterogeneous coalition was a desire to defend the state apparatus against internal and external threats. 'Without external and internal security, any other kind of political reconstruction seemed pointless' (Hale 1994: 13).

The course of historical events does not provide us with a clear turning point from which the decline of the Empire could be traced. As a complex interplay of social forces and structural changes, the dismantling of the Ottoman Empire becomes a linear process only in retrospect. Nevertheless, there are a number of instances indicating the wind of change. Bernard Lewis, for example, sees in the Treaty of Carlowitz (1699) the end of one epoch and the beginning of another: 'This was the first time that the Ottoman Empire signed a peace as the defeated power in a clearly decided war, and was compelled to cede extensive territories, long under Ottoman rule and regarded as part of the House of Islam, to the infidel enemy' (Lewis 1961: 36). According to Carl Brown, the Treaty of Kücük Kaynarca (1774) marks the turning point. Ending the Ottoman Russian War (1768–74), this treaty deprived the Empire of the Crimean Khanate, which was declared independent, and of supremacy over the Black Sea (Brown 1984: 23). From the Ottoman defeat at Vienna (1683) to the Greek War of Independence (1821–29) a whole series of historical events could be chosen to mark the beginning of the dissolution of the Ottoman Empire. It is historically evident, however, that from the eighteenth century onwards the Ottoman Empire was dragged progressively into the European power struggle, increasingly to its disadvantage.

In changing alliances and confrontations the Ottoman Empire became the sixth player of the European pentarchy, alongside Russia, the Habsburg Empire, Great Britain, France and Prussia. Since the Treaty of Kücük Kaynarca, the Ottoman Empire had been the stage for constant internal and external warfare, leading to dramatic territorial losses and eventual collapse after the First World War.[11] It would be misleading, however, to ascribe the Ottoman reforms exclusively to the impact of the European power struggle. There was also a strong internal stimulus behind the efforts to centralise state power and modernise the army, caused by the social transformations within the Empire (Karpat 1972: 243). The major internal impulse for the reforms came from what Caglar Keyder calls a 'patrimonial crisis', the centrifugal forces which arise in the peripheral administration of a mainly agrarian patrimonial Empire (Keyder 1997: 30-31). So, while it was struggling to find its new role in the emerging international system, the Ottoman state was internally endangered by a process of feudalisation. Confronted with the centralised power resources of European nation-states, it was the deficiencies of its patrimonial structure that shifted the Ottoman Empire from a powerful challenger to an ailing state at the mercy of the European powers.

The traditional social order and the impact of European modernisation
Given that the Ottomans were able to sustain a remarkably strong central state against the structural perils of patrimonial administration for so long, this change of fortune was striking. The basic social stratification of the Empire divided its people in two main groups. The first group, called *askeri* (military), represented the Ottoman state elite, 'to whom the sultan had delegated religious or executive powers through an imperial diploma, namely, officers of the court and the army, civil servants, and *ulema*'. The privileged *askeri* class was entirely exempt from taxation. The second group, the *reaya*, comprised the bulk of Muslim and non-Muslim subjects who were taxed (Inalcik 1964: 43–4).

Besides this horizontal stratification, the society of the Empire was also characterised by a vertical differentiation, the so-called *millet* system. Based on Islamic law, monotheistic religious communities had the right to organise their internal affairs autonomously. The religious leaders of the communities represented their people *vis-à-vis* the central administration. It was their obligation to guarantee public order and the payment of taxes. Only in the case of violation of this order was the central administration allowed to interfere in the affairs of a *millet* (Shaw 1971b: 91).

The traditional system of checks and balances under the control of the central state could cope with the decentralising forces that resulted from the necessity to administer the Empire through intermediaries. The Ottoman rulers eliminated the regional aristocracy in the conquered lands and entrusted executive functions only to military, civil or religious appointees. In terms of legitimacy and material means, all three functional groups were dependent on the centre. Under the supreme leadership of the sultan, the *ulema*, the civil servants, and the two professional parts of the Ottoman army, the infantry (Janissaries) and the cavalry (*sipahi*), formed together the hegemonic bloc of the classic Ottoman state institutions.

As an alternative to salaried services, the sultan also offered his intermediaries land, as a fiefdom from which to extract economic surplus. However, according to the principle that all land belongs to the sultan (*miri*), the fiefdoms, which were assigned mainly to the members of the cavalry, were of a temporary nature. This assignment of land, known as the *timar* system, played a major role not only in providing the economic foundation of the state, but also in controlling the peasant population (Karpat 1964: 74).

The system of checks and balances and the non-heritable character of fiefs were parts of the general policy of the Ottoman state administration to prevent the accumulation of autonomous power resources in the hands of its functionaries and officers or local notables. This policy guaranteed the supremacy of the sultan and therefore his relative control over the political, economic, and cultural means of social reproduction.[12] The tendency of the administrative staff of patrimonial systems of domination to appropriate the means of administration was thus effectively contained. This specific administrative structure of the Ottoman Empire had a comparative advantage over the feudal character of competing European patrimonial states that additionally had to cope with the political competition of the church.

Yet the relatively high degree of central control exerted by the traditional Ottoman state was closely linked to a specific mode of reproduction. This was symbolised in the warrior (gazi) image of the Ottomans: the acquisition of material means by war and conquest.[13] 'The rapidity of Ottoman expansion provided dynasts and ruling elites with an unprecedented "patrimonial reserve" in the form of conquered lands, tribute, booty, and other resources' (Salzmann 1993: 396). From the late sixteenth century onwards, mounting war costs, inventions in technology and logistics of inter-state war in Europe, changes in the major routes of trade, and fiscal crises due to the flow of precious metals from Latin America to Europe strongly affected this mode of material reproduction. The change of external political and economic conditions thus contributed significantly to the erosion of the classical institutional setting of the Ottoman state.

In explaining the decay of the Empire, however, the distinction between internal and external makes sense only for analytical purposes. In reality, internal and external developments were inseparably linked. The structural constraints under whose impact the Ottoman state elite had to act were more and more a result of the modernisation process itself.[14] Moreover, as a political entity whose history was characterised by an intensive interaction with Europe, the Ottoman Empire took part in the modern social transformation which began in Europe and subsequently spread over the globe. If modern Europe emerged in a thousand-year-long historical process, in which political communities acquired the form of nation-states in concentrating and accumulating the means of coercion and capital (Tilly 1990), then the Ottoman Empire was from its beginning a part of this war-prone historical process. From the signature of the Peace of Buda in 1503, the Ottomans played an important role in the development of a distinctive system of states, linked by treaties, embassies, marriages, declared wars and formal peace settlements (Tilly 1990: 162–3).

In this emerging system of states, we can theoretically locate the turning point for the Ottoman role in the consolidation of European nation-states. Once the basis of its former strength, the patrimonial system of checks and balances, preventing the accumulation of independent power resources, now became a decisive factor weakening the Empire's position in the competitive European state system. Nation-states, as territorially bounded administrative 'power containers' (Giddens 1985: 13), monopolise the power resources of the political, economic, and cultural functions that, according to Norbert Elias, a society has to provide. With its effective monopolies of physical force and of taxation, the nation-state acquires a high degree of internal pacification and, at the same time, is able to concentrate its military means for inter-state competition.

In the centuries-long competitive historical process of modern state formation, the survival of political entities depended on their ability to meet the demands of the modern nation-state. Based on indirect rule and military conquest, it was the dilemma of empires that they could not match these standards without destroying their own social foundations (cf. Lieven 1999). While from the perspective of the nation-state modernisation means accumulation, centralisation and monopolisation of power, the same social transformation can historically be translated into the feudalisation and dissolution of traditionally structured empires. This was exactly the Ottoman experience: that in the long run all the attempts to centralise and strengthen the Ottoman state ended in its disintegration.

Destruction of the traditional order and feudalisation of the state

One hundred years earlier than the reform attempts of Selim III, the Ottoman government had already had to curb tendencies towards feudalisation. Under *Grand Vezir* Fazil Mustafa Köprülü (1689–91), the central government undertook reform measures to prevent the abuse of state-delegated authority by provincial governors and to discipline the Janissary regiments (Matuz 1985: 187–90). However, the necessary limitation of the power of provincial governors, who became plunderers of their own society (Mardin 1973: 174), also facilitated the rise of a new group of local magnates, the so-called *ayan*. The *ayan* were regarded as natural representatives of local communities who performed public services and could influence the decisions of the central government.[15] Their local power positions rested on a combination of traditional authority with material positions such as merchants, traders, artisans, guildsmen or landowners.[16] In fighting the autonomous aspiration of state functionaries in the periphery, the centre unwillingly strengthened the influence of the *ayan*.

Albert Hourani divides these local magnates according to their sources of authority into three groups: religious functionaries such as *ulema*, *qadis* or *muftis*; leaders of local garrisons and of the Janissaries; and *ayan* and *agas* whose authority was rooted in the social prestige of their noble families (Hourani 1981: 44–5). Obviously, local magnates emerged either from the group of administrative functionaries in the central government or from local noble families. The inconsistent usage of the term *ayan* in academic literature, however, indicates that a precise distinction between both groups of local magnates is not possible. It is important for this study that ayanship meant a certain control over local revenues and security forces. Amid the financial and administrative strains of the eighteenth century, the central government increasingly delegated administrative functions to these intermediaries, and the *ayan* 'began to resemble a freeholding landed gentry which partly was able to maintain private armies, to levy taxes, and to dispense justice' (Lewis 1961: 447).

Another group of local power holders, the *derebeys* ('lords of the valleys'), emerged in Anatolia during the decline of Ottoman provincial administration in the seventeenth century. 'Unlike the notables, who were primarily an urban phenomenon, their power was concentrated in the mountains', where they taxed the villagers and levied tolls on caravans. Toward the end of the eighteenth century, parts of Rumelia, the European provinces of the Empire, and almost the whole of Anatolia were under the control of *derebeys*, who also had substantial physical force at their disposal. The central government treated them, as members of 'tribal nobility', alternately as rebels or as useful intermediaries. Ruling over autonomous, hereditary principalities, the *derebeys* reached the summit of their power during the reign of Selim III. However, owing to transitions between the two groups, a clear distinction between them and the *ayan* was often hard to make (Gould 1976: 486).

The increasing feudalisation of the Ottoman administration reflected the dramatic transformation engulfing all three elementary functions. As a result of military defeats, loss of territories, and rising expenses in holding the frontier areas, both the security situation and the economic conditions of the Empire deteriorated. Concerning the control of the means of physical force, the phenomenon of the *derebeys* or the appearance of irregular armies and mercenaries under the control of provincial magnates clearly indicated the loss of central control. The appropriation of the means of violence by local power-holders was further enhanced by the need to dispatch substantial numbers of troops from the core lands of the Empire to its multiple military fronts. This deterioration of internal and external security was interdependent with a dramatic change in the political economy of the Ottoman state: the gradual shift from the state-controlled *timar* system to a semi-autonomous system of tax-farming.

Under changing economic conditions, the state had to secure quick and easy cash returns. Consequently, the sultan dispensed fiefs to the upper strata of society, opening them for both official functionaries and *ayans*. At the beginning these tax-farms were granted for only a brief term; however, 'later the practice spread of granting the tax-farmer a life interest which, by abuse, became heritable and alienable' (Lewis 1961: 446). While its European competitors consolidated the state monopolies of physical force and taxation, the Ottoman state slowly but surely lost central control and became more dependent on its intermediaries. These political and economic developments also affected the legitimacy of Ottoman rule. The social stratification of Ottoman society rested on a traditional symbolic order in which justice (*adalet*) was the key concept of a stable order. 'It meant that within society, each group and each individual should remain in his place ... without trespassing on the rights of others' (Zürcher 1993: 15). The privileges of the ruling elite were legitimate only if they could maintain this order and defend the Islamic community against the outer world (cf. Salzmann 1993: 402–3).

The military defeats, the weak internal security, and tax-farmers who increasingly levied taxes for personal enrichment without government control challenged the legitimacy of the central power. The uneven integration of the Empire into the economic structures of an evolving world market had a further impact on its traditional order. With the Ottoman lands becoming an import market for European manufacturers, many Ottoman artisans became jobless. In the Balkans, Turkish Muslims were gradually transformed from the backbone of the handicrafts into unskilled labourers, where 'a new group of Christian traders, agriculturists, shippers and craftsmen, sprang up and gained wealth, education, and power' (Issawi 1980a: 3). Whereas the basic political and economic structures of Ottoman society were still of a traditional nature, modernisation had already become visible and was experienced in the destruction of the traditional Ottoman order.

Until the reign of Selim III, modernisation took place largely as a result of the interdependencies between the Ottoman Empire and Europe, and the Empire was almost entirely passive under its impact. Being one major source behind the structural changes of Ottoman society and thus behind the decay of the traditional order, modernity had not yet reached the minds of the ruling elite. In opening up the country to modern ideas of training and education as well as in applying modern organisational devices in the administration in the period of early reforms, Selim III and Mahmud II spearheaded a process whereby modernisation found its indigenous social actors. But the historical example showed that modernisation as an active reform process was not possible without the initial participation of traditional forces. Apparently, modernisation means at the same time carrying on features and social forces of the past. In 1808, for example, Sultan Mahmud II was brought to power with the help of a coalition of *ayan* under the leadership of Bayraktar Mustafa Pasha, who turned into a supporter of reform after the deposition of Selim III. In a compromise with the *ayan*, the sultan acknowledged officially the *de facto* power that the *ayan* had already acquired in many provinces. In return, the *ayan*, whose position was now hereditary, formally approved the reorganisation of the Ottoman army and the supremacy of the Sultan in the military and in taxation.[17]

The higher ranks of the *ulema* were another force of the traditional Ottoman elite supporting the reforms of Mahmud II. The *ulema* formed a 'powerful corps of Muslim learned men who dominated the religious institutions, the judiciary and education of the Empire and, in addition, held most important positions in public administration, diplomacy and politics' (Heyd 1961: 63). Although many leading *ulema* had made common cause with the Janissaries in previous revolts, a basic hostility existed between the learned orthodox *ulema* and the mostly illiterate Janissaries, affiliated as they were to the heterodox Bektasi order.[18] As an integrated part of the ruling class with personal ties to the court, the higher *ulema* sanctioned the reforms as required 'for the sake of religion and state' (Heyd 1961: 95). They tempered unrest in their own lower ranks and in the population by bestowing their religious authority upon the major reforms. It is a characteristic feature of the reform process that these important actors, the *ayan* and the *ulema*, were gradually deposed from their positions of power although never completely.

The Tanzimat and the 'Eastern question'

The interrelation between the modernising process and the structural problems of patrimonial domination presented here is salient to the understanding of the dilemma that the Ottoman rulers had to face during the nineteenth century's 'Eastern question'. The autonomous aspirations of the Janissaries, provincial governors, the *ayan*, or *derebeys* clearly indicate how far the internal feudalisation of the Empire had gone. In some cases this process led to the loss of entire provinces. Regional leaders monopolised the political and economic power resources at hand and initiated processes of regional state formation. Hence, what from the Ottoman perspective must be called feudalisation can also be seen as a process, or processes, of monopolisation. Within the international framework of an evolving system of states, the feudalisation of the Ottoman Empire was one of the driving forces for modern state formation in the Middle East and the Balkans.[19]

The expansion at the turn of the century of the Saudi kingdom, whose religiously motivated tribal troops seized the holy cities of Mekka and Medina in 1806, the *de facto* independence of Egypt under Muhammad Ali (1805–48) and his occupation of Ottoman provinces in Syria and Cilicia (1831–40), the search for autonomy of the Lebanese Emir Bashir Shihab II (1788–1840), and the modernisation and formation of an independent Tunisia under Ahmad Bey (1837–55) are examples of the interrelation between the dissolution of the Ottoman Empire and the emergence of the modern political landscape of the Middle East. Even more dramatic than in the Arab territories were the events in the Empire's European provinces. The Serbian Revolts of 1804–6 and 1815–17, the Greek War of Independence (1821–29), the rebellions in Bosnia and the Herzegovina in 1857 and 1875, and the subsequent uprising in Bulgaria (1876), are cases that indicate the precarious state of Ottoman rule in the Balkans.

Beginning with the Greek War of Independence, a particular structure of diplomatic and coercive interaction evolved in which the analytical distinctions between the levels of international, regional and local forces became totally blurred. From an international perspective this 'Eastern question system', as Carl Brown called it, was characterised by a contradictory pattern. While the European powers, especially Britain, were following a policy of settling the minority problems in the Balkans at Ottoman expense, they were at the same time supporting the Empire as 'a would-be bulwark' against the expansionist ambitions of Russia (cf. Brown 1984: 54). This contradiction was due to the fact that events in the Balkans were no longer a matter only for the European balance of power, but also for the European public, now supporting nationalist movements and pushing their governments to intervene.[20] From the Ottoman perspective, the ailing Empire was dragged into a multilateral power struggle among political entities – states, proto-states, local principalities, ethnic and religious groups – all of which justified their violent action for independence by drawing heavily upon the newly established nationalist discourse. Moreover, in their struggle against the Ottoman state, foreign and domestic forces were coalescing, and the Ottoman elite in Istanbul saw itself beset by external conspiracy and internal betrayal.

Given this historical and structural background, it comes as no surprise that the reform efforts of the Tanzimat were not guided by any long-term strategy to modernise society, but rather determined by the political events of the day. Confronted with a deteriorating external and internal security situation and with the integrity and sovereignty of the state at stake, the Ottoman reforms were a classic example of what was called 'defensive modernisation'.[21] Yet the military reform was insufficient to enable it to face external threats, and the modernisation of the Ottoman administration was unable entirely to contain the internal feudalisation of the state. In retrospect, the Tanzimat were rather helpless against the structural constraints that modern social transformation imposed on Ottoman society.

The major reform edicts: from traditional to legal authority
If the Tanzimat aimed at stopping the downward spiral of the Ottoman state, they failed from a twentieth-century perspective. None the less, we have to be aware that the reforms caused massive changes in the social fabric of Ottoman society. The new social forces, whose foundations had been laid by the reforms of the administrative, military and educational institutions of the Ottoman state, later played an essential role in the formation of the Turkish Republic. Furthermore, many of the reforms of the Tanzimat period, as well as the cultural and political debates under the Ottoman intelligentsia, found their continuation in the Turkish nation-state, although with different trends and emphases from those under the imperial order. The major political–administrative trends of the Tanzimat can be summarised as follows:

1 the abolishment of the patrimonial system of tax-farming and the creation of a monetised and rationalised system to levy taxes;

2 the secularisation and formalisation of education and of the administration of justice;

3 the functional differentiation of branches of government;

4 an increasing division of the powers of government leading to the establishment of an Ottoman parliament and an Ottoman constitution;

5 a differentiation of the means of physical force according to the separate realms of internal and external security;

6 the introduction of a new system of provincial administration.

All of these are indicators of a transformation from a traditional system towards a legal system of domination, but they were, nevertheless, initiated by imperial decrees. This top-down character applies to the reforms under Selim III and Mahmud II, as well as to the reform edicts of the Tanzimat. The imperial decree that marks the beginning of the Tanzimat period, the *Hatt-i Sherif* of Gülhane, was a late result of Mahmud's reform efforts. He appointed a commission to work out comprehensive reforms under the leadership of his Minister of Foreign Affairs, Reshid Pasha, 'in many ways the real architect of the nineteenth-century Ottoman reforms' (Lewis 1961: 105). Only a few months after the death of Mahmud II, the *Hatt-i Sherif* was promulgated by his son and successor, Sultan Abdülmecit I (1839–61) in November 1839.

The *Hatt-i Sherif* of Gülhane and the subsequent *Hatt-i Hümayun* of March 1840 aimed at a complete reconstruction of the Ottoman state along Western lines. The text of the first reform edict reminds the people of the past glory of the Empire, its strength and greatness, based on observance of the rules of the holy Koran. The decline of the Empire, which in a 'succession of accidents led to weakness and poverty in the last one hundred and fifty years', is ascribed to the disregard for sacred codes of laws and regulations. In order to improve this situation, the reforms stipulated in the imperial decree should be based on a 'thorough alteration and renewal of ancient customs'. The reform edict thus targets the problems caused by the feudalisation of the state. It aims to improve the situation in the provinces and criticises the corrupt system of tax-farming. The introduction of a regular and fixed system of taxation is suggested, in order to contain the autonomous aspirations of corrupt tax-farmers and to guarantee resources for the defence of the country. New institutions were to stop a further deterioration of security, because in the absence of security 'everyone remains insensible to the voice of the Prince and the country'.

The *Hatt-i Sharif* of Gülhane perfectly reflects the structural changes in the political and economic foundations of the traditional order, and the threats these changes posed for the legitimacy of Ottoman domination in general. The remedies proposed resemble the legal order of a modern state: a guarantee of property and civil rights for all subjects of the Sultan, 'of whatever religion or sect they may be'; the introduction of universal conscription and the reduction of the term of military service to four or five years; the reorganisation of provincial administration, based on functionaries with fixed salaries and on a clear division between private property and the means of administration. The reorganisation of the provinces according to the French model was followed by a series of other legal innovations. In the 1850s and 1860s, state courts and new secular penal, commercial, and maritime codes were introduced alongside the religious *sheriat* courts – which were based on Islamic Law – and new trade laws were enacted, all of them modelled on European examples.[22]

The second Tanzimat period, associated mainly with the political roles of Ali Pasha and Fuad Pasha, starts with the *Hatt-i Hümayun* of 18 February 1856. In this edict Sultan Abdülmecid confirms the reform measures of the *Hatt-i Serif* of Gülhane and the Tanzimat in general, with a strong emphasis on religious liberty and equality for his non-Muslim subjects. The status of the non-Muslim minorities was stipulated according to a legal status of citizenship with general individual rights. Religious freedom, equal rights for admission to public employment and public schools, generally applicable tax regulations and property laws, and laws against corruption, extortion, and torture are major features of the edict. It also takes steps to improve the infrastructure of the Empire, with regulations to guarantee unimpeded commerce and trade (Hurewitz 1956a: 149–53).

Besides the political-administrative reforms, further opening the Ottoman Empire to international trade and foreign capital was another essential element of the second Tanzimat period. Free-trade agreements, such as the one approved between Mahmud II and Britain in the Commercial Convention of Balta Limani in 1838, were confirmed and extended to other European states, opening the Ottoman lands to foreign investment. The Ottoman market was now freely accessible for the sale of European commodities, depriving the Ottoman government of mercantile instruments such as monopolies, taxes, and tolls that could have been used to stop a further deterioration of the financial situation of the state (Zürcher 1993: 49–50). In 1854, two years before the promulgation of Abdülmecit's reform edict, the Ottoman government had already begun borrowing abroad in order to meet the financial difficulties created by the Crimean War (1853–56). Only 16 years later, the Ottoman state found itself completely dependent on foreign loans, while debt servicing consumed one-third of its treasury income (Zürcher 1993: 67–8). Increasing integration in the capitalist world market, based on terms of trade which were to the extreme disadvantage of the Ottoman economy, and the related failure of attempts to reform the financial administration of the Empire led to national bankruptcy in 1875.[23]

It is necessary to analyse the two well-known Tanzimat edicts against the background of both the inter-state competition of the European state system and the power struggle within the Ottoman Empire. As described earlier, the Ottoman rulers had to deal simultaneously with a multiplicity of relatively autonomous actors on the inter-state and the intra-state level.[24] The drawing up of the Hatt-i Serif of 1839 belonged to an era in which the feudalisation of the Empire already threatened its territorial integrity. The Serbian revolts, the Greek War of Independence, the rise of Muhammad Ali and his willingness to challenge even the legitimacy of the Ottoman ruler in Istanbul are cases in point to explain under what intense pressure the reform edict was drafted. In the light of this historical context, the modernising push of the Ottoman reforms of the 1830s and 1840s is easily explicable.

In the Hatt-i Hümayun of 18 February 1856, the external pressure on the Sultan is even greater. The reform edict was promulgated only eighteen days after Russia had accepted preliminary terms to end the Crimean War. Since October 1853, British, French and Ottoman troops had been fighting against Russia, which had occupied the Danubian provinces of the Ottoman Empire in July 1853.[25] The Hatt-i Hümayun was designed to facilitate the admittance of the Ottoman Empire to the 'Concert of Europe' at the Paris Peace Conference, which terminated the Crimean War on 30 March 1856. Article seven of the Paris Peace Treaty contains the declaration that 'the Sublime Porte is admitted to participate in the advantages of the public law and system (*concert*) of Europe' and that the signatories respect the independence and territorial integrity of the Ottoman Empire. Furthermore, the Treaty orders the restoration of 'all parts of the Ottoman territory of which the Russian troops are in possession'. The linkage between the Paris Conference and the reform decree becomes obvious in article nine:

> His Imperial Majesty the Sultan, having, in his constant solicitude for the welfare of his subjects, issued a firman which, while ameliorating their condition without distinction of religion or of race, records his generous intentions towards the Christian population of his Empire, and wishing to give a further proof of his sentiments in that respect, has resolved to communicate to the Contracting Parties the said firman, emanating spontaneously from his sovereign will.[26]

Taking into account the net of constraints in which the Sultan and the Sublime Porte had got caught up, the reference to the 'spontaneous and sovereign' will of the Sultan is almost cynical. While the official admission of the Ottoman Empire to the European state system formally granted the Empire equal rights, it took place at the mercy of the great powers. However, this does not mean that the Tanzimat were just a reaction to the outer and inner constraints the Ottoman government had to face. The Ottoman reformers who acted in this web of power relations were driven not only by structural conditions but also by two other important sources of social action: first, their conviction of the dire necessity of the reforms; second, personal interests. An amalgam of interests and ideas was also behind the new social forces which, as supporters of the reforms, began to endanger the imperial order of the state. The rise of the opposition movement of the 'Young Ottomans', the Ottoman constitution of 1876 and the short parliamentarian experience between December 1876 and February 1878 are indicators that the modern legal content of the reform edicts had developed in a framework of reference for political discourse and action. The political conflicts and intellectual debates of the late Ottoman Empire were increasingly dominated by the new power struggle among modernising forces and by the frictions within the hegemonic bloc that dominated the reform process in the first half of the nineteenth century.

Opposition from within: Ottoman supremacy challenged by modern forces

In the previous chapter we discussed the prominent role of a class of modern functionaries such as officers, administrative clerks, teachers and the intelligentsia. This specific kind of educated bourgeoisie, whose societal power resources were cultural rather than economic and who were directly linked to the institutions of modern statehood, grew in number and kind with the reform process and demanded further participation in state and society. In its reform efforts the Ottoman state depended on the professionalisation of the administrative system and therefore on modern education. Naturally, the traditional lack of interest that Ottoman rulers usually showed toward literacy campaigns underwent a dramatic change during the Tanzimat period.[27] Furthermore, 'the expansion of state activities into new spheres, which included the building of a new educational system, required that Turkish become an all-purpose language, easy to learn and easy to understand' (Kushner 1977: 56).

The modernisation of the Ottoman state entailed the creation of a standardised language accompanied by the emergence of a literate public in the urban centres of the Empire. In the second half of the nineteenth century, this literate public became, through newspapers and books, an essential part of the political discourse. Moreover, since the 1860s a new genre of Ottoman novel developed, revolving around social, cultural and political questions posed by the modernisation of Ottoman society (Mardin 1974: 403). The rise of constitutional and representational ideas, the dissemination of political and nationalist ideologies among the religious minorities of the Empire and the ascent of pan-Turkist, pan-Arab, or pan-Islamic ideologies among the Muslim population of the Empire was associated with the social role of a literate public which from its beginning was interacting with its European counterparts.

In 1865, a group of young intellectuals – westernised bureaucrats, journalists and some modern-oriented ulema – belonging to the lower stratum of the educated bourgeoisie, began to spread their ideas among the literate public (Mardin 1988: 31). The ideas of those young intellectuals, known as 'Young Ottomans', were characterised by an attempt to synthesise Islam with the ideals of the Enlightenment. Kemal Karpat divides their thoughts into three categories. Firstly, the institutional ideas of the Young Ottomans concerned the introduction of a constitutional order and representative institutions, which were to be based on Islamic principles. Secondly, they supported the concept of a strong central state against the autonomous aspirations of ayan and derebeys. Finally, they promoted the idea of a new political identity in which the traditional loyalty to the millet, the religious community, was to be replaced by the vatan, the fatherland, which is above religious, ethnic or regional divisions (Karpat 1972: 262–5).

The Young Ottomans formed a modern political opposition which was nationally minded, liberal in its institutional concepts, and reverted to the legitimate power of traditional Islamic symbols. In agitating against the over-westernised bureaucratic elite of the country, who had almost completely monopolised the resources of the modern state apparatus, the Young

Ottomans combined both a critique of the 'aristocratic' political establishment of the Empire and their own aspirations to participate in the power
resources provided by the modern sectors of Ottoman society. They can be
considered as the Ottoman pioneers of a modern discourse of constitutionalism, a representational system of government, the modern division of
power, and national language reform. This discourse, which grew out of both
the societal changes of the Tanzimat period and the legal spirit of the reform
edicts, was later incorporated into the Turkish Republic.[28]

Together with a group of bureaucrats and officers under the leadership of
the former *grand vezir* Midhat Pasha, the Young Ottomans formed the core of
the Ottoman constitutional movement. In December 1876, this movement,
backed by diplomatic pressure and parts of the Ottoman army, achieved the
promulgation of an Ottoman constitution and the establishment of a
representative assembly. Basically, two main political objects triggered the
short constitutional phase of the Ottoman Empire. On the one hand, it was an
attempt on the part of the bureaucrats and the intelligentsia to curb the power
of the sultan. On the other hand, the introduction of a representational system
was a reaction to the changes in Ottoman society that the modernisation of
the Empire had caused. 'The need and place for a parliament were determined
not by culture but by the functional necessities stemming from a diversified
social structure and a differentiated political system' (Karpat 1972: 267–8).

Ottoman society, under the impact of modernisation, became much more
diversified than under the traditional social order. Influential traditional
forces, such as the sultan himself, provincial notables, tribal leaders, or
traditionally oriented *ulema*, still made up an important part of the Ottoman
social mosaic. Yet genuinely modern forces evolved during the Tanzimat to
play progressively major roles in the economic, political and cultural sectors
of the Empire. Furthermore, individual social groups such as the *ulema*, the
bureaucracy or the army were internally fragmented into forces with different
interests and committed to either modern or traditional values. As is typical
for modernising societies in general, the Ottoman social mosaic resembled
what Ernst Bloch called the contemporaneity of the non-contemporaneous
(Bloch 1985).

The Ottoman parliament, in which essentially the economic interest
groups confronted functionaries of the government, was certainly far from
being a democratic body of representation. However, its debates showed
clearly that the modernisation of the Empire had acquired its own dynamic,
and the idea of a legal system of domination had superseded the legitimacy
and sanctity of traditional authority. The parliamentary representatives
claimed a just and efficient system of taxation, guarantees for the freedom of

the press, and a legal framework for economic transactions and for curbing corruption and favouritism in the administration. In short, the legislative body demanded legal control over the executive power of the state (Karpat 1972: 268–9). Although the parliamentarian phase lasted for only a short period, the fifteen months of constitutional rule marked a turning point. A deep rift had developed within the hegemonic bloc that had dominated the reform process since the destruction of the Janissaries. The genuinely modern forces of the bureaucracy, the army and the intelligentsia were breaking away from the traditional claim to power of the Ottoman dynasty.

In the course of the Tanzimat, the court had lost control of the reforms to the bureaucracy. The bureaucrats of the Tanzimat 'had liberated themselves from the shackles of a slave bureaucracy and had taken into their own hands the reins of the modernization movement' (Mardin 1974: 407). The instrument of domination gradually became the power behind the traditional authority of the sultan. In this social process, however, the new bureaucratic elite took over the pretension of the sultans; to restore the past glory of Ottoman power. Moreover, they also became assimilated into the aristocratic social habitus of Ottoman court society and of the diplomatic aristocracy of Europe which was the social environment in which many Ottoman officials became westernised (cf. Findley 1989: 188ff). Held together in a hegemonic bloc by a coalition of interests, the aristocratic values and elitist attitudes of the Ottomans became a part of the social fabric of the new bureaucratic elite. Thus the bureaucrats of the Tanzimat themselves acted like potentates (Mardin 1962a: 108–12).

As a result of the joint hegemonic bloc initiating the Ottoman reform process, the modern elite of the Empire, whose power resources were grounded in the structural changes caused by modernisation, incorporated major features of the social habitus of the traditional Ottoman elite. As Ilter Ortayli put it, 'they continued the world view and life style of the old masters of society'.[29] The social habitus of the modern reforming elite still carried the aristocratic dualism of Ottoman society, with its contempt for the mass of ordinary people. Although the Young Ottomans and later the Young Turks criticised this neglect of 'the people', the stark dichotomy between the rulers and the ruled, which over time acquired an ever stronger notion of cultural superiority, they later adopted this attitude of the bureaucratic elite of the Tanzimat (Mardin 1969: 274–81).

Concerning the political culture, this habitus was symbolised in the military title of *pasha*, which designated a leading representative of the Ottoman Empire and of the Turkish Republic. In this term the division between civilian and military aspects of state power is blurred, and the fact that it has continued to be used indicates to a certain degree the authoritarian notion of statehood in Turkey (Birand 1991: 178).

Hamidian absolutism and the end of the Ottomans

The more than thirty years of Sultan Abdülhamid's reign (1876–1908) are usually referred to as a period of absolutist or despotic rule, and indeed, while the Tanzimat were characterised by the growing power of the bureaucracy and the rise of constitutional forces, Abdülhamid II dissolved parliament and suspended the Ottoman constitution in 1878. He cracked down on any kind of opposition to his rule, built up a repressive network of information services, and muzzled the critical journalists and novelists who had just started to spread their ideas to the literate public. Ironically the same autocratic ruler, who turned against all legal and social checks to his power and who temporarily restored the supremacy of the palace over the bureaucracy, had to proclaim constitutional rule twice. The Hamidian period began with the proclamation of the Ottoman constitution three months after Abdülhamid's succession to the throne in September 1876, and it ended on 23 July 1908 with the restoration of the constitution by Abdülhamid after the so-called Young Turk revolution, a sign that the social forces aroused by the legal spirit of the Tanzimat could only temporarily be suppressed.

Whether Abdülhamid's reign was a continuation or a deviation from the Tanzimat is a matter of interpretation. He continued the attempts of the Tanzimat reformers to modernise and centralise the administration and to enforce central state control over the provinces. Furthermore, he extended educational reforms considerably and enhanced the Empire's communication facilities. Although they were under heavy censorship, the dissemination of newspapers, periodicals, and books increased further, as did the influence of Western ideas owing mainly to members of the literate public in exile (Lewis 1961: 181–94). Hence, the reforms under Abdülhamid perfectly served the mobilisation of the administrative power of the state. Subordinating the reforms to 'unity and survival' (Duguid 1973: 139), he used the modernised state apparatus as a means of surveillance. In this respect Hamidian absolutism was a culmination of the reform process from above, which had created the necessary means for the state to monitor its populace more closely and to secure the sultan's domination through 'enlightened despotism'.[30]

A break with the tendencies of the Tanzimat can be seen in Abdülhamid's instrumentalisation of Islam as an ideology of unity. While the Tanzimat period saw a gradual decline in the role of religious dignitaries within the state elite, Abdülhamid II surrounded himself with ulema and sufi sheikhs, the latter the traditional leaders of Islamic orders (Zürcher 1993: 83). Although dedicated to further modernising the Ottoman state, he reintegrated these traditional religious dignitaries, who still had a strong influence on the people, into the ruling elite.[31] Selim Deringil argues that Abdülhamid's pan-Islamic rhetoric and appeals to Muslim solidarity were a reaction to a legitimacy crisis of the Empire that began with Mahmud II and culminated in Hamidian times:

> This was a crisis that had both external and internal dimensions. The external dimension was the uphill struggle to secure the acceptance of the Ottoman State as a legitimate polity in the international system. The internal dimension was the struggle to overcome the 'legitimation deficit' that accrued as the state permeated society physically and ideologically to an unprecedented extent. (Deringil 1998: 166)

According to the external and internal dimensions that Deringil mentions, the need to reconfirm the legitimacy of Ottoman rule resulted from a paradoxical development: that the nineteenth-century reform process in the Ottoman Empire led to a strong state in a weak Empire. While the politics of centralisation and modernisation of the state apparatus provided the sultan with the necessary instrument for his autocratic rule, the pan-Islamic ideology of Hamidian rule proves its growing dependency on ideological power resources. In the face of continued weakening of the Empire in economic and political terms, the state had to resort to the authority provided by the symbolic power of Islam. Deringil's study tells us how the late Ottoman state attempted to dominate the means of symbolic reproduction and to acquire the third 'key monopoly', the control over the religious symbolic order. Being trapped in the 'no-man's land' between traditional and legal authority, the politicisation of Islam was one measure to safeguard the integrity of the state. The other was to hyper-centralise power in the hands of the sultan, not only as a curb on the internal opposition,[32] but also as a reaction to the humiliations caused by the economic and political emasculation of the Empire from outside. In order to understand how Hamidian absolutism reflects the downward spiral of the Ottoman state, we must take a final glance at the economic and political developments that culminated in the late nineteenth century.

Culmination of economic and political decline

In economic terms, the establishment of a foreign Public Debt Administration in 1881 was one of the most humiliating events in the early years of Abdülhamid's rule. Set up to serve the interests of investors in Ottoman government securities, the debt administration controlled a large and growing share of the revenues of the Ottoman state (Findley 1980: 223 and 281). The incapacitating institutionalisation of foreign control over the political economy of the Empire, however, was somehow a logical step in its unfavourable incorporation into the world economy. The integration of the material reproduction of Ottoman society into the capitalist world market happened despite an almost complete exclusion of the Ottoman state. In this alienation of the state from the economy, the interplay of three factors was essential: intrinsic contradictions between political centralisation and the monetisation of the economy; the neglect of economic reforms by the state elite; and uneven ethnic and religious integration into the modern economy.

Contrary to traditional modes of production, a modern economy is based on the commercialisation and monetisation of material reproduction. As an abstract power resource, money also serves as means of exchange, linking production, distribution, and consumption of material goods and so establishing abstract social relations. Thus the monetisation of the economy contributes to the functional separation of political and economic realms, as well as to the social separation of the individual from society.[33] The attempt by the Ottoman state to achieve monopoly of taxation, and therefore to enhance the material resources necessary for its political centralisation, was counteracted by the individualising tendencies that resulted from the abstract character of money. While the state was increasingly dependent on money as an abstract and freely transferable power resource, the monetisation of administration and economy also supported the autonomous aspirations of local magnates. Basing their material power on money, they were able to consolidate their regional strongholds and to escape direct state control. Given the particular historical conditions of the reforms, the Ottoman government was confronted with the paradox that their policy of centralisation at the same time contributed to the feudalisation of the state.[34]

The economic alienation of the Ottoman state was further intensified by the general attitude of its ruling elite, almost neglecting economic reforms and the application of mercantilist policies to protect or stimulate the economy (Zürcher 1993: 18). The state's few economic initiatives were characterised by their exclusive devotion to the manufacturing of goods for governmental and military use, and an ignorance of the role of raw materials and economic infrastructure (Clark 1974: 66 and Issawi 1980b: 472). After a failed initiative to build up manufacturing facilities in the Istanbul and Marmara regions during the early Tanzimat period (Clark 1974: 67), the pace of industrialisation slowed down again, as shown by the fact that in 1913 only 17,000 workers were employed in factories that used power.[35] The Ottoman state's salient exclusion of the civilian market ran parallel with European commodities conquering the Ottoman market. Consequently, the

Empire's traditional manufacturing economy faced a rapid decline. In moving European goods more quickly to formerly remote areas, the modernisation of the Ottoman infrastructure further accelerated the deterioration of local production (Issawi 1980b: 470). Thus, the reforms had a contradictory effect on the economy and helped to increase the Empire's economic dependence.

Given the insignificance of inter-regional trade and the dominance of manufacturing for local markets, we can hardly see the Ottoman Empire as an economic unit that entered the world market (Zürcher 1993: 20). In addition to stark regional disparities, a sharp religious division developed in the Ottoman economy as a consequence of the traditional millet system. In the nineteenth century, its more traditional agrarian wing consisted mainly of Muslims, whilst the modern capitalist sector was made up mostly of non-Muslims (Karpat 1972: 260). One reason behind this division was the close association of landownership with military service. As the non-Muslim millets were traditionally excluded from the right to carry arms, they were not able to acquire land in exchange for military service. Thus the economic attention of non-Muslims was directed rather to trade and finance. Another reason goes back to the autonomy rights that the millet system provided, which opened early channels of trade and communication between Christian communities and European states.

Based on the legal framework of the millet system, the so-called 'Capitulations' became an instrument for European interference in the economic and political affairs of the Empire. From the Treaty of Amity and Commerce, concluded between the Ottoman Empire and France in 1535, the Capitulations developed into a class of commercial treaties under which Western nationals enjoyed extraterritorial privileges (Hurewitz 1956a: 1). Under the impact of the Eastern Question, Capitulations were granted for all European nations, and the inner autonomy of the Christian communities achieved a degree of formal institutionalisation unknown to the traditional order. The Capitulations not only opened doors for tax evasion, but also strengthened political and economic ties between the Christian minorities and the West. The modern sector of the Ottoman economy therefore acquired a Christian and an extraterritorial face, obstructing the efforts of the Tanzimat reformers to integrate the minorities politically. Towards the end of the nineteenth century, 'over 90 per cent of the industrial establishments with more than ten workers were owned by non-Muslims' (Zürcher 1993: 89–90).

In political terms, the intensification of the Eastern Question completed the disintegrative tendencies of the economic development. Abdülhamid's accession to the throne had been preceded by nationalist revolts in Herzegovina and Bulgaria, and soon the Empire was again embroiled in a disastrous war with Russia (1877–78), which led to the humiliating Treaty of San Stefano in March 1878. Only the intervention of the great powers prevented the almost complete loss of Ottoman territory in Europe. At the Berlin Congress in July 1878, the Ottoman Empire was allowed to retain its formal supremacy over an autonomous Bulgaria. But Serbia, Romania and Montenegro became independent, and Austria–Hungary was allowed to occupy Bosnia and Herzegovina. Finally, the Russians were granted the northeastern Anatolian provinces of Batum, Kars and Ardahan (Matuz 1985: 238–9).

After parcelling out the European provinces at the Berlin Congress, European interference drifted from the Balkans into the Anatolian heartland of the Ottoman state. At Berlin, the British government has assumed a direct interest in the welfare of the Armenian population in eastern Anatolia, and two European-inspired reform programmes were forced on the Empire in 1879 and 1896 (Duguid 1973: 141). Sultan Abdülhamid was confronted with British plans for Armenian autonomy in the eastern provinces, implying European supervision over tax collection, judicial procedures and the gendarmerie (Salt 1990: 308–10). While the Ottoman government was trying hard to centralise state power, European interference was pressing for a decentralisation of the provincial administration. Moreover, the British reform plans encouraged Armenian aspirations for autonomy in a region with an entirely mixed population.

This renewed European interference coincided with Abdülhamid's attempt to re-establish state control over eastern Anatolia. In successfully subduing most of the derebeys and Kurdish tribal leaders in the 1830s and 1840s, the Ottoman state was able to establish its relative control over the eastern parts of Anatolia.[36] However, the security situation completely deteriorated during the Ottoman–Russian War. In order to regain government control, Istanbul used the existing rivalry between the Kurdish agas in the countryside and urban notables. The government tried to manipulate the various groups so that none was powerful enough to challenge Ottoman sovereignty (Duguid 1973: 144–5). As a mechanism of supervision and control, as well as in order to be prepared for another war with Russia, the hamidieh cavalry corps had been formed in 1891. They consisted of Kurdish tribesmen attracted by exemption from conscription and taxation. At the same time Armenian revolutionary forces, encouraged by the European reform proposals, began their militant activities, 'provoking Muslim reprisals and causing suspicion to fall on the Armenian communities in general' (Salt 1990: 312). Eventually, the central government lost control over the tense situation and the Kurdish *hamidieh* regiments, acting autonomously, became the major force in the violent escalation leading to the Armenian massacres of 1895–96.[37]

Again, Ottoman attempts to impose state control found themselves within the constraints of the Eastern Question system and ended in collective violence. There is no doubt that as far as the economic and political causes behind the Ottoman decline are concerned, the reign of Abdülhamid II can be seen as a culmination of previous developments. Yet, Abdülhamid's despotic attempt to keep things firmly under control also finally failed. Unable to contain the external forces of decay, in the long run the despotic regime lost its legitimacy and even strengthened internal forces of opposition. Therefore, the period of Hamidian absolutism itself became the stage for the formation of social actors and political ideas that were eventually to put an end to Ottoman rule. A brief examination of those domestic developments will lead us to the conclusions of this chapter.

Turkish nationalism and the Young Turk revolution

When the Eastern Question system reached the Anatolian heartland of the Empire, Anatolia became at the same time the heartland of a new political ideology. In the course of the Tanzimat, the territorial notion of the Ottoman Empire had undergone a change. The relation between adminstrative modernisation and identity formation was reflected in the replacement of the classical notion of *dar al-islam*, the 'Abode of Islam', by the modern concept of the territorial nation-state and its people. As we have seen, the Young Ottomans were the first political group to promote the new concept of political loyalty to the fatherland (*vatan*). Yet, while the constitutional movement of the 1870s aimed at an integration of the different *millets* under the umbrella of an Ottoman nation, in Hamidian times the concept of *vatan* acquired a more pronounced Muslim and Turkish connotation, and Anatolia became its territorial core. It was under the reign of Abdülahmid II 'that Ottoman identity assumed an increasingly Turkish character, even if this identity was packaged in universalist Islamic terms' (Deringil 1998: 11).

The rise of Turkish nationalism took place in the international intellectual climate of historical, racial and linguistic thinking of the late nineteenth century. The burgeoning interest in Turkish history was 'coupled with the growing awareness that Turkish history was in effect one's own history'. Intellectual circles developed an idealised history of the Turks and their 'inborn capacity to become civilized and to civilize others' (Kushner 1977: 29–31). Against the background of Armenian and Greek nationalist separatism and foreign intervention, this historical reasoning and the ongoing language discussion, revolving around the purification of the Turkish language, supplied the intellectual justification for a culturally based Turkish nationalism and the concept of an essentially Turkish Anatolia (Kushner 1977: 52–80). As in the Armenian and Greek cases, Turkish nationalism developed as an ideology and as a social movement in a close interplay between domestic opposition groups and exiled communities in Europe.

Between the formation of the first organised opposition group in 1889 and the Young Turk revolution, Abdülhamid II was able to keep the revolutionary forces at bay with a mixture of coercion and co-option.[38] From its foundation in 1895, however, the organisation behind the Young Turk Movement – the Committee of Union and Progress – gained strength and was increasingly able to rally support within the ranks of the armed forces. The mülkiye and the harbiye schools,[39] the two training centres for the bureaucracy and the military, developed into the main breeding grounds for the Committee's clandestine activities. Thus the two cornerstones of Abdül-hamid's educational reform undermined the very foundations of his absolutist rule. At the turn of the century the centre of internal opposition had moved from Istanbul to Salonica, from where a group of young officers, civil servants and intellectuals controlled the activities of the opposition in the Empire. Triggered by the discussions about a Russian–British intervention in Macedonia, the Ottoman troops posted there mutinied, and the Young Turk Movement demanded in July 1908, in a co-ordinated campaign, the restoration of the constitution.

Sultan Abdülhamid's attempt violently to crush the insurgence failed, as the troops he had despatched showed signs of refusing to do their duty. Finally, the Sultan had to give in; the servants of the Ottoman reforms, the new educated professionals in the military and the civil service, had deposed their imperial masters. Although the Ottoman monarchy formally existed until the proclamation of the Turkish Republic in 1923, the Young Turk revolution marks the end of the imperial order. The social and political dynamics of the reform process eventually destroyed the foundations of the sultanate and put an end to more than 500 years of Ottoman rule. From the perspective of the palace, the apprehension of external conspiracy and internal betrayal, expressed most vividly in the paranoid character of Abdülhamid II, had seemingly been proven right. While the European powers had frequently broken their promises to guarantee and respect the integrity and sovereignty of the Ottoman state, social forces within the new army and the modern bureaucracy, built up to secure that state, finally turned against the symbol of the Empire.

Conclusions: demise and survival of the Ottoman Empire

Our analysis of the Ottoman modernisation process shows that it comprised two dimensions: first, the structural transformation of traditional Ottoman society caused by the general modernisation process; second, the deliberate political action of a reforming state elite. In the eighteenth and nineteenth centuries these interrelated passive and active dimensions of social transformation caused dramatic changes with regard to the elementary functions of the social reproduction of Ottoman society. Political involvement in a competitive system of states, economic integration into the rising world market, and the dissemination of the political and scientific thoughts of a modern global culture undermined the social foundations on which the Empire had rested for centuries. Reacting to symptoms of this fundamental structural change, and in order to cope with the inherent weaknesses of patrimonial administration, the palace and the higher echelons of the Ottoman bureaucracy instigated reforms that focused chiefly on the reorganisation of the control of the means of physical force, according to standards given by the model of the modern European nation-state. In the words of Charles Tilly, the modernisation of the Ottoman Empire took an almost purely coercive trajectory with little space for the accumulation and concentration of capital (cf. Tilly 1990: 137–3).

The reformers' attempts to monopolise the means of physical force and to reorganise the traditional political structure of the Empire, which was based on a cluster of semi-autonomous survival units, led to a process of political competition among monopolising and feudalising forces. In this process the monopoly formation at central state level was counteracted by the aspirations of regional powers, which tried in turn to monopolise the resources of political and economic power. What has to be explained as feudalisation from the perspective of the central state can be interpreted from a regional perspective as the formation of monopolies, albeit on a lower level. Contrary to Elias' theoretical definition, however, this first phase of monopoly formation was a process, historically, not of free competition, but of the complex and interdependent action among a multiplicity of players in the so-called Eastern Question system. The difficult situation for the Ottoman government was further aggravated in the second half of the nineteenth century: with the rise of a literate public and the constitutional movement, a new internal front emerged, which signalled the overlapping of the first phase of monopoly formation with its second phase, the nationalisation of the state monopoly. From now on the differentiation between foreign enemies, traditional or modern separatism, and internal opposition became blurred.

The almost total neglect of economic reforms and the regional and religious disparities of the Ottoman economy intensified disintegrative tendencies in the political realm. The historical experience of the Ottomans contradicts Elias' theoretical assumption that the monetisation of economic exchange generally supports the formation of a stable central authority. Although the Ottoman policy of centralisation had to rely on taxes by money payment, the monetisation of the economy was in the long run and in the particular historical context rather to the advantage of decentralising forces. Furthermore, as shown by the absolutist reign of Abdülhamid II, the coercive path of modernisation led to a growing crisis of legitimacy for the traditional system of domination on which the sultanate still rested, despite all reforms. The defensive modernisation of the Ottoman rulers had finally undermined its initial purpose: to safeguard the traditional order through reforms from above.

Against this background, several specific patterns of Ottoman modernisation can be discerned that had an impact on modern Turkey in general. This impact concerns both the institutional structures of the Turkish state and the social habitus of its political elite. The instruments of modern state domination, the army and the bureaucracy, triggered by military security concerns, became not only the foci, but also the driving forces of Ottoman and Turkish modernisation. The institutions of the modern state came not through bargaining among different social actors, but through imposition by the ruling elite. The authoritarian character of the Ottoman reforms and their coercive trajectory are reflected in the strict hierarchy of state institutions and the almost complete identification between state apparatus and state elite. Turkish modernisation, driven by security concerns, acquired two distinctive faces. On the one hand, it became a strategy of adjustment to external constraints; on the other hand, it was conducted internally as an educational programme imposed by an authoritarian elite.

As we have seen earlier, the temporary coalition of interests between the traditional elite and the rising modern state elite led to a merger of their attitudes and values. The social habitus of the military–bureaucratic elite, and of parts of the Ottoman intelligentsia, incorporated aspects of the patriarchal elitism of the Ottoman rulers. The huge gap between the court and the people was thus perpetuated in the habitus of the new elite, which saw itself in the position of enlightened teacher. Despite this distinct elitism, the world-view of the modern Ottoman elite was deeply influenced by the Empire's precarious security situation. Later we will discuss the fact that the atmosphere of conspiracy and betrayal, in which the Ottoman state elite was fighting on multiple fronts, also made a remarkable impression on the world-view of the Turkish republican elite.

Although the Ottoman Empire disappeared as a traditional patrimonial state, as a political unit without unity, it has survived not only in the political structures of the Turkish state and in the social habitus of its elite, but also in the political culture and the conflict structures of both the Middle East and the Balkans, where traces of the processes of monopolisation and feudalisation described earlier, and of the specific features of the modernisation of Ottoman society, can be observed. The decline of the Ottoman Empire was simultaneously accompanied by the rise of a new order, which incorporated a multiplicity of patterns developed under the impact of Ottoman modernisation. Temporarily hidden behind the dominant international structures of imperialism and later the Cold War, the Ottoman legacy has now become visible again in an emerging Greater Middle East. How the successor of the Empire, the Turkish Republic, has been dealing with this new situation will be examined in the following chapters.

Notes

1   See Jorga (1990: 313–16); Lewis (1961: 78–80); Matuz (1985: 218); Zürcher (1993: 32–7).

2   The *grand vezir* can be described as the acting head of the Ottoman government, who executed the will of the sultan and met with the high ranks of the Ottoman administration at the Sublime Porte, the latter became in the terminology of the nineteenth century a synonym for the Ottoman government.

3   Cf. Inalcik (1964: 49–53), Karpat (1972: 251) and Mardin (1988: 30).

4   For a different assessment of the role of Selim III, see Shaw (1968: 31).

5   Clark gives an example of Selim's incognito visits to inspect newly established factories (Clark 1974: 75).

6   The Translation Chamber was set up in 1833. During the Greek War of Independence (1821–29), the predominantly Greek translators (*dragomans*) of the Sublime Porte fell under suspicion and were dismissed.

7   This periodisation follows that of Serif Mardin (1962a: 3).

8   Here, the adjective 'modern' refers to the functional role, the power resources, and the related social interests of those actors who constitute themselves in relation to processes such as the textualisation, centralisation and administration of knowledge rather than to the social habitus of a group or of individuals.

9   Behind the Eastern Question was the intensive interplay of two processes: the Ottoman role in the state system and its increasing internal feudalisation. A short definition of the Eastern Question is given by Zürcher: 'The question of how to satisfy competing Balkan nationalism and the imperialist ambitions of the great powers without causing the destruction of the Ottoman Empire, or if its destruction was inevitable …, to dismember it without upsetting the balance of power in Europe and causing a general war, was known throughout the nineteenth century as the "Eastern Question"' (Zürcher 1993: 40).

10   This becomes clear in view of the educational reforms of Mahmud II. The schools

established under his reign aimed not at instructing the populace at large, but at creating an educated class of bureaucrats to increase the efficiency of a centralised state administration (Karpat 1972: 256).

11 Issawi, for example, gives a list of 25 'major wars' in which the Empire was involved between 1768 and 1923. He omits to list a number of 'important expeditions' of the Ottoman army against insurrections in the Balkans and in its Arab territories (Issawi 1980a: 3–4).

12 Cf. Inalcik (1964, 1977), Kellner-Heinkele (1987) and Salzmann (1993).

13 About the *gazi* image in Ottoman history, see Kafadar (1995).

14 According to the theoretical framework of this book, it must be stressed again that modernity is not to be considered as an immanent quality of European societies. The equation of modernisation with Westernisation is rather a result of the historical fact that the 'breakthrough' of the 'Great Transformation' (Polanyi 1957) happened to take place in Europe, from which it spread over the globe. That precursors of modern political and economic institutions, as well as modern ideas, could be observed in other parts of the world was one of the major incentives for Weber's world historical studies. For a still valuable account of indigenous modern developments in the world of Islam, see the study by Maxim Rodinson (1966).

15 Cf. Inalcik (1964: 43–4 and 1977: 27) and Matuz (1985: 187).

16 Cf. the introduction in Naff and Owen (1977).

17 See Lewis (1961: 74–6), Matuz (1985: 214–16) and Karpat (1964: 79–80).

18 The Bektasi order is a mystical Islamic brotherhood founded in Anatolia by Haji Bektas Vali in the thirteenth century. With its Shia (Alevi) background and the incorporation of Christian elements, the Bektasi order is of a syncretistic nature and has therefore been opposed by the Sunni Muslim orthodoxy.

19 For an account on the moulding forces of the Arab state system, see Harik (1990).

20 A more precise description of this argument can be found in Anderson (1966: 53–87) and Brown (1984: 46–56).

21 The German historian Hans-Ulrich Wehler defined the term 'defensive modernisation' as a political strategy of the traditional elite of a country to adjust to outer constraints imposed by the dominant power of a revolutionary country. One purpose of this strategy is to safeguard the traditional order through reforms from above against revolution from below. Defensive modernisation is the attempt to prevent major changes in the political, economic and social power relations of a society by limited reforms (Wehler 1989: 345, 532–3).

22 Quotations are all from Hurewitz (1956a: 113–16); see also Lewis (1961: 106–28), Matuz (1985: 224–26) and Schölch (1987: 384 ff).

23 According to statistics presented by Issawi, 45 per cent of the gross amount of money borrowed between 1854 and 1914 was used to liquidate previous debts of the Ottoman governments (Issawi 1980a: 362–3).

24 On the inter-state level, Britain, France, Russia, Austro-Hungary and Prussia (later Germany) played the major roles. On the intra-state level, the Ottoman government had to deal with separatist movements in the Balkans and the Arab provinces, as well as with domestic opposition forces.

25 In January 1855, the King of Sardinia joined the allies against Russia (see

Anderson 1966: 125–45).

26 All quotations from Hurewitz (1956a: 154).

27 The introduction of printing presses in the Empire gives us a good example. The Jewish community, for instance, was allowed to introduce a press as early as 1493–94, but only on condition they did not print in Turkish or Arabic. While the Armenian community soon followed, the first printing press for the dissemination of papers and books among the Muslim population came as late as 1727. Before 1830 the number of books printed did not exceed one hundred; see Karpat (1964: 255–7).

28 For a comprehensive study of the Young Ottomans, see Mardin (1962a).

29 As cited in Deringil (1998: 169).

30 See Lewis' chapter about Abdülhamid (Lewis 1961: 175–209).

31 One should not forget that we are here mainly concerned with structural change and social action within the ranks of the elite. Although the reform process had a strong impact on the Ottoman society as a whole, in Hamidian times most of the populace was still living within the confines of the traditional millet system, and they perceived the world in the moral categories derived from the symbolic orders of religion.

32 In this respect the deposition of Sultan Abdülaziz in 1876 and attempts to depose Abdülhamid II in the early years of his reign belong to the personal background of Abdülhamid's move to despotic rule (cf. Lewis 1961: 175–80).

33 Still one of the best sociological studies of this process is that by Georg Simmel (1989).

34 With regard to the contradictions inherent in the Ottoman policy of centralisation, this study rejects Deringil's criticism and agrees with Salzmann's view 'that the Ottoman state became a victim of its own policies of centralization'. See Deringil (1998: 9) and Salzmann (1993).

35 See Issawi (1980a: 56). The figure must be compared with a general population of fifteen million.

36 The letters written by the Prussian General Helmuth von Moltke, who was involved in Ottoman military activities at that time, give an interesting account of the applied methods of coercion and co-option, as well as of the general security situation in Anatolia during the 1830s (Moltke 1981).

37 There are different points of view about Abdülhamid's role in the Armenian massacres. Whereas Zeidner claims that one reason behind the building up of the hamidieh regiments was the sultan's intention to suppress the Armenians violently, Jeremy Salt explains the escalation of the events by a complex interplay between the Ottoman sultan, the British government, Christian missionaries, Armenian nationalists and Kurdish tribes, see Zeidner (1976) and Salt (1993).

38 Concerning the co-option of members of the Young Ottomans, see Mardin (1962a: 398).

39 The harbiye school was the major training centre for the officers of the Ottoman army and can be translated as 'War College'. The term mülkiye stems from the department of internal affairs first established by Mahmud II in 1836, and was then used for the non-military and non-ecclesiastical servants of the Ottoman state (Lewis 1961: 374).

4 National Resurrection
The Early Turkish Republic

The Republican state and its cultural revolution

On 29 October 1923, the Grand National Assembly in Ankara accepted a draft amendment of the constitution that had been prepared by Mustafa Kemal Pasha and Ismet Pasha (Inönü) the night before. In the amendment it was stipulated that the Turkish state have a republican form of government and that the Grand National Assembly elect as head of state a president from among its own members. The resolution was passed by 158 votes with more than 100 abstentions at half past eight in the evening. Fifteen minutes later the deputies elected Mustafa Kemal, later named Atatürk ('father of the Turks'), as the first President of the Turkish Republic. Mustafa Kemal then appointed Ismet Inönü as his prime minister. With a 101-gun salute the proclamation of the Republic was announced throughout the whole country the same night.[1]

The final termination of dynastic rule marks a radical turning-point after many centuries of Ottoman political history. Yet this profound change was not as enthusiastically received as Mustafa Kemal's own account of the events would lead one to believe (cf. Atatürk 1963: 673). Even within the National Movement there was strong support for a constitutional monarchy, and it was not by chance that some of its leading proponents happened to be in Istanbul while the amendment to the constitution was being pushed through. It was not until late September 1923 that Mustafa Kemal had used the word 'republic' for the very first time in an interview with the *Neue Freie Presse* in Vienna (Dumont 1983: 145). The response that the interview provoked made clear that the political future of Turkey had not yet been decided and that a long debate on this issue might be counterproductive to republican aspirations. With the constitutional amendments of October 1923, the tactician Mustafa Kemal confronted the political scene with a *fait accompli*.

59

The proclamation of the Turkish Republic was the final step towards abandoning the patrimonial identity of the Empire, and was the key event in a series of political and cultural reform implemented during the fifteen years of Mustafa Kemal's presidency. The main aims of these reforms were, first, the complete destruction of the political symbols and institutions of the Ottoman Empire, and second, the formation of a Turkish nation-state and the construction of a Turkish nation. The political reforms had already been started in November 1922 with the abolition of the Ottoman sultanate and the subsequent flight of Sultan Mehmet VI, who left Istanbul for Malta on a British warship (Lewis 1961: 259). Only a few months after the proclamation of the Republic, Mustafa Kemal went further with the demolition of the political institutions of the Ottoman Empire. In March 1924, the Caliphate was abolished and the Ottoman dynasty was forbidden to reside in the Turkish Republic. In the same month, the religious courts and Islamic schools, the juridical function of the chief mufti, and the ministries of religious affairs and of pious foundations were dissolved. In 1926, the government finally enforced new secular law codes drafted according to Swiss, German and Italian models.

The iconoclastic character of the cultural reforms can best be documented in Mustafa Kemal's own words. In his famous five-day speech to the congress of the Republican People's Party from 15–20 October 1927 in Ankara, regarding the prohibition of the traditional head-gear of Ottoman bureaucrats, the fez, he declared:

> Gentlemen, it was necessary to abolish the fez, which sat on our heads as a sign of ignorance, of fanaticism, of hatred to progress and civilisation, and to adopt in its place the hat, the customary headdress of the whole civilised world, thus showing, among other things, that no difference existed in the manner of thought between the Turkish nation and the whole family of civilised mankind (Atatürk 1963: 738).

The enforcement of this hat-law (1925) went parallel to the closure of religious brotherhoods, convents, sacred tombs and other places of worship. Moreover, the government abolished religious titles such as sheikh or dervish. In 1926, the Gregorian Calendar came into effect, and two years later the Latin alphabet and Western numerals were introduced.[2] In 1934, Ankara enforced a new law requiring Turks to adopt surnames, and the pilgrimage to Mecca was prohibited. Finally, in 1935, Sunday became the official day of rest instead of the Muslim Friday. This cultural transformation of Turkish society was accompanied by striking changes in the role of women in public life. As early as 1924, the coeducation of girls and boys was introduced, and ten years later the regime granted active and passive female suffrage (Göle 1996: 14).

The introduction of political equality for women went along with other bold and symbolic events, such as the first Miss Turkey contest in 1929 and the opening of public beaches for women in the early 1930s (Ahmad 1993: 87–8).

The deliberate dissolution of Ottoman–Muslim culture was completed with the establishment of two institutions that served the purpose, under the personal leadership of Mustafa Kemal, of national identity building: the Turkish Historical Society (1931) and the Turkish Linguistic Society (1932). The Turkish Historical Society's task was to write a national history in order to enable the people to imagine a common historical culture. This national history was grounded on a universal idea that all civilisations are based on the ancient Turkic civilisation. The 'Turkish Historical Thesis' holds that the Turks had been forced by natural disasters to leave their ancient homelands in Central Asia and migrate to different parts of the world. In the Middle East the Sumerians and the Hittites should be considered as predecessors of the Anatolian Turks, linking the history of their ancient empires with the national history of the Turkish Republic. In keeping with these claims, the Turkish Linguistic Society invented the so-called 'Sun Language Theory'. This theory proposed that 'pure Turkish', as an ancient language uninfluenced by Middle Eastern cultures, had been the foundation stone for the development of many, if not all, other languages.[3]

There is no doubt that these drastic iconoclastic measures – especially language reform, which severed future Turkish generations from the written Ottoman cultural heritage – can be described as a cultural revolution. For the republican elite, modernisation became synonymous with Westernisation or Europeanisation. In this respect the Kemalists followed the ideas of Ziya Gökalp (1876–1924), whom Mustafa Kemal himself called the 'intellectual father of the new Republic' (Özelli 1974: 81). In The Principles of Turkism, Gökalp responded to the political and cultural threats of a Muslim world faced by European imperialism as follows: 'There is only one way to escape these dangers, which is to emulate the progress of the Europeans in science, industry and military and legal organization, in other words to equal them in civilization. And the only way to do this is to enter European civilization completely' (Gökalp 1968: 45–6). In the light of Gökalp's appeal to emulate the European example, the proclamation of the Turkish Republic was as much a political turning-point as the starting-point of both a cultural revolution and Turkey's deliberate march from the Middle East towards the West. However, this radical picture of the Kemalist reforms also served as a smokescreen to hide the continuities between Ottoman modernisation and the formation of a Turkish nation-state. The Ottoman state and its society did not just disappear, and modern Turkey was much more than an 'invention by Mustafa

Kemal' (Dumont 1983). The foundation of the Turkish Republic was rather the national resurrection of social, political and cultural patterns of Ottoman society, although in a new Western guise.

It was not only that the early Republic inherited the complex and precarious security context of the Empire, but also that Mustafa Kemal followed the example of imposing reforms from the top. Like Ottoman modernisation, the Kemalist reforms were designed to defend the state apparatus against external and internal threats and to secure the position of the military–bureaucratic elite. Moreover, both the social background of the republican state elite and their world-view and political ideas rested on the previous reform process and the social change it had stirred in Ottoman society. In three sections, we will examine this continuity of state-centred modernisation and its impact on the political and social structures of the Turkish Republic and on the social habitus of the Kemalist elite.

In the first part, the formation of the republican state will be analysed against the background of both the outer constraints imposed by the European power struggle and the internal resistance that Kemalists had to face. The security predicaments imposed by this violent struggle with external and internal foes are reflected in the Kemalist world-view and in the authoritarian structures of the republican state. Furthermore, they became incorporated into the foundational myth and political culture of Turkey. The second section analyses the social and personal background of the iconoclast Mustafa Kemal Atatürk, and the relationship between Kemalist principles and the ideas of the Tanzimat; it shows that both the individual and his ideas were strongly moulded by the Ottoman heritage. The concluding part will discuss the question of continuity vis-à-vis revolution.

Security predicaments behind the foundation of the Turkish Republic

From Empire to nation-state: the external consolidation of Turkey

After the revolution of July 1908, hopes of stopping the dismemberment of the Empire soon faded. In October 1908, the island of Crete declared its incorporation into Greece, Bulgaria cut its formal ties to the Ottoman Empire, and Vienna announced the annexation of Bosnia and Herzegovina (Matuz 1985: 251–2). A series of regional insurrections in the Balkans followed in which not only the Christian population but also Muslim Albanians became involved. The revolts in Albania (1910), Kosovo (1910, 1912) and Monte-negro (1911), caused mainly by traditionally motivated resistance against the centralising policies of the Young Turk regime, increasingly adopted a nationalist posture (Zürcher 1993: 109).

In its Arab provinces, the Empire was confronted with Italy's colonial ambitions and embroiled in small-scale warfare in Yemen. Whereas with the latter Istanbul agreed on an autonomy scheme in 1911, in the same year Italy declared war against the Empire. In October 1912, the Ottoman government had to sign a peace treaty with Italy, ceding its last province in North Africa and the Dodecanese islands to the Italians (Anderson 1966: 288–91).

Encouraged by this evident military weakness of the Empire, an alliance of the Balkan states of Serbia, Montenegro, Greece and Bulgaria declared war against Istanbul on 8 October 1912. The two rounds of the Balkan War (1912–13) ended with the loss of the richest and most developed areas of the Empire: Albania, Macedonia and Thrace. Even the ancient Ottoman capital of Edirne had to be temporarily ceded, but was retaken by Ottoman troops before a final settlement took place in September 1913 (Zürcher 1993: 111–14). The point of no return was reached as the Young Turk regime, under the Ottoman Minister of War, Enver Pasha, decided to overcome international isolation and entered the First World War on the side of the central powers, Germany and Austria.[4]

Being militarily, economically and in terms of internal communications in no condition to fight a major war, Istanbul soon found itself surrounded on multiple fronts (Zürcher 1993: 117). Ottoman troops were fighting in Galicia, Macedonia and Romania. They had to defend the Empire against Russia in the Caucasus, against Britain in Iraq and at the Suez Canal, and in the Dardanelles against the allied forces of France and Great Britain (Matuz 1985: 264–5). Despite singular military successes, the First World War ended for the Ottoman Empire in an absolute fiasco. On 31 October 1918, Sultan Mehmet VI had to accept the truce of Mudros, an unconditional capitulation. Only one day later the leadership of the Young Turk regime fled Istanbul aboard a German submarine (Zürcher 1993: 139).

For the last time, political power rested on the Ottoman sultan and the older bureaucrats of the Sublime Porte. However, Sultan Mehmet VI Vahideddin (1918–22) did not truly rule over an Empire, but was almost a puppet in the hands of the Entente. His power hardly went beyond Istanbul and its vicinity (Matuz 1985: 269). In this situation of political emasculation, an Ottoman government delegation reluctantly signed the Treaty of Sèvres in August 1920. The articles of the Treaty comprised all issues that for more than one hundred years had constituted the Eastern Question. Contrary to the promises given in Paris (1856) and Berlin (1878), at Sèvres the Empire eventually had to surrender the territorial integrity and political sovereignty of the Ottoman state.

Istanbul now had to recognise French protectorates in Morocco, Tunisia,

Lebanon and Syria, and British rule in Egypt, Palestine and Iraq. It was compelled to renounce its rights over the Arab province of Hedjaz, with the holy cities of Mecca and Medina. Articles 115–117 of the Treaty announced the British annexation of Cyprus and the naturalisation of its Turkish residents. Smyrna (Izmir) and parts of western Anatolia remained formally under Turkish sovereignty, yet administration and maintenance of order was to be the responsibility of the Greek government. In north-eastern Anatolia, the establishment of a free and independent state of Armenia was proclaimed. Those Anatolian territories inhabited mainly by Kurds were to be given local autonomy, with the right to address the Council of the League of Nations to apply for independence after one year. Finally, freedom of navigation in the Bosphorus, the Dardanelles and the Sea of Marmara was put under an international 'Commission of the Straits', composed of representatives of the United States, Britain, France, Russia, Greece, Romania, Bulgaria and Turkey (Hurewitz 1956b: 81–7).

From a Turkish perspective, the clauses of Sèvres, though never implemented, marshal evidence for the great conspiracy behind the dismemberment of the Ottoman Empire. Regarding the incentives and purposes behind the Ottoman reforms, Sèvres can be interpreted as a proof of the complete failure of Ottoman top-down modernisation. In retrospect, the attempt to defend the Empire and to save the state by modernising its political and societal structures accelerated rather than hindered dismemberment. The inherent contradiction of the Ottoman reforms – to modernise state structures according to the standards of modern nation-states while maintaining the imperial, multinational and religious identity of an Empire – turned to the benefit of centripetal forces. Furthermore, it weakened the Ottoman position among the members of the European state system, with their dominant discourse of national identity and self-determination. Accordingly, the Treaty of Sèvres is also a document that proves the Ottoman state elite's failure to adjust itself to the discursive reality of the international system.

Yet this negative reading of the Ottoman reforms is too one-sided. More than one hundred years of defensive modernisation created fertile ground for the Turkish National Movement. Moreover, out of the dismemberment of the Empire, with its territorial losses and its change in the ethnic and religious composition of the populace, emerged both the territory and the people necessary to claim an independent Turkish nation-state. Ironically, the darkest moment of Turkish history, the Treaty of Sèvres, gave the National Movement a chance to establish a Turkish nation-state whose right of existence was no longer questioned, but guaranteed by the international system of states. In applying modern nation-state discourse and promoting not the integrity and sovereignty of the Ottoman Empire but the national rights of the Turks, the National Movement could turn the disadvantages of the Eastern Question system to its advantage. The Turco–Greek war (Turkish War of Independence, 1920–22) eventually marks this turning-point in Turkey's role in the particular structure of diplomatic and coercive action which characterised the Eastern Question system.

In 1915, contradicting territorial promises earlier given to Italy, Britain offered the Greek government territorial concessions around Izmir as an inducement to enter the war. In May 1919, the Greek army occupied this area with the consent of the allies. However, the Greek troops did not stop with the occupation of Izmir, but moved forwards into western Anatolia. This offensive seemed promising, because the remaining Turkish troops were occupied with the French advance in Cilicia, the Italian landing in Antalya and the nascent Armenian state in eastern Anatolia. Parallel to the Greek occupation, on 19 May 1919, Mustafa Kemal arrived, as newly appointed inspector-general of the ninth army, in the Black Sea Coastal town of Samsun. Only two months later, he cut his ties with the Ottoman government in Istanbul and began to organise the national resistance in Anatolia.

Under Mustafa Kemal's leadership, the Turks were able to profit from diverging interests among the allies, and play them off against each other by concluding bilateral agreements. After the Armenian defeat in November 1920, the Turkish National Movement in March 1921 signed a treaty of friendship with the Bolsheviks. This move enabled the nationalists to withdraw troops from the eastern front and to secure material support from Bolshevik Russia (Zürcher 1993: 160). In October 1921, agreements with France and Italy followed, with both pulling their troops out of Anatolia and both supporting the Turkish nationalist course from this time on.

The decisive battle with the Greek army took place in late August 1922. Turkish troops stopped the Greek advance at the Sakarya river north of Eskisehir, and were able to drive the Greek forces back to Izmir in less than one month.[5] On 11 October 1922, Ismet Inönü signed the armistice of Mudanya with the allied representatives of Britain, France and Italy. The agreement handed eastern Thrace over to Turkey and confirmed formal Turkish sovereignty over the Straits (the Dardanelles, the Sea of Marmara and the Bosphorus), although they remained under British control. It was further decided that a final treaty had to be negotiated at an international conference, which took place between November 1922 and July 1923 in Lausanne. The Treaty of Lausanne replaced the clauses of Sèvres and secured the integrity of Anatolia, confirmed the abolition of the Capitulations and sanctioned Turkey's participation in any regime concluded for the Straits. In exchange for full sovereignty, the Turkish side had to renounce all rights over the Arab provinces and Cyprus, as well as grant non-Muslim minorities full rights and freedom of emigration (Hurewitz 1956b: 119–24).

The Lausanne Peace Treaty ended the classical Eastern Question and marked Turkey's full integration into the system of states. After more than a century of violent struggles, the Ottoman Empire, deprived of its Arab and European provinces, rose again in the only legitimate form an independent polity then could take, as a nation-state. On the eve of the conference of Lausanne a British General Staff memorandum expressed Turkey's successful change from empire to nation-state as follows:

> This change is due to the creation of a national spirit in Turkey, and this in turn has resulted in the recent successes of the Turkish Army, with the result that we can no longer treat the Turks as a conquered nation to whom it is possible to dictate any terms we wish.[6]

In Lausanne the European powers applied the same standards in favour of Turkey which had been applied against the Ottoman state. In claiming the right of national self-determination and fighting for it by military means, the Turkish National Movement found the adequate response to the dramatic security predicaments the Empire faced in 1918. Furthermore, Mustafa Kemal's clear rejection of pan-Islamist or pan-Turkist ideas, which were part of the ideological outlook of former Ottoman governments, facilitated the integration of a territorially based Turkish nation-state into the post-war order. Thus the security and integrity of the state not only stood at the centre of the Ottoman reform process, but was the key political question of the foundational phase of the Turkish Republic. From the early reforms under Selim III till the foundation of the Republic, Turkish modernisation continued its coercive path. Its major concern was the integrity of the state, and the republican elite inherited from its Ottoman predecessors the precarious state of external security, as well as the complex structure of competing domestic forces. After the guarantees of Lausanne, it was against these domestic threats that Mustafa Kemal and his associates had to consolidate their power. The integrity of the state and the interests of the ruling elite again became equated.

Unionists and nationalists: the internal consolidation of Turkey

In order to understand the success of the National Movement and later the Kemalists, we have to look briefly at the political experiences of their immediate predecessors. When the Young Turks seized power in 1908, they justified their move against Istanbul by citing the inability of the Ottoman government to defend the Empire against external threats. Yet as a hetero-geneous movement that was held together only by the desire to overthrow the Hamidian regime, its internal fragmentation soon became visible. Broadly, the Young Turks can be divided into two main groups: the Liberals and the Unionists, the latter being members and followers of the Committee of Union and Progress. This division resembled the social divide among the modernised part of Ottoman society. While the liberal faction represented the higher stratum of Western-educated bureaucrats and professionals who supported a constitutional monarchy, the typical Unionist belonged to the lower middle class of civil servants, officers and young intellectuals. Their aspirations were also directed against the establishment of the Tanzimat – the power circles around the palace and the Sublime Porte – and towards more radical and centralised reforms of the Empire's social and political structures (Ahmad 1993: 33–5).

The political struggle within the Young Turk movement was decided by the increasing militarisation of politics and society, a development which reflected the external security constraints. Eventually, the Balkan War gave the Unionists a chance to seize power. After the Ottoman government had shown signs of accepting a proposal by the great powers to hand over the former Ottoman capital of Edirne to Bulgaria, the Unionists launched a *coup d'état* in January 1913 (Zürcher 1993: 113–14). Under the leadership of the so-called triumvirate of Enver, Talat and Cemal Pasha, the Unionists, in close alliance with the army, controlled the state and established a dictatorial regime that left the palace with only formal responsibilities. They established an infrastructure of local party branches and a network of special security and information units. The regime instigated a radical reform programme, including steps to secularise the law, to improve the status of women, to organise elections (albeit controlled), and to introduce a policy of economic nationalism, the idea of a state-created capitalist economy (Kazancigil 1981: 49–50). Both the organisational infrastructure and the reform programme of the Unionists provided a major platform for the later success of the National Movement.

In the years after the First World War, four main players were involved in the internal political strife of Turkey: Sultan Mehmet VI, who tried to re-establish the influence of the palace; the liberal opposition, which had been silenced under Unionist rule; the representatives of the Entente powers; and the Unionists themselves. Although their leadership had left the country, the Unionists' organisational structures and communication networks still existed. Furthermore, they dominated the Ottoman parliament, the security forces and other remaining parts of the state infrastructure (Zürcher 1993: 139–40). The political forces were soon divided into two major factions. While in Istanbul several small parties around the Sultan were seeking to save what was left of the Empire, in Anatolia the National Movement was built up around the Association for the Defence of the Rights of Eastern Anatolia (Payaslioglu 1964: 417). In July 1919, the Association assembled in Erzerum with Mustafa Kemal as its elected chairman and drafted a first version of the so-called National Pact, expressing the determination to maintain the integrity of the country against all territorial claims of the Entente (Lewis 1961: 248–50).

Although the National Pact proposed to 'save the Ottoman state, with its sultan-caliph, and the constitution', the rift between the National Movement and the government in Istanbul deepened quickly (Payaslioglu 1964: 417). In January 1920, the Ottoman parliament in Istanbul adopted the National Pact and thus isolated the sultan, who collaborated with the representatives of the Entente. After the allies had formally occupied Istanbul in March 1920 and deported a larger number of nationalist representatives to Malta, the parliament prorogued itself indefinitely, and the remaining nationalist activists left for Ankara. The sultan finally dissolved parliament on 11 April. In opposition to the sultan, Mustafa Kemal called for elections to a new parliament, the Grand National Assembly, which met for the first time on 23 April 1920 in Ankara (Ahmad 1993: 49–50). Now, the sultan and his government in Istanbul used all political, religious and military means at hand to destroy the National Movement. The chief mufti issued a fetva that it was a religious duty to kill members of the rebellious group, and in May 1920 a court martial in Istanbul condemned Mustafa Kemal and other prominent nationalists to death (Lewis 1961: 252). Accordingly, the Turkish state's struggle for survival and the internal power conflict were knitted closely together.

The final victory of the National Movement was due largely to two interrelated factors: first, the gradual deterioration of the political legitimacy of the Istanbul government and the sultan; second, the ability of the National Movement to monopolise the means of physical force in its hands. The prestige of the palace and of the bureaucrats of the Sublime Porte had already been weakened under unionist rule. With the flight of the Unionist leaders, their domination over the palace was replaced by the domination of the Entente. In the light of the occupation of Istanbul, the Greek offensive in western Anatolia and the conclusion of the Treaty of Sèvres, the close collaboration with the occupational powers of the Empire's traditional political institutions – the palace and the Sublime Porte – further eroded their political legitimacy. While the sultan and his bureaucrats lived at the mercy of the Entente, the Nationalists gained legitimacy in their heroic strife against external foes.[7]

Complementary to this legitimacy deficit, the Istanbul government had almost completely lost control over the means of physical force. Only the Entente and the nationalists had substantial coercive means at their disposal. The political split between Istanbul and Ankara was thus reinforced by the fact that 'the Allies kept enough troops in Istanbul to deprive the sultan of his freedom of action, but not enough in the hinterland to establish effective authority in Anatolia' (Rustow 1959: 519). As we saw in the previous section, the Turkish War of Independence gave the National Movement a historic chance to acquire both monopoly of physical force and legitimate authority for political leadership. As in the example of the Young Turks, the political struggle moved now to within the confines of the victorious movement.

Royalists and republicans: the consolidation of Kemalist power

The consolidation of Kemalist power rested on two processes: the monopolisation of the means of symbolic reproduction and the monopolisation of the means of physical force. The major political instrument in the acquisition of those monopolies was the Republican People's Party (RPP), which Mustafa Kemal founded in summer 1923.[8] The first monopolisation process was manifested in the iconoclastic reforms described at the beginning of this chapter. The cultural revolution, which was already a feature of the Unionist reform measures, was radically pushed through after the establishment of the Republic. Both the Unionists and the Kemalists could draw on their particular power resource: the organisational and cognitive knowledge of their Western-style education. The officers, bureaucrats and professionals of the republican elite based their legitimation to rule on knowledge (Mardin 1971: 201). Consequently, the cultural reforms created the necessary symbolic resources on which the legitimacy of the Kemalist power monopoly rested.

The interrelation between the symbolic character of the reforms and the monopolisation of physical force becomes transparent in the events that followed the abolition of the sultanate. With the signing of the Treaty of Lausanne, the nationalists lost their major common denominator – the preservation of the Turkish state – and the internal fragmentation of the movement became apparent. The majority of this loose alliance of army officers, bureaucrats, professionals, merchants, and landlords and clerics of Anatolia still saw the national struggle as a means to restore the power of the sultan and the Ottoman dynasty (Ahmad 1993: 52). Moreover, during the War of Independence, Islam had served the National Movement as a major means of cohesion and mobilisation (Heper 1981: 350).[9]

Mustafa Kemal and his republican wing had now to defend their claim to power against different competitors. On the one hand, traditional forces such as local notables, ethnically or religiously constituted groups and conservative forces intended to restore the political institutions of the Ottoman Empire. On the other hand, internal fragmentation and personal rivalries among members of the modernising military–bureaucratic elite had developed into a major source of internal conflict.

The rift among the nationalists became apparent with rising tensions between Mustafa Kemal and conservative officers even before the Republic was proclaimed. Already during the First Assembly (1920–23), the Ankara Parliament was split into two major factions. While the so-called 'First Group' chiefly comprised wholehearted supporters of Mustafa Kemal's radical course, the 'Second Group' tended to promote a constitutional monarchy and to oppose the abolition of the sultanate. As a result of a 'candidacy test' imposed by Mustafa Kemal, only three out of 118 representatives of the Second Group were re-elected to the Second Assembly in July 1923 (Frey 1965: 306–27). Shortly after this elimination of the Second Group, the Assembly passed a law obliging officers to resign their commissions if they wanted to play a role in politics. Whereas Kemalist officers could stay in the army without losing political representation, opponents of the Kemalist course were rather inclined to resign in order to promote their political ideas (Ahmad 1993: 57). This disengagement of the army from politics can be interpreted as the Kemalisation of the military and was, hence, the first step to monopolising the means of physical force in the hands of the Kemalist movement.[10]

The second step towards the consolidation of Kemalist power was the promulgation of the Law on the Maintenance of Order in March 1925. Under this emergency law, which expired only in March 1929, 'the government was able to impose and enforce its will through the armed forces' and specially established courts, the so-called "independence tribunals"' (Lewis 1961: 270). Although released as a reaction to the Kurdish insurgency led by the Naksibendi Sheikh Said,[11] the Law on the Maintenance of Order and the independence tribunals effectively served the Kemalist regime in crushing political opposition, silencing critical journalists and rushing through the cultural reforms. In her account of the events, Halide Edib, a contemporary witness, makes clear how the internal security threat was used to establish and justify the power monopoly of the RPP under Mustafa Kemal: 'The Kurdish rising was attributed to foreign intrigue, and political anxiety was formed almost into panic at the possibility of another armed struggle' (Adivar 1930: 220).

The short life of the Progressive Republican Party (PRP), an opposition party formed in the Second Assembly, provides another example of Mustafa Kemal's tactical skills in playing off the different forces that resisted his claim to absolute power. The PRP was founded by a number of 'able, disgruntled, and still very influential former associates of Mustafa Kemal' (Frey 1965: 324), who left the RPP over the way the government under Premier Inönü handled the resettlement of Muslims from Greece (Zürcher 1993: 175). It included military and civilian leaders, as well as notables and former members of the Second Group.[12]

The motives behind the opposition within the military–bureaucratic elite were twofold. In the first place, fundamental programmatic differences, concerning issues such as the idea of maintaining a constitutional monarchy, the position and strength of the legislature, and the role of the localities, had grown since the proclamation of the Republic. In the second place, strong personal rivalries existed among leading members of the independence movement, in which the 'edginess of several illustrious generals towards Mustafa Kemal's ascendancy' was of great importance (Frey 1965: 325–6).

Being aware of dissatisfaction with the government, Mustafa Kemal did not intervene when the PRP was officially constituted in November 1924. He even replaced his close associate, Prime Minister Ismet Inönü, who faced heavy criticism and was known to be rather radical, by the moderate Fethi, in order to prevent mass desertions from the Republican camp (Zürcher 1993: 176). The Sheikh Said rebellion in February 1925, however, gave Atatürk the chance to correct this conciliatory approach: 'With the parliamentary session ended on April 20th, and the independent press silenced since March 6th 1925, the two main checks on the government's activity had been removed. What remained was the opposition's party organisation and it was against this that the government now moved' (Zürcher 1991: 90). Under the impact of the religiously inspired Kurdish rebellion north of Diyarbakir, Prime Minister Fethi lost a vote of confidence on 2 March and was replaced by Ismet Inönü, who, with Mustafa Kemal's support, enforced the Law on the Maintenance of Order. In June 1925, an Independence Tribunal accused members of the PRP of backing the rebellion and exploiting religion for political purposes. The party branches were closed down at the same time (Zürcher 1993: 180). The final blow against the opposition came in the following year with the so-called Izmir Plot. On 15 June 1926, shortly before Mustafa Kemal was expected to arrive in Izmir on an inspection tour, an assassination attempt against him was discovered. The plotters were arrested and with them 21 members of parliament from the former PRP. In two show trials in July and August 1926, the arrested politicians and 50 former Unionists were accused of supporting the plot and planning a coup d'état. Based on very weak evidence, if any at all, a number of prison and death sentences were passed and four of the accused were executed.[13]

Despite the short experiment with the Free Republican Party,[14] the Izmir plot and its show trials mark the beginning of twenty years of authoritarian one-party rule in Turkey. The Kemalists saw the RPP primarily as 'a mechanism for social control from above'. Vested with enormous power in the hands of the party leader, it was an instrument of both social control and the implementation of the decisions of its leadership. Now the Kemalist leadership and the close union of party, army and state administration formed a hegemonic bloc that looked upon the state as their personal domain, just as the palace and the higher bureaucrats of the Sublime Porte had in Ottoman times. Thus, the authoritarianism of the Ottoman state became an essential element of the political culture of the Turkish Republic. Moreover, the RPP set the example for the Turkish party system, with its extreme party loyalty and partisan type of politics (Frey 1965: 303–4).

However, contrary to its dictatorial inclinations, the early Republic never developed into a totalitarian state. There was still room for the articulation of different opinions, although to a limited degree (Robinson 1963: 87–8). Even the old opposition leaders were allowed to return as elder statesmen in the 1930s and 1940s (Zürcher 1991: 93). The dictatorial leadership of Mustafa Kemal has to be assessed against the historical background of the events presented here. It is this interrelation between historical context and individual which melted together in the foundational myth of the Turkish Republic and which in its ideological forms, Kemalism or Atatürkism,[15] has played a decisive role in Turkey's political life. It is the social and ideological background behind the creation of this myth that we now examine.

The man and his principles

Mustafa Kemal Atatürk: 'The Father of the Turks'
In Mustafa Kemal, an almost classic representative of the late Ottoman modernisers came to the head of the National Movement. He belonged to the social stratum whose evolution is closely linked to the structural change of the Tanzimat and which broke away from the Ottoman dynasty in Hamidian times. In this respect, he stands for the continuity of self-bred opposition that leads from the Ottoman Constitutional Movement through the Young Turk revolution to the Kemalist Republic.[16] Mustafa Kemal was born in 1881, the son of a customs officer in Salonika. As a vehicle of social advancement and education, the military had a crucial impact on moulding his life. He attended the military schools in Salonika and Monastir before enrolling in the War College in Istanbul. In 1905, he graduated as general staff captain from the

Staff College in Istanbul and was, one year later, a founding member in Salonika of the Committee of Union and Progress. Involved in the Young Turk revolution, Mustafa Kemal appeared in 1908 among a handful of leading Unionist officers on the balcony of the Olympus Hotel from which they proclaimed victory (Macfie 1994: 34).

Like other Unionists, Atatürk represented perfectly the well-trained, knowledgeable military–bureaucratic elite of the late Ottoman Empire, guided 'by a view of the interests of the state' (Mardin 1973: 180). The self-image of the officer corps as vanguard of a new enlightenment was based on the adoption of Western techniques and thoughts, and characterised by an almost complete identification of the army with the state (Hale 1994: 2). Mustafa Kemal was deeply influenced by the positivist spirit of the modern Ottoman army and by the philosophical ideas of Comte, Montesquieu, Voltaire and Rousseau, whose books are still on display in the presidential villa in Ankara (Gronau 1995: 22). This personal and educational background made him an ideal representative of the republican wing of the National Movement. Indeed, the typical Kemalist came from Macedonia, Thrace or one of the areas occupied after the First World War. He was a younger member of the military–bureaucracy without strong affiliations to any locality and, consequently, an ardent supporter of radical Turkish nationalism.

It certainly goes without saying that Mustafa Kemal was a remarkable personality. It can be further assumed that the existence of the Turkish Republic is essentially due to his political awareness and tactical skills, even though the founder of the Republic could not have played his role successfully without the backing of other prominent figures in the Nationalist and later in the Kemalist movements. Amongst his closest associates, Ismet Inönü was one of the most crucial contributors and somehow a necessary complement to Atatürk (Heper 1998: 9). In spite of the fact that Inönü played an eminent role in Turkish politics for over half a century, he could not match the charismatic qualities of Mustafa Kemal. According to Dankwart Rustow, 'none of the highest army commanders ... could have equaled the personal courage, resoluteness, and even ruthlessness, combined with patience, foresight, and judgement, which Kemal displayed' (Rustow 1959: 537). Where did these charismatic qualities and tactical abilities come from which made Mustafa Kemal the 'father of all Turks'?

From a sociological point of view, Atatürk's extraordinary character was neither the result of a 'godlike mission', nor due to a 'narcissistic disturbed personality structure' (cf. Volkan and Itzkowitz 1984). The legends about his providential abilities – according to which he predicted not only the territorial boundaries of the Turkish Republic in 1907, but also the course of the

Second World War and the demise of the Soviet Union – and the psychologisation of his role contributed heavily to the ideological smoke-screen of total change. Behind the remarkable qualities of Mustafa Kemal, we can detect a social collage in which the essential cultural, political and social streams of Ottoman modernisation converged.

As is still reflected today in the large range of postcards featuring his portrait, Atatürk combined the characters of teacher and officer, intellectual and bohemian, and of enlightened educator and rigid bureaucrat. Whereas his life-style resembled that of the Westernised top bureaucrats of the Tanzimat, his military successes gave him the image of a *gazi*, the religiously inspired traditional warrior of the Ottoman Empire. In stark contrast to his liberal attitude in gender affairs, his Western attire and his propensity to enjoy operas, theatres, ballrooms and alcoholic drinks, Mustafa Kemal used the title *gazi* until he took the name Atatürk in 1934 (Ahmad 1993: 63).

Mustafa Kemal's personal abilities and his tactical finesse, which helped him to assert himself in the complex web of internal and external power relations, were completed by his profound knowledge of local, regional and international conditions. As a result of his military career he was aware of the power relations in both the Empire and the international system. He experienced the last years of the Empire as Ottoman officer in Damascus (1905), Macedonia (1907), Tripoli (1908, 1912), Albania (1910), and Diyarbakir (1916). Atatürk gained tactical skills and fame in a series of successful military campaigns, such as the defence of the Straits (1915) and the re-occupation of the eastern provinces of Bitlis and Mus (1916). He commanded the Seventh Army at the Syrian front (1917 and 1918) and was the victorious leader in the War of Independence. Moreover, he was familiar with foreign views and diplomatic practices, owing to his post as military attaché in Sofia (1913), his close collaboration with the Prussian officer Liman von Sanders, who organised the defence of the Straits, and his visit to Germany together with the Ottoman Crown Prince (1917).

It is against this background that we have to understand the tactical alliances and the interplay of coercion and concessions that characterised Atatürk's political moves and which led eventually to the establishment of the Turkish Republic under the power monopoly of the Kemalists. The consolidation of the Turkish Republic was not the work of a single man, but it depended heavily on the outstanding leadership of an officer–politician equipped with both 'a sense of realism and excellent timing'.[17] The multiple facets of Mustafa Kemal's personality resembled somehow the mosaic of Ottoman society, and his personal qualities are made explicable by the fact that his social background was deeply rooted in Ottoman modernisation. It is not by chance that his method of divide and rule, as well as his authoritarian ambitions, remind us of the kind of political conduct we have experienced on the part of Ottoman sultans and their *grand vezirs*.

The six arrows: the principles of Kemalism

Not only in the individual Mustafa Kemal is the continuity between the Empire and the Turkish Republic visible, but also in the six Kemalist principles. Paul Dumont even claimed that 'there is an unbroken continuity in Turkish modernist doctrine from the ideology of the Tanzimat to the six Kemalist arrows' (Dumont 1984: 41). It was in May 1931 that the third congress of the RPP adopted the six principles – nationalism, statism, revolutionism, populism, republicanism and secularism – and made them, in the form of six arrows, the symbol on the party emblem. In February 1937, they were incorporated into the Turkish constitution (Ahmad 1993: 63). As a central source of Kemalist ideology, these principles largely shaped the modern political history of Turkey, and this section will demonstrate how they built a bridge between the Ottoman reforms and modern-day Turkey.

As we have seen, the main ideas behind Turkish nationalism – Anatolia as homeland and Turkish history and language as its cultural foundations – developed in the intellectual debate about the political future of the late Ottoman Empire. The rise of a specific national consciousness of the Turks was mainly due to two factors. On the one hand, there was the experience of progressive isolation that the Turkish Muslims faced in their attempts to safeguard the Empire. On the other hand, the dissemination and discussion of the linguistic and historical findings of modern science provided the necessary philosophical framework for the evolution of nationalist ideas. The official doctrine of the early Republic, that the Turkish nation has its roots in early Anatolian history, was thus a construct that emerged from the combined discourses of Ottoman and European intellectuals. However, in the writings of the late nineteenth-century Young Ottomans, the word 'nation' (*millet*) still had a strong religious connotation. In Kemalist nationalism it was then purified of religious, ethnic and racial aspects in order to provide an ideological platform for a territorial nationalism (Kazancigil 1981: 51).

As with its political heritage, the Turkish Republic inherited the economic problems of the Ottoman state in a radicalised way. It was argued that the state-centred top-down modernisation of the Ottoman reformers reflected the absence of an economically strong middle class. Furthermore, the economically active part of the Empire belonged mostly to the Christian minorities, who were seeking political independence. The early Republic inherited this weakness in its economic sector, aggravated by the Armenian massacres (1915-16) and the expulsion and resettlement of Anatolian Greeks after the War of Independence.[18] Kemalist statism was, firstly, a reaction in consequence of this structural condition. Secondly, it was the resumption of the nationalist economic policies originally launched by the Unionists – the creation by the state of a Turkish bourgeoisie.

While the Kemalist regime was not particularly concerned with economic development during the 1920s, the World Depression and the country's general economic situation in the early 1930s spurred the formulation of the statist concept. Hemmed in by regulations and restrictions, Turkish production had not yet reached the pre-war level of 1913. Although committed to the principles of capitalist enterprise, the Kemalist regime saw the world market as an imperialist order, hampering the economic development of modernising states and thus justifying political primacy over the economy (Herschlag 1968: 68–70).

In resorting to state intervention, the regime formulated two economic five-year plans in the 1930s, displaying a clear preference for industrialisation and state entrepreneurship (Herschlag 1968: 80). Although the Soviet and German examples of the time are detectable behind Kemalist statism, its implementation by decree and the tight control of the state over the economy were no less in line with Ottoman precursors. Moreover, even in pre-republican times, the 'Turkish part' of Ottoman manufacturing was largely in the hands of the state (Robinson 1963: 101; Mardin 1973: 172). Hence, 'it can be argued that important aspects of étatism under Atatürk originated in the otherwise largely ill-fated industrialisation efforts of the Tanzimat' (Clark 1974: 76). The Ottoman heritage is further stressed by the educational policies of the early Republic. In the beginning, focused on the supply of manpower for the state bureaucracy, the state displayed no increase in efforts to expand secondary vocational education until the first five-year plan (Özelli 1974: 86–7).[19] In short, Kemalist statism can be looked upon as a merger of the Ottoman heritage with the statist development models prevalent in the 1920s.

The other four principles can also be traced back, albeit less visibly, to the Ottoman reforms. French philosophy, which is behind the principles of revolutionism, republicanism and populism, was already a force in the intellectual discourse of the late nineteenth century, and many of the exiled opposition to Sultan Abdülhamid resided in Paris. Yet it was the collapse of the Empire after the First World War and the collaboration of the Ottoman political establishment with the Entente that enabled the lower ranks of the military-bureaucratic elite finally to depose the Ottoman dynasty.

The three principles mentioned, together with the Kemalist secularisation drive, have to be explained against the background of this transformation of elites and the establishment of an entirely new basis of legitimacy for the republican regime. While the term revolution (*inkilab*) as an expression of the dynamics of reforms entered the political vocabulary of Turkey in the late Tanzimat era (cf. Lewis 1961: 156), both populism and revolutionism served as means to mobilise the population under a revolutionary leadership during the War of Independence. After the establishment of the Republic, Kemalist populism expressed the unitary notion of society whose corporate view denied the social fragmentation of Turkish society. Elitist and solidarist in its character, populism became a major ideological force to justify the authoritarian single party system (Dumont 1984: 32–3; Kazancigil 1981: 51).

Comprising the ideas of popular sovereignty, freedom and equality before the law, republicanism represents what Weber called legal authority. It was one of the instruments to grant legitimacy to the new regime against the resistance of traditional forces. Republicanism stands for the final moves from frontiers to borders, from the Islamic *umma* to the Turkish nation, from religious to national symbols, from the fragmented control of physical force to the legitimate claim of a state monopoly. In spite of these clear deviations from the formal structure of the Ottoman polity, republican ideas were none the less not as new as they appeared. Several of the Young Ottomans had already pleaded in favour of republican institutions, yet not in open opposition to the Caliphate and the sultanate (Dumont 1984: 26–7). From this perspective, the move from empire to republic was rather the logical completion of the legal and administrative reforms of the Tanzimat than a clear 'turning-point in the political philosophy of the Turks' (Karal 1981: 16).

The crucial role that the secularist principle plays in Turkish modernisation becomes apparent in Niyazi Berkes' definition. According to him, secularisation in non-Christian countries should not be read in the narrow context of a relationship between church and temporal authorities. Given the extent of domination that religious rules and symbols exert over all areas of life, it is rather the basic conflict between the forces of tradition and the forces of change that stand behind secularisation (Berkes 1964: 6–7). Consequently, secularism represents the essential doctrine for Turkey's modernising forces, and the iconoclastic reforms were a bold expression of both the irreversible character of Kemalist modernisation and the destruction of political legitimacy based on religion. However, the primordial social function that religion had for the Turkish population could not be simply decreed away. It was not folk-religion, but official religion and its influence in politics that were replaced by secularism. Secularisation was a means to erase the possibilities of political resistance by religious means against the modernising elite and the central state (Mardin 1971: 208–9).

The introduction of secularism did not separate state and religion, but was rather a move to take religion out of politics while keeping the state involved in religious affairs (Adivar 1930: 231). Behind Atatürk's iconoclasm and the pivotal role of secularism in the Kemalist project, we can detect the way 'confessionalisation' took place in Turkey. The suppression of religious symbols and institutions, as well as the strict adherence of the Kemalist state elite to the secularist principle, expresses confessionalism in its theoretical sense: the imposition of state control over the symbolic reproduction of society.

In this respect, the Directorate of Religious Affairs (Diyanet), set up in 1924 as a 'department for the administration of mosques and the appointment of imams and preachers' (Landmann 1997: 215), became the major instrument of state interference. However, it characterises the dialectical relationship between secularism and Islam in Turkey that the Diyanet has developed into a powerful bureaucratic institution that meanwhile promotes Islam in Turkish society (Steinbach 1996: 332). In spite of secularist dogma, Islam had and still has an impact on Turkish politics, and is regaining political strength under the conditions of an emerging Greater Middle East.

Conclusions: revolution and continuity

'The Turkish revolution was launched in order to achieve the qualities of nationalism and a modern state in a fundamentally medieval, theocratic empire, and to throw off the pre-existing institutions and concepts' (Karal 1981: 12). It was the purpose of this chapter to disclose the ideological character of this official tenor of Kemalist historiography. Not that there is no case to be made for bold deviations from the Ottoman past: the iconoclast measures, the application of the nation-state discourse and the abolition of both the sultanate and the Caliphate are cases in point. Yet in the light of the strong continuities of Turkish modernisation, the application of the mere term 'revolution' to the Kemalist reforms appears highly questionable. Instigated by an authoritarian and elitist-minded group of officers, the Kemalist reforms corresponded in their spirit and state-centred tendencies to the modernisation project of the Ottoman reformers, and most of the specific patterns of Ottoman modernisation were still features of the early Turkish Republic.[20] While the former ruling class was almost entirely displaced by modernised members of the secondary elite (Eisenstadt 1984: 9), most social structures, especially in the periphery, remained untouched.

In stark contrast to the Kemalist denigration of the Hamidian period, Mustafa Kemal's enlightened absolutism resembles in many respects the authoritarian rule of Sultan Abdülhamid II. His centralist policies, as well as the enhancement of the surveillance capacities of the Ottoman State, are clear precursors of Unionist and later Kemalist authoritarianism. Telling are the parallels between Atatürk's cultural revolution and Abdülhamid's attempt to monopolise the resources of symbolic reproduction and to use them as a major source of legitimacy for his regime. Ironically, from a theoretical point of view Hamidian 'Islamism' appears to be almost a blueprint for Kemalist secularism. However, while Abdülhamid drew on indigenous religious symbols, Atatürk and his associates used their cultural capital of Western knowledge. They not only successfully applied the nation-state discourse to the outer world, but they were able to monopolise the domestic production of a national culture. Thus they provided themselves with the necessary symbolic means to legitimise their system of domination. If we add the statist economic plans of the 1930s, the Kemalist regime achieved control over all three elementary functions of social reproduction, and finalised the Tanzimat's institutional change from traditional to legal authority.

Yet the foundation of the Turkish Republic took place as part of an intra-bureaucratic struggle which, with the exception of the War of Independence, lacked mass support (Mardin 1971: 199). Despite our focus on this elite transformation, we should not forget that the greater part of Turkey's populace was hardly touched by the reforms. Whereas Ankara displayed all the formal requirements of modern legal authority, large parts of the country were still deeply rooted in traditional life. From the very beginning, the Kemalists compromised with traditional forms of domination and had to rely on traditional leaders as intermediaries between centre and periphery. Like the Unionists before, the Kemalist movement was organised around traditional notables in the countryside, and their influence 'was amply felt in parliamentary politics and party activities' (Sayari 1977: 106). Under the umbrella of the nation-state, the Republican regime sustained major patterns of Anatolia's traditional society. Indeed, its policy of co-optation and coercion was not very different from the Ottoman example. This applies equally to the social habitus of the Kemalist elite, which reflected the enormous gap between centre and periphery in the perpetuation of Ottoman elitism. Nobody proves that better than Atatürk himself:

> If I obtain great authority and power, I think I will bring about by a coup – suddenly in one moment – the desired revolution in our social life. Because, unlike others, I don't believe that this deed can be achieved by raising the intelligence of others slowly to the level of my own. My soul rebels against such a course. Why, after my years of education, after studying civilization and the socialization processes, after spending my life and my time to gain pleasure from freedom,

should I descend to the level of common people? I will make them rise to my level. Let me not resemble them: they should resemble me.[21]

In conclusion, the Kemalist project was confronted with social constraints similar to those of its Ottoman predecessor. Nevertheless, the similarity of both the external and internal constraints imposed by the international system and by the heterogeneous structures of Turkish society did not determine the historical course that Turkish modernisation has taken. In order to explain how the move from empire to republic was possible, we have to consider not only the historical and social context, but also the influence of concrete actors. This encompasses the individual action of Mustafa Kemal and his social environment: in the described situation of permanent warfare and radical change it was first of all the charismatic authority of Atatürk that could legitimise breaks with the past. In contrast to other potential political leaders, Mustafa Kemal escaped the Ottoman collapse as a highly respected officer who was identified neither with the palace nor with the Unionist leadership. Criticising the conduct of the war, he stood aloof from the Unionists during the First World War, and his rivalry with the Ottoman Minister of War, Enver Pasha, was proverbial (Rustow 1959: 522). Furthermore, the military success in the War of Independence against the Greek invasion gave Atatürk the reputation of 'saviour of the nation', making him literally sacrosanct (Zürcher 1991: 41).

In being a war hero, an iconoclast and a revolutionary at the same time, Atatürk combined all the attributes of the exceptional sanctity Max Weber ascribed to the typical charismatic leader. His model of charismatic domination can therefore best explain the successful implementation of the Kemalist reforms. Similarly, we can look upon the institutionalisation of the republican system as the inevitable process of routinisation that a charismatic system of domination has to take on in order to overcome its transitory character and establish itself permanently. In establishing the Republic, Atatürk used both modern and traditional sources of authority. In this respect the party, the army and the bureaucracy represent the key instruments of legal or rational authority, while the personal, patriarchal and hierarchic character of the relationship within these institutions and among the Kemalist leadership, their intermediaries and the people resembles traditional aspects of domination. Just as in the late Ottoman Empire, the society of the early Republic was a patchwork of traditional and modern societal structures, though with a different pattern in which the modernist face dominated.

The veneration of Atatürk, which took place after his death on 10 November 1938, makes clear how strongly the image of the Turkish Republic was knitted to his image. In '*Paris Soir*' the then French Interior Minister Albert Sarraut declared: 'The death of President Atatürk is an immense loss to this admirable Turkey; his heroism and his genius achieved at the same time both independence and renewal.'[22] The charisma of Mustafa Kemal captivated not only the Turkish populace, but also representatives of formerly hostile great powers. The dramatic change of image that characterises the move from empire to republic further concealed the continuities of Turkish modernisation. The following chapter will show how both the Ottoman heritage and rationally routinised aspects of Atatürk's charismatic domination were incorporated into the institutional and ideological setting of post-Second World War Turkey.

Notes

1 See the descriptions in Atatürk (1963: 665–73), Gronau (1995: 220), Kinross (1964: 380–1) and Lewis (1961: 261–2).

2 From the Turkish perspective the numerals used in Europe were Western, albeit they are Arabic in origin.

3 See Alici (1996), Zürcher (1993: 198–9) and Mardin (1981: 211–12).

4 It is not the place here to discuss the reasons behind this decision, which was certainly not only made on the basis of the almost one century old cooperation between the Ottoman Empire and Germany. For a discussion of the political and strategic considerations behind the Ottoman-German alliance, see Anderson (1966: 310–15), Haley (1994a and 1994b), Matuz (1985: 262–5) and Zürcher (1993: 116–18).

5 For a short overview of the Greco–Turkish war, see Jensen (1979).

6 Quoted from Macfie (1979: 211).

7 For a detailed historical account of cultural and political developments in Istanbul under five years of allied occupation, see Criss (1999).

8 The party was founded as the People's Party, and soon renamed the Republican People's Party.

9 According to Paul Stirling, a social anthropologist who conducted field studies in two Anatolian villages between 1949 and 1952, 'the majority of the Turkish villagers think of the War of Independence as a triumph of Islam over the infidels, rather than as the national victory of a secular Republic' (Stirling 1958: 400).

10 The importance of this step cannot be overestimated. Due to the low educational level of the ordinary soldier, the officers performed the decisive role of intermediary between the armed forces and the political leadership. Bound by personal ties, it was the allegiance to their officers rather than to political leaders or ideologies on which the loyalty of the troops rested (cf. Mardin 1981: 201–3).

11 The Sheikh Said rebellion, which broke out in February 1925, is considered more closely in the second part of the book, when the Kurdish question is discussed.

12 Among its founding members were some of the leading figures of the National Movement such as Rauf Orbay, Ali Fuat Cebesoy, Refet Bele and Adnan Adivar,

who were in Istanbul when the proclamation of the Republic took place.

13 For a detailed analysis of these events, see Zürcher (1991).

14 The Free Republican Party was a loyal opposition party that Mustafa Kemal set up in 1930 as a valve for social discontent. The party was closed down in the same year after it received an unexpectedly popular response (cf. Ahmad 1993: 59–60).

15 In Turkish the equivalent to Kemalism is 'Atatürkcülük'.

16 It is important, however, to mention that the Young Ottoman theories behind the Constitutional Movement were partly of Islamic origin. In the ideas of the Young Turks, this Islamic substratum becomes weaker and it disappears completely in Kemalism (Mardin 1962a: 404).

17 Introduction to Landau (1984: xi).

18 For an overview and an extended bibliography on the Armenian massacres and the Istanbul trials related to them after the First World War, see Akcam (1996) and Dadrian (1991).

19 About the modernisation of the educational system under Atatürk, see Winter (1984).

20 Such as the following characteristics: security centred, army and bureaucracy as foci and driving forces, imposition of change from above, educational programme, identification of state apparatus and state elite, patriarchal and elitist in mind, implemented in an air of conspiracy and betrayal.

21 Entry in an unpublished diary of Atatürk from 6 June 1918, quoted in Volkan and Itzkowitz (1984: 104)

22 Quoted in Dumont (1983: 177) and translated by the author.

5 Western Integration
The Multi-Party Period

'The Return of the Janissaries': Turkish military in politics

In the early hours of 27 May 1960, parts of the Turkish armed forces started a successful military coup with the occupation of strategic spots in Istanbul and in the capital, Ankara. Following the 'grammar of mid-twentieth-century coups' (Rustow 1964: 373), the army seized cabinet members, took control of radio stations, and broadcast at 7 a.m. a 'breakfast communiqué', in which Alparslan Türkes, a then unknown colonel, announced as follows:

> Honorable Fellow Countrymen: Owing to the crisis into which our democracy has fallen, and owing to the recent sad incidents and in order to prevent fratricide, the Turkish armed forces have taken over the administration of the country. Our armed forces have taken this initiative for the purpose of extricating the parties from the irreconcilable situation into which they have fallen and for the purpose of having just and free elections, to be held as soon as possible under the supervision and arbitration of an above-party and impartial administration, and for handing over the administration to whichever party wins the elections. Our initiative is not directed against any person or class. Our administration will not resort to any aggressive act against personalities, nor will it allow others to do so.[1]

As promised in the communiqué, the officers immediately started re-engineering Turkey's polity. On the very same morning, the military junta commissioned seven faculty members of the Istanbul School of Law to work on a new constitution (Giritli 1962: 5). One day later, this group of law professors released a declaration that justified the coup on the grounds of unconstitutional acts having been committed by the former civilian government of the Democratic Party under Prime Minister Adnan Menderes (Zürcher 1993: 254). General Cemal Gürsel, the former commander of land forces, was announced chairman of the junta and served for the next 17 months simultaneously as president, prime minister and commander-in-chief. For this transitional period, Turkey was governed by the so-called 'National Unity Committee' (NUC), a heterogeneous junta of, initially, 38 members, which appointed a 17-man cabinet of technocrats in order to execute the officers' decisions.

The military intervention of 1960 ended the democratic experience of what is now known as the First Turkish Republic (1923–60). However, in contrast to many other military interventions around the world, the junta kept its promises given in the breakfast communiqué and facilitated a quick return to civilian rule. In January 1961, the ban on political activities was lifted and new parties could register for the elections that were to take place ten months later. On 6 January 1961, the convention of a constituent assembly marks the beginning of the Second Turkish Republic (1961–80). The assembly approved a new constitution on 27 May 1961, exactly one year after the coup. In the new constitution, the former principle of unity of power was replaced by a system of checks and balances to prevent the majority group in the Assembly from having an almost free hand. Despite the introduction of an upper house (Senate) and of proportional representation, the juridical control over state activities was enhanced. Furthermore, the new constitution contained a 'full bill of civil liberties' and manifested a 'social character' (Giritli 1962: 10; Zürcher 1993: 257). Ironically, a military coup brought about the most democratic constitution Turkey had ever had whose general principles stated 'that the Turkish Republic is a democratic, secular, social and nationalistic State based on human rights' (Giritli 1962: 7).

Yet this military-guided top-down democratisation of Turkey's polity did not provide what its instigators sought: political stability. On the contrary, the new constitution gave the diverging forces of Turkey's continuing modernisation a framework for political expression. The 1960s saw the formation of labour unions, student movements and extremist parties whose focus of activity became the rapidly growing cities.[2] This politicisation of the populace met with a parliamentary stalemate caused by Turkey's uncompromising political elite, expressed particularly in the inability of the Justice Party and the Republican People's Party (RPP) to form a grand coalition. Due to its extreme partisanship and rampant nepotism, the political establishment produced no more than a series of inefficient, short-lived coalition governments. Thus the Second Turkish Republic became increasingly a stage for social conflict and a series of political crises that resulted in two further military interventions (1971 and 1980). In retrospect, the 1960 coup did not put an end to the crisis of Turkish democracy, but set a precedent for what has been called Turkey's 'military democracy', the fact that 'the court of last resort

in Turkish politics is not the ballot box but the military' (Salt 1999: 72).
The Turkish army, simultaneously object and subject of the Ottoman
reforms, and the essential institution during the foundation of the Turkish
Republic, was in almost every respect the most suitable body to take up the
Kemalist and Ottoman legacies (cf. Karabelias 1999: 131). Contrary to Dankwart Rustow's assumption that the 1923 disengagement of the army from
politics put an end to all military interventions in Turkey (Rustow 1959:
513), this Kemalisation of the Turkish military laid the very foundations for
the militarisation of Turkish politics after the Second World War. As
guardians of the Kemalist State, the armed forces have acquired a unique role
in Turkey's polity. The political decline of the RPP, which lost its dominant
position under the dynamics of the multi-party system and the impact of
Turkey's rapid economic transformation, counterbalanced the rise of the
army's political role. Thus, the three military interventions (1960, 1971,
1980) can be seen as subsequent steps in which the army took over the classical functions of social, political and ideological control from above, which the
RPP had held under single-party rule. In the political and economic context
of the second half of the twentieth century, the Turkish officer corps evolved
as the sole legitimate heir of Kemalist authority and as a distinct political force
apart from and above the everyday quarrels of democratic politics.

In the light of its autonomous role in Turkish politics, the thought and
actions of the army are, none the less, full of contradiction. On the one hand,
the generals are staunch promoters of Westernisation, democratisation and
the rule of law; on the other hand, as guardians of Kemalist principles, they
uphold the authoritarian traditions of Ottoman statehood. While the military
wants to spearhead the modernisation of Turkish society, the officers despise
its inevitable social and cultural fragmentation (cf. Karaosmanoglu 1993:
24). Based on the national republican myth around Atatürk, the ideology that
justifies military intervention also obliges the army to restore civilian rule as
soon as possible. The political role of the Turkish army therefore reflects not
only internal fragmentation,[3] but also the inherent contradictions of Kemalist
ideology. Turkey's integration into supra-national institutions of the Western
world put further constraints on the military.[4] Since 1945, Turkey's political
elbow room was limited by its strategic importance as a 'Cold War warrior'
(Gözen 1995: 74) and the demand by its Western allies that it apply certain
formal democratic rules. Under the impact of these contradictions and
constraints, the Turkish armed forces have developed into both a guardian of
and an obstacle to Turkish democracy.

This crucial but paradoxical role of the Turkish military will first be
analysed against the socio-political background of the military interventions.

The three coups of 1960, 1971 and 1980 serve as focal points to examine the return of the 'new Janissaries' and the stabilisation of their autonomous political role. In the following section we try to explain current patterns of military action in Turkish politics. How are the political functions of the military embedded in the legal and social structures of Turkey? How do generals, politicians and society interact? We will see that many of Turkey's current political problems are linked to the fact that under the authoritarian umbrella of the armed forces, Turkey's modern elite has established a cartel of interests that excludes rising 'counter-elites' from fair participation in the economic and political resources of the country.[5] It is striking that in its social habitus the modern Turkish establishment still resembles Ottoman high society in its traditional elitist attitudes. The chapter concludes with a brief summary of Ottoman–Turkish continuities in light of new geo-strategic framework of an emerging Greater Middle East.

The guardians in action: socio-political developments and military intervention

Democratic rule and the army: the foundations of military autonomy
Turkey's transition to multi-party politics began immediately after the Second World War with President Inönü's decision to abandon the power monopoly of the RPP. In January 1946, three prominent defectors from the RPP, Celal Bayar, Adnan Menderes and Fuad Köprülü, formed the Democratic Party (DP), which soon became a melting pot for various groups dissatisfied with authoritarian Republican rule. More important, however, the DP was able to capitalise on the aspirations of both the newly emerging groups of well-educated professionals and businessmen and the hitherto neglected masses of Turkey's traditionally oriented countryside. 'It was not until 1946 that the peasant emerged as an important political factor' (Szyliowicz 1962: 431).[6] Ironically, it was within the framework of the policy of economic and political liberalisation, which Ismet Inönü himself initiated, that the DP assumed power. The general elections of 1950 delivered a 'devastating verdict' on almost three decades of Republican rule, granting the Democrats 408 parliamentary seats against 69 for the RPP (Ahmad 1993: 108–9, Zürcher 1993: 231).[7]

In the economic field, the first half of Democratic rule (1950–55) was characterised by large but rather uncoordinated investments in agriculture, regional infrastructure and primarily state-owned industries. While the government under Prime Minister Menderes distributed material resources in order to please its electorate, most of Turkey's post-Second World War boom was financed by foreign aid and by the economic boost associated with the Korean War. Within the international framework of the Cold War, Menderes used Turkey's new strategic position to the utmost to get financial assistance from the USA and Western Europe (Zürcher 1993: 239). Yet the politically inspired economic policies of the DP soon proved that 'rapid industrialization, agricultural increases and massive capital construction do not necessarily equal economic development' (Simpson 1965: 151). In 1958, Turkey's economy was in an appalling condition, calling for a major adjustment programme to cope with the effects of high inflation, a mounting trade deficit, a decline in real incomes and the extremely unbalanced accounts of the public sector. With the cost of living having risen by 150 per cent since 1953, the economic burden was now on the shoulders of ordinary people (Simpson 1965: 150).

Confronted with the mounting economic crisis, the Menderes government increasingly resorted to authoritarian and ideological means to maintain its power. Given that the DP leadership's political socialisation took place during the single-party era, the adaptation to the authoritarian style of their Republican predecessors came as no surprise. Politics under the DP government was characterised by extreme partisanship and a 'profound intolerance of each political faction for its rivals' (Harris 1970: 439). The landslide victory of the DP in the 1954 elections almost annihilated parliamentary opposition and gave Menderes full power over the state apparatus.[8] Thus the government was able and willing to suppress the opposition as political tensions rose during the second half of the 1950s. The increasing violation of democratic rights and individual liberties, as well as concessions to traditional and conservative forces, completely alienated the intelligentsia of the cities who had earlier supported the Democrats (Weiker 1962: 281). The political exploitation of religious sentiments among the population accompanied this suppression of public criticism and led to open charges that the DP regime was undermining the secularist principles of the Turkish State (cf. Zürcher 1993: 243–5).

It was in the light of this aggravated economic and political crisis that the Turkish army intervened and toppled the Menderes government. But it would be short-sighted to take at face value the impartial role the military claimed in its breakfast memorandum. From the time of its foundation, a gradual alienation of the army from the DP was taking place. Moreover, the social and political developments under Democratic rule increasingly undermined the powerful position that the Turkish armed forces had inherited from Ottoman and early Republican times. Therefore, the military intervention of May 1960 was both a reaction to the critical situation into which the DP had brought the country, and an attempt to restore the leading role that the Turkish military had played in the modernisation and formation of the Turkish state. A brief glance at the changing balance of power among Turkey's elite proves how close the army had come to being subordinated to civilian domination.

As indicated before, the DP became the political vehicle to give voice to an unequal coalition of peasants, provincial town dwellers, professionals and the business community, the latter evolving from the Kemalist policy of national economy. So far this coalition of traditional and modern civilian forces had been objects rather than subjects of the political process. The periphery in its social forms – peasantry, urban lower strata and petty bourgeoisie – was excluded from political participation under the single-party system (Keyder 1979: 13). The introduction of multi-party politics gave them the opportunity to promote their interests against the military–bureaucratic Kemalist establishment and its political voice, the RPP. In this social process the DP government enhanced in two respects the rift between the classical forces of Turkish modernisation and the civilian part of a modern middle class associated with the countryside. On the one hand, the DP leadership increasingly made use of traditional religious symbols in appealing to the voters of the periphery. On the other hand, it stressed its civilian background, in contrast to the Republican military–bureaucracy.[9] 'The DP represented the first ruling party to emerge under leaders who had not won their spurs in the military', and who only thinly veiled their contempt for the officer corps (Harris 1970: 441).

In the Democratic Party era (1950–60), the military suffered a dramatic decline in parliamentary representation, with professionals and merchants replacing retired officers and state officials as the most powerful group. Deputies with a military background tended to be backbenchers or in junior government posts. In the late 1950s, nearly one half of the top governmental leaders came from the legal profession, while only three per cent were from the military (Frey 1965: 268). This was a stark contrast to the single-party period, in which retired officers were clearly over-represented in the top leadership. That the new government replaced the chief of the general staff only a few weeks after the 1950 elections (Harris 1965b: 169) and that five of six defence ministers under Menderes had a civilian background (Frey 1965: 290), further proves the attempt of the DP regime to subordinate the military to the civilian power structure. Although a direct involvement of officers in politics had been prohibited since 1923, under the previous Republican rule a military career was the almost natural precursor to a leading position in Turkish politics.

In sharp contrast to this decline of political influence, the military's image as spearheading modernisation was strengthened by the American aid programme in the light of the Truman Doctrine. Young Turkish officers encountered Western technical and military training, and modern political and social concepts. These new skills widened the gap between them and senior officers, whose position was based on seniority rather than ability (Lerner and Robinson 1960: 28–9). Adding the fact that the Democrats were filling the highest military posts with officers amenable to their policies (Rustow 1964: 367), it comes as no surprise that the conspiratorial activities against the Menderes government started among the middle and lower ranks of the officer corps.[10] In 1955, a group of young officers formed the secret 'Atatürkist Society' in Istanbul, expressing their dissatisfaction with the senior commanders and demanding social and military reforms (Harris 1965b: 171). Justified by their ideological self-perception as the 'vanguard of the intelligentsia' and the 'defender of Atatürk's reforms' (Harris 1965a: 66), these young officers were the driving force behind the 1960 military intervention and its attempt to reconstruct Turkey's polity.

The overthrow of the Menderes government was therefore triggered not only by concerns about the country's political situation, but also by the fact that the privileged position of the Turkish military was at stake, and more particularly the personal and professional aspirations of some of its young officers. This becomes clear with the so-called 'retirement of the 5,000' – the decision of the junta to retire 235 of the 260 generals and admirals, as well as some 5,000 lower-ranking officers, in August 1960. Behind this 'rejuvenation' of the army was a more radical group of young officers under the leadership of Alparslan Türkes, the 'voice' of the breakfast communiqué. This faction within the NUC pledged itself to more radical measures and a complete reconstruction of Turkish society under the political leadership of the military. From summer 1960 onwards, the army was torn by this internal strife between radical and moderate forces. In November 1960, fourteen radical officers around Türkes were excluded from the NUC and posted to Turkish embassies abroad. It took the senior commanders two years, in which two more abortive coups were launched, to re-establish their supremacy over the 'radical youth' within the armed forces (Zürcher 1993: 254–6).[11]

During the multi-party period of the First Republic, we can observe an overall decline in the power that the Turkish military had previously enjoyed. Although Atatürk banned the officer corps from any direct involvement in politics with the foundation of the Republic, the officer–politician was the leading figure under single-party rule, and together with the RPP the military formed the backbone of Kemalist authority. With the coup in 1960, the Turkish army re-established its political role and based it on a new legal footing. 'The key to the willingness of the military to "return to the barracks" was the adjustment of the political system to legalize a more prominent role for the senior commanders than had existed in the past' (Brown 1989: 389). It is not by chance that this adjustment was anchored in the same constitution that is otherwise striking for us with its liberal and democratic character. Two cases in point are the creation of an upper chamber and the re-location of the position of the chief of the general staff. Whereas the introduction of the Senate provided retired officers with an opportunity of non-elected representation, the role of the chief of the general staff was strengthened, moving him from a position subordinate to the ministry of defence to a post reporting directly to the prime minister.

More important than these constitutional provisions, however, was the introduction of a new political body, which since then has developed into a key instrument of the military's influence on political decision-making. Section two of the 1961 constitution, which deals with the executive power, stipulated the formation of a National Security Council (NSC). Consisting of representatives of both the government and the military, NSC must 'communicate the requisite fundamental recommendations to the council of ministers with the purpose of assisting in the making of decisions related to national security and coordination'.[12] This new constitutional body opened an avenue for the generals to assume executive functions without being embroiled in party politics. As we shall see later, the NSC in its present form demonstrates the critical civil–military relationship in Turkish politics, where the military is not accountable to civilian rule, but the politicians seem to be accountable to the generals.

While the 1960 intervention laid the foundation stone for the specific political role of the military in Turkey's democracy, it also set the precedent for further intervention. In this respect, two salient points have to be made. In the first place, the initiative of the young officers showed that the military top brass need to remain aware of the aspirations of its subordinates and the privileges of the army as a whole. If the senior commanders do not want to lose control, they have to take their rank and file into account and, if necessary, to take the lead in political action. In the second place, the coup established a specific pattern of intervention, in which the military does not assume direct political power, but intervenes from above as a neutral, enlightened force of adjustment, legitimised as the guardian of democracy and of the Atatürk revolution. This heritage of the Ottoman spirit of decree was apparent in the thinking of the National Unity Committee, whose members justified their intervention by their aim to set basic political, economic and educational goals and directions for the Turkish nation (Weiker 1963: 120).

Politicians, officers and social unrest: the decline of the Second Republic
In order to understand Turkey's political history after the Second World War,
one has to recognise that the introduction of multi-party politics coincided
with dramatic social changes. Turkish modernisation, triggered by the
Ottoman and Kemalist reforms, gained momentum after the authoritarianism
of the early Republic was gradually lifted. The industrialisation of the
economy, the mechanisation of agricultural production, the spread of
modern education and the revolution of the means of transportation and
communication entailed two major social developments, which gradually
undermined the power monopoly of the Kemalist modernisers. First, as the
social forces behind the DP proved, a new modern elite was rising whose
power resources were no longer directly linked to the state. This emerging
elite, itself a result of the economic and educational reforms of the early
Republic, challenged the power monopoly of the social forces that formed the
hegemonic block under Republican rule. Second, and even more crucial, for
the first time in Turkish history, modern change strongly affected the life of
the periphery and transformed the traditional patterns of social reproduction
in economic, political and cultural fields still prevalent there.

With regard to the second development, the process of rapid urbanisation
in particular reflects the dissolution of Turkey's traditional society, ending
'the strict physical separation of urban metropolis from rural village' (Ülman
and Tachau 1965: 153). The high rates of population growth and the
modernisation of the economy led to massive waves of rural migration into
the big cities and abroad.[13] In the period 1960–94 more than 1.63 million
people left Turkey under state-controlled programmes (Unbehaun 1996:
88). However, working emigration was an insufficient valve for rural
migration. Since 1945, Turkish cities have faced dramatic population growth,
with more than 50 per cent of residents finding their homes in a *gecekondu*, the
squatter settlements that have become a major feature of Turkey's cities.[14]
Within less than three decades, the modernisation process had destroyed the
strict physical separation between the centre and the periphery that had
characterised Ottoman and Turkish society for centuries.

In the light of these crucial social developments and the fact that the
Democratic Party made a large political profit out of them, the military
intervention of 1960 was also an attempt to stem the rising power of newly
emerging socio-economic groups (Ülman and Tachau 1965: 162). 'The
military coup of 1960, however, emphasized that the real power within the
country was not in the hands of the peasants but was still concentrated in the
same classes that had always controlled Turkish society' (Szyliowicz 1962:
441). This was dramatically shown in the execution of Prime Minister Adnan

Menderes in September 1961. Although the junta tried to maintain a legal face in the tribunals against the DP government, the death sentence against Menderes was carried out against the will of the public, as well as against protests from Ismet Inönü and foreign governments (cf. Zürcher 1993: 261). Yet the impact of this bold sign of strength was limited. While the political power of the army was re-established, the attempt to stem the rising power of the masses was doomed to fail. In this respect, the twenty years of the Second Republic were a sad chapter of Turkish history, in which social dislocation and political extremism coincided.

The military intervention of 12 March 1971 marks the first attempt to stop the deterioration of the Second Republic's political structures. The high command of the Turkish military directed a bold communiqué to the National Assembly. Prompted by strikes, student demonstrations, urban guerrilla actions and parliamentary stalemate, the 'March 12 Memorandum' threatened the political elite with inevitable military intervention if a strong and capable government able to deal with the mounting anarchy and the fratricidal strife in the country was not formed. The ultimatum forced the resignation of Prime Minister Süleyman Demirel and the formation of a non-partisan cabinet under the indirect rule of the high command. Nihat Erim, prime minister from March 1971 to April 1972, justified the crucial role of the military with the following words:

> The situation which had worsened gradually after 1963, entered a new phase in 1968 when student protests degenerated into armed fights between the rightist and leftist extremists. Professional agents, trained, armed and directed from outside Turkey, were able to transform some leftist student organizations into urban guerrilla units,... preparing for the establishment of a Communist People's Republic in Turkey (Erim 1972: 248–9).

Between March 1971 and October 1973, Turkey was ruled by three consecutive cabinets of technocrats, whose main task was the restoration of law and order (Erim 1972: 250). They declared a state of emergency and implemented martial law in the areas most affected by the turmoil: Turkey's largest cities and some of its provinces with a high percentage of Kurds (Nye 1977: 209–12). There, leftist and rightist commandos tried to rally the politicised youth for their own purposes (Burnouf 1972: 102). It was one of the major tasks of those cabinets to crack down on left- and right-wing groups, as well as on the newly established trade unions (Brown 1989: 389). Furthermore, a number of constitutional amendments were made in order to 'curtail the "abuses of freedom" which the 1961 Constitution had liberally granted' (Nye 1977: 213).

Although the political repression of the 1971 coup by communiqué 'depoliticized the student unrest and delivered a crushing blow to the leftist movement' (Olson 1973: 197), the political turmoil soon resumed. In the second half of the 1970s, clashes between left- and right-wing militants escalated into a wave of terror and urban guerrilla warfare, in which nearly 4,500 Turks lost their lives (Sayari and Hoffman 1994: 168).[15] At the same time as the Turkish state was in danger of losing its monopoly of physical force, the parliamentary system was becoming increasingly paralysed by electoral politics, personal rivalries among political leaders, and a bureaucracy heavily infiltrated by partisanship. Especially, the ultra-nationalist National Action Party under Alparslan Türkes used its participation in several coalition governments to infiltrate its adherents into the state administration and the security services. What is more, its commandos, the so-called Grey Wolves, became notorious in stirring up and participating in violent clashes along ideological, ethnic and sectarian lines, thus enhancing the ethno-nationalist notion of Turkishness (Argun 1999: 91).

This tense political atmosphere was aggravated by the deteriorating economic situation of the country, whose creditors demanded an IMF-guided 'austerity package' (Keyder 1979: 39). The oil-price shock in 1973–74 and the subsequent recession in Europe derailed Turkey's state-controlled economy, whose industrial sector relied heavily on the availability of foreign reserves and technical input (cf. Zürcher 1993: 278–82). The political turmoil hence coincided with the collapse of Turkey's economic strategy of import-substitution, which characterised the period between 1963 and 1978 (Önis 1991: 163). In the winter of 1979, the financial and economic crises materialised in daily power cuts, bare shelves, breakdowns of central heating and road transport, and factories that worked a mere 30 per cent of their capacity (Birand 1987: 45). Confronted with Turkey's 'rapid slide into social disorder, political deadlock and economic insolvency' (Birand 1987: viii), the generals decided again to oust the civilian administration and to take power by military coup.

According to Mehmet Ali Birand's sources, the preparations for the carefully calibrated 'Operation Flag' began as early as December 1979 and found the silent approval of Turkey's Western allies. On 12 September 1980, General Kenan Evren, then chief of the general staff, announced that the military had taken control of the government. In his keynote speech, Evren declared that in the severe crisis besetting the country, 'the Turkish armed forces have been obliged to take over the running of the state in order to protect the integrity of our nation and its territory' (Birand 1987: 193). Parliament was dissolved, political leaders taken into custody, political parties and trade unions directed to disband and martial law declared country-wide. (McFadden 1985: 69). The military held both the political structures introduced with the 1961 constitution and the politicians themselves responsible for the failure of the Second Republic. The generals, therefore, proposed not only a transitional programme, but also a long-term project to rebuild totally the political and economic structures of the Turkish state (cf. Tufan and Vaner 1984: 193).

The Third Turkish Republic began with 38 months of military rule, under which the terror of the commandos was eradicated, but also many citizens allegedly associated with leftist or Islamist views suffered.[16] Again, the military supervised the drafting of a new constitution, following more or less the same process as twenty years before. On 7 November 1982, a referendum approved the new constitution by an overwhelming majority. However, in making the vote compulsory and prohibiting by decree any critique of the new constitution, the military regime did not take any risks (cf. Zürcher 1993: 293–6).[17] Although not formally abrogating basic democratic liberties, new provisions curtailed the right to enjoy them and enhanced the military's role in the realms of politics and jurisdiction. Moreover, a series of laws enforced under both military rule and the subsequent civilian government of Turgut Özal violate established democratic practice in such matters as political parties, trade unions, collective and individual freedoms, the press, and higher education (Ahmad 1985: 213).[18] It was this reconstruction programme that finally institutionalised the political autonomy of the Turkish military, and that still forms a major legal obstacle to the democratisation of Turkey's society.

The army, multi-party politics and the Turkish elite: modern diversification, patronage and traditional elitism

The Turkish armed forces: a state within the state

The previous sections elucidated how the Turkish armed forces established themselves in Turkey's polity as an autonomous political force whose political role is not subject to the imponderables of electoral processes. According to Ümit Cizre-Sakallioglu, this political autonomy can be defined as the ability of the military 'to go above and beyond the constitutional authority of democratically elected governments'. The Turkish generals frequently issue demands, policy suggestions, and warnings on political matters (Cizre-Sakallioglu 1997: 153). Since 1970, the army has had unquestioned autonomy to determine defence policies, and the defence budget has been subject neither to parliamentary debate nor to a critical discussion in the press (Cizre-Sakallioglu 1997: 159–60). Yet this political autonomy is not restricted to matters of national defence. Owing to an enlarged security conception that does not distinguish between external and internal threats, the Turkish military acquired the power to draw the limits of politics in a much more general way (Candar 1999: 131).

Beginning with the 1961 constitution and continuing through the amendments of 1973 until the writing of the 1982 constitution, Turkey has developed a 'double-headed' political system whose executive and juridical functions are characterised by parallel civilian and military systems (Cizre-Sakallioglu 1997: 157).[19] In the political realm, the power position of the army is fixed in the National Security Council, 'the institution that really runs the country' (Candar 1999: 131). As stipulated in article 118 of the 1982 constitution, the NSC is composed of the prime minister, the ministers of defence, interior and foreign affairs, the chief of the general staff, and the four commanders of the army, the navy, the air force and the gendarmerie. Under the chairmanship of the president of the republic, the NSC meets together with the director of national intelligence and the secretary-general of the NSC, who is a high-ranking officer responsible to the chief of the general staff.

The NSC's task is to guarantee the formulation and implementation of a national security policy. According to the 'Law on the National Security Council' of November 1983, national security entails protecting and safe-guarding the state against any foreign or domestic threats, including any aspect of political, social, cultural and economic life. Since its inception as a constitutional body in 1961, the NSC has developed from an institution that provides information to the government to one that issues policy recommendations to which the council of ministers has to give priority. So far, the recommendations of the NSC on the economy, foreign policy, education, human rights and university administration have obtained approval without exception.[20]

While the NSC highlights the political influence of the Turkish army, the foundation of the 'Army Mutual Assistance Association' (OYAK) in September 1961 marks the emergence of the military as entrepreneur. With the creation of OYAK, the army departed from its previous anti-business attitude and established military–business relations. Supported by subsidies, legal privileges and tax exemptions, OYAK, with more than 25 companies, has developed to become the fourth or fifth largest holding in Turkey, involved in supermarket chains, real estate development, joint ventures in industry and agriculture, and stock, bond and insurance operations (Parla 1998: 30, 42). In 1987, the 'Foundation for Strengthening the Turkish Armed Forces'

(TSKGV) was created. This second economic pillar of the military aims at the development of a national defence industry. In the 1990s, OYAK and TSKGV together employed more than 40,000 people, and their investments in 55 joint ventures indicate the integration of military and private capital, as well as the mutual dependence of army, state and capital (Parla 1998: 44–9).

The autonomous status of the military is further strengthened by its own educational system, which provides the army elite with both academic knowledge and military ethics based on the values of Kemalist ideology. The system educates a military caste socially and ideologically formed into a group which stays apart from and above the rest of society (Karaosmanoglu 1993: 27). To be an officer is an elite career, which, with its military high schools and academies, also provides an upward avenue for people from lower economic strata. Recruitment patterns indicate a clear continuation of Turkey's classical military–bureaucratic elite, since, according to the statistics, most officers come from families of military or civil service background (Brown 1989: 400).

Like the Janissaries, who were loyal directly to the sultan and the Ottoman state, the modern Turkish officer serves to Atatürk and the Kemalist Republic. In a genealogical spirit, tracing a direct line from Atatürk, the military conceives itself as guardian and trustee of the Turkish state (Birand 1991: 23). Military training is based on the Prussian principles of absolute loyalty to the motherland, rigid discipline, blind belief in the commanders and unquestioned obedience; the officer corps is committed to a form of ideological Atatürkism that in its claim to cover all fields of human activity is of a fundamentalist character (cf. Birand 1991: 31, 53–6).

The striking autonomy that the Turkish military has developed in the political, economic and educational realms makes it virtually a state within the state. Holding the monopoly of physical force, the army additionally has substantial economic means, and socialises its officer corps within its own symbolic order. Although the military career does not lead to a brilliant material future, the army is able independently to provide its members with all the societal resources that Norbert Elias considered to be elementary for social reproduction.[21] In addition, the soldier's moral superiority is constantly emphasised, and civilian society is looked upon with contempt. Not surprisingly, the elitist notion of Ottoman statehood has survived within the Turkish army, and the military conceives of itself as the institutional incarnation of the Turkish state.

The army's most recent political intervention, the so-called '28 February Process', was another example of the political subordination of elected representatives to the military. This 'postmodern coup', as Cengiz Candar puts it (Candar 1999: 130), started with a meeting of the NSC on 28 February 1997, at which the generals launched 'a carefully calibrated campaign of destabilization' against the coalition government of Welfare and True Path parties (Salt 1999: 72). The generals demanded via the NSC that the government implement of measures to protect the secular nature of the state. During the campaign, the army identified 'religious fundamentalism' along with 'separatist terrorism' as the main threat to the political integrity of the Turkish Republic, and politicians, bureaucrats, judges, journalists and academics were frequently called in to receive 'briefings' on the subject (cf. Salt 1999: 74–6). Hence the eventual resignation of Prime Minister Erbakan in June 1997; the closure of his Islamist Welfare Party by the constitutional court in January 1998 took place under massive pressure from the military.

However, military interventionism continued after Erbakan's resignation. Although the succeeding minority government of Prime Minister Yilmaz came to power with the blessing of the army, it soon had to face the power of the generals. Owing to the influence of conservative and religious circles in Yilmaz's Motherland Party, the government showed a certain reluctance to implement measures such as the closure of religious schools and the prohibition of beards and headscarves on university campuses, as demanded by the generals. This hesitant implementation of the recommendations of the NSC stirred a severe war of words between the government and the high command, in which the politicians once more surrendered. Nothing displayed this more boldly than the 'briefings on fundamentalist threats' which Prime Minister Yilmaz and President Demirel received in March 1998 at the general staff headquarters in Ankara. According to the press, the 'briefings' took place at the request of the two politicians, who as political representatives of the Turkish state rank quite clearly formally above the chief of the general staff.[22]

Party politics and patronage: electoral politics under military tutelage

A full understanding of the political dynamics behind the specific military–civil relationship in Turkey makes it necessary to look at the historical and social conditions behind the evolution of the Turkish party system. Although Turkey's competitive multi-party system has developed since its inception in 1946, the ideological roots of the major parties still reflect the basic split in the National Movement, which was divided into the Kemalist camp and a bloc of conservatives and Liberals. In this respect, the foundation of the Democratic Party was a personal and ideological continuation of the two abortive attempts to found an opposition party in the Atatürk era. From 1945 onwards, the DP and its successors have represented the centre-right tendency in Turkish politics. Under the impact of the social changes of the 1960s and 1970s, the RPP moved from its authoritarian statist posture to a centre-left position. Particularly under the leadership of Bülent Ecevit, who succeeded Ismet Inönü as chairman of the party in 1972, the RPP was distancing itself from the military and developed a clear left-of-centre policy in order to seek votes among the growing urban migrant and working-class population.

Twenty years after the 1980 coup, the centre-left is divided into Ecevit's Democratic Left Party and the relaunched RPP, while the DP has found two heirs in the True Path Party and the Motherland Party. Furthermore, the Welfare Party and its successor, the Virtue Party, represent religiously oriented defectors from the former Democratic camp, whereas the National Action Party, founded in February 1969, developed under the leadership of the former colonel Alparslan Türkes into a virulently anti-Communist and Turkish nationalist party that glorifies the Turkish State and its national culture (cf. Arikan 1998: 123–5). Interestingly enough, the reconstruction after the military interventions failed to sever these lines of political tradition. It is even more striking that the political leaders of the Second Republic, who had been banned from politics between 1980 and 1987, returned as major political actors in the 1990s. The continuing leading role of these old men of Turkish politics – Süleyman Demirel, Bülent Ecevit, Alparslan Türkes[23] and Necmettin Erbakan – indicates another area of continuity in Turkey's political modernisation.

We are reminded of the basic conflicts of the late Ottoman Empire and the early Republic, not only by the ideological division between the Turkish parties, but also by their organisational structure, which contains both hyper-centralisation previously observed to be characteristic of Turkish modernisation and extreme personal leadership. Originally founded on a national level, Turkish parties have only gradually established themselves in the localities and provinces. The national party leader hovers above all local branches, and the latter communicate with the national centre rather than among themselves (Turan 1994: 236). The actual number of active party members is small, and the party leader tends to control all intra-party processes, resulting in a marked lack of democratic procedure within the party structure. 'The difficulty and even the impossibility of changing the leader and the leadership, coupled with weak intraparty democracy, leave opponents usually with no choice other than resigning from the party. The only serious alternative is expulsion.'[24]

Consequently, it is the jealous political leaders and their sympathisers rather than competing concepts and ideas that shape the political landscape of Turkey. Political parties are therefore not instruments to formulate a political will, but clientelistic organisations for the distribution of material and legal resources acquired via the state apparatus. 'It is evident that politics in general has been reduced to a game of capturing public resources and then redistributing them through legal and illegal means. There is an almost complete absence of meaningful debate among the political elite' (Beriker 1997: 449). Against this background, the dissatisfaction of the Turkish population with party politics is understandable, as is the fact that the military capitalises on the negative image of politicians. Yet behind rampant corruption and patronage in Turkish politics, we can detect more than low morals among politicians. In contrast to the self-reliance of the armed forces, political parties have to work within society and are therefore open to outside pressures and demands. Furthermore, with the integration of the periphery into politics, the multi-party system has also become a stage for the competition between traditional and modern social forces. The political parties have had to adjust to the societal condition of both accelerated modernisation and the persistence of traditional structures.

The clientelistic character of Turkish parties thus resembles the well-established forms of social conduct that can be observed in modernising societies in general and in Turkish society in particular. In a society in which modern forms of social organisation do not yet encompass a majority of the population, clientelistic networks and patronage are convenient systems for the exchange of resources (Özbudun 1981: 252). While the Ottoman rulers and Atatürk used the traditional structures of the periphery as intermediaries, competitive politics made it salient to recruit traditional notables, sheiks and tribal leaders directly into party ranks. Given the heterogeneous character of Turkish society, it comes as no surprise that, according to a survey in the 1960s, most local party cells were based on kinship and traditional solidary groups.[25]

Moreover, the political awakening of the periphery and its sheer numerical weight in national elections set the trend whereby political life increasingly became focused on the demands of the villages (Leder 1979: 87–90). In the new multi-party system, the extreme gap between centre and periphery, which for two centuries had characterised Turkish modernisation, developed into a key question in Turkish politics. Turkey's large peasantry equated the RPP with central state oppression, and the centre-right parties exploited this view by representing the Republicans as elitist bureaucrats and by furnishing the countryside with roads, waterways, mosques and a variety of public services (Özbudun 1981: 260). Thus it was the DP and its successors who capitalised heavily on this development and exercised political patronage in return for votes (Heper and Keyman 1998: 261).

Within the framework of multi-party politics, patterns of traditional clientelism and modern party-based patronage became major features of

Turkey's political life. Since the inception of competitive politics, we can observe both the stabilisation of traditional forms of leadership and the evolution of new forms of urban patronage by political machines.[26] In one way or another, all political parties had to adopt systems of patronage in order to acquire and distribute resources provided by the state. Only the army was able to stay aloof and thus to enhance its image as a neutral force, set apart from the bargaining of a political marketplace that was becoming characterised more and more by morally questionable practices. On the one hand, the political role of the military was thus accomplished by its image of moral superiority. On the other hand, it was the political role of the army itself that contributed to the degeneration of Turkish party politics. In depriving the parties of power to give political directives, the military depoliticised them and strengthened their tendency to become state-related power blocs for the distribution of public resources. It is the central dilemma of Turkish politics that the negative image of Turkish parties and the positive reputation of the Turkish armed forces are two sides of the same coin.[27]

Ottoman elitism and the modern elite: Turkey's Kemalist establishment

So far, this chapter has focused on the Turkish army as the key institution that holds up the authoritarian, state-centred and paternalistic spirit of the Turkish modernisation process. However, it would be wrong to locate the heritage of Ottoman elitism only within the higher ranks of the armed forces. Almost two hundred years of top-down modernisation have left their imprint on Turkish society as a whole. The social habiti of the different forces that Elias marked as the central source of national cultures, the hegemonic bloc on which state power relies, are all in one or another way affected by this Ottoman legacy. Not only the officer corps, therefore, but also Turkey's social establishment in general shows the insignia of an inherited elitism. Whether officers, politicians, bureaucrats, journalists or entrepreneurs, many representatives of Turkey's elite display attitudes which developed within the hegemonic social block of Ottoman reforms. Given the prominent role of the military–bureaucratic elite in Ottoman modernisation, it is understandable that not only the military, but also the upper echelons of Turkey's bureaucracy exhibit this inherited elitism.

In a clear analogy with still vivid forms of patriarchal authority, high-ranking Turkish bureaucrats view the state as a father figure acting with compassion and justice towards its children. Although an initiator of democratic procedures, the bureaucracy perceives democratic rules in merely juridical terms. From the bureaucratic perspective, it is the bureaucracy itself that designates democratic structures as a formal set of rules. Democracy therefore has to facilitate policies through enlightened debate rather than organise conflicting ideas and interests through adversarial politics. Consequently, the bureaucratic detestation of party politics resembles that of the military, and, like the generals, bureaucrats consider themselves as being apart from and above the rest of society (Heper 1993: 39–42).

In his analysis of Turkey's post-1980 bureaucrats, Metin Heper discovered that the intrabureaucratic change left the elitist and anti-democratic views of bureaucrats almost untouched. He concludes that 'those bureaucrats who are most strongly for Westernization … are farthest away from a notion of a liberal-democratic state; instead, they are the most earnest partisans of the non-liberal State' (Heper 1993: 67). This contradiction in the bureaucratic attitude towards democracy and Westernisation applies equally to the military's concept of being democracy's guardian. In both concepts we can easily discern the legalistic bias of the Tanzimat and the Kemalist reforms. From the perspective of a corporate world-view that denies existing social and cultural fragmentation, the military and the bureaucracy view a democratic society not as pluralistic, but as a unitary community based on legal authority.

Besides its competitive party system, post-Second World War Turkey has developed ever-expanding media whose influence on the political discourse is not to be underestimated. As we have previously seen, Turkey's journalistic sector also has its roots in the late years of the Tanzimat. Between 1922 and 1925, the early Republic saw a short period of open press discussion, which ended with the promulgation of the Law on the Maintenance of Order (Zürcher 1991: 7). The freedom of the press was for the first time legally established in the 1961 constitution. Since the abrogation of the state broadcasting monopoly in April 1994, private radio and TV programmes with different political and commercial interests have been mushrooming.

Although we have to group Turkish journalists in their majority within the Republican and modernist camp, they share a clear resentment against the West. Like many generals and politicians, they like to put the demise of the Ottoman Empire down to Western conspiracy. In referring to the Treaty of Sèvres, they keep alive the late Ottoman sense of conspiracy and betrayal, which maintained that there was a plan made by Western powers to weaken and dismember Turkey. This topos and the accusation that Turkey was discriminated against on religious grounds accompanied media discussion around the ups and downs of Turkey's application to become a candidate for full membership of the EU. Until the mid-1980s, a general mistrust of democratic institutions and processes was widespread among Turkish journalists, who generally accepted the model of top-down modernisation represented by the military–bureaucratic elite (cf. Alpay 1993: 70–78).

Despite their fight for freedom of the press, which has repeatedly been curtailed by military interventions, the journalists have only slowly developed a democratic culture. On the one hand, they have shared an authoritarian spirit that does not tolerate the liberties of others and tries to manipulate the masses from the perspective of a holder of ultimate truths (Heper and Demirel 1996: 121). On the other hand, the limitations to the freedom of the press have contributed to a culture of self-censorship, according to which sensitive topics such as religious liberties, the cult of Atatürk, the Armenian massacres, Kurdish identity and the role of the military have been deliberately avoided for many years (Alpay 1993: 83). For most of the period since 1945, the Turkish press has lacked an adequate level of reflection concerning Turkish political history. The liberalisation policies of the 1980s led to the growth of the popular mass press and to power conflicts between big media companies, such as Dogan and Sabah, rather than to an improvement in the quality of press discussion. Additionally, the 28 February process showed that the Turkish press is still willing to support the military in ousting a civilian government, as the massive press campaign against Prime Minister Erbakan showed.[28]

Unlike bureaucrats and journalists, Turkey's economic elite has no tradition linking it directly with Ottoman times. As discussed previously with the economic role of religious minorities in the Ottoman Empire, the Muslim Turkish entrepreneur is a latecomer among Turkey's modern social groups. Based on family businesses, industrial holdings such as Koc or Sabanci emerged in the 1960s. Since 1971, the leading industrialists and businessmen have been associated in the 'Turkish Industrialists' and Businessmen's Association' (TÜSIAD). TÜSIAD is a driving force behind Turkey's full integration into the EU and stands for a clear Western and market-economy-oriented course. In accordance with its liberal attitudes, TÜSIAD repeatedly criticises the legal and political deficits of Turkey's democracy. None the less, the economic elite is closely tied to the military and the political and bureaucratic state elite. With the legacy of Kemalist statism and more than twenty years of state-controlled policies of import substitution, Turkey's big business has developed a strong dependency on the state (cf. Ilkin 1993: 179–81, 189–91).[29] A further point to be made is that many holdings are involved in joint ventures with the military's economic pillar OYAK, thus establishing an institutional compromise with the state elite (Parla 1998: 38–41).

Although statism was abolished in the 1980s, the policies of liberalisation have not abandoned the role of the state as a key economic actor and major distributor of subsidies and economic rents to the private sector. The close interrelation of political and economic interests under a neo-liberal aegis rather caused widespread tax evasion, a growth of the underground economy and the politicisation of economic rent distribution (Önis 1997: 752). Politically, these developments were accompanied by the rise of political Islam and by confrontation between the Kemalist establishment and Erbakan's Welfare Party. This political dichotomy finds an economic equivalent in the division between TÜSIAD, representing big business located mainly in the Istanbul and Marmara Sea area, and the 'Independent Industrialists' and Businessmen's Association' (MÜSIAD), which represents the more Islamic-oriented small businesses of Anatolia. One conflicting issue between the two economic associations is the fact that big business has preferential access to state subsidies.

The political and economic dichotomies briefly mentioned here signal the rise of a 'counter-elite' that is challenging the established power of Turkey's modern hegemonic bloc in the political, economic and cultural fields (cf. Göle 1997). Since the foundation of the Republic, an elite of specifically modern actors has evolved around the institutional core of Ottoman–Turkish modernisation: the military–bureaucratic establishment. Based on a cartel of particular interests, this modern elite of officers, bureaucrats, politicians, journalists and representatives of big business controls access to the power resources of Turkey's modern society and legitimises this position with the remnants of Kemalist ideology. As the self-proclaimed guardian of the Atatürk Revolution, the military dominates this hegemonic bloc, and, in contrast to its civilian counterparts, has access to all three elementary societal functions, making it relatively autonomous with regard to its political, economic and symbolic power resources. Yet while the socio-structural background of this elite is specifically modern, it is characterised by an elitist social habitus that cannot hide its Ottoman legacy. The Kemalist establishment preserved several patterns of traditional social conduct and essential aspects of a world-view whose historical and social roots are to be found in the demise of the Ottoman Empire and the formative phase of the Turkish Republic. Thus the institutional stagnation of Turkey's democracy is complemented by an anachronistic social habitus on the part of the country's classical Kemalist elite.

Conclusions:
Ottoman–Turkish continuities and the Greater Middle East

The first part of this book investigated the question of how important aspects of Ottoman modernisation and of the foundational phase of the Turkish Republic have been incorporated into the political and social structures of present-day Turkey. Yet these elements of Ottoman–Turkish continuity do not exclude change. On the contrary, in the historical process continuity appears as change, and the Ottoman legacy is only one force that has shaped modern Turkey. From this perspective, the introduction of multi-party politics and the association with the West set limits and constraints on post-Second World War Turkey, engendering two salient processes. First, the incorporation of the periphery into the political system was the political answer to the ending of the physical separation of centre and periphery caused by the accelerated modernisation of Turkish society. Second, the rise of the military as a relatively autonomous political, economic and social force led to its becoming the major institutional heir of Ottoman and Kemalist reforms.

Theoretically, we can locate these conditions and processes of Turkish state formation within Elias' conceptualisation of the monopoly mechanism. While the Ottoman struggle of the nineteenth century almost entirely reflected the competitive elimination contests of the first phase of the monopoly mechanism, post-1945 developments indicate the dominance of the second phase of the monopoly mechanism, in which the monopolised resources pass from individuals to institutions, and the relatively private monopolies become public. Both phases converged under the leadership of Mustafa Kemal Atatürk in the foundation of the Turkish nation-state. This major move to fully accepted member of the state system was consolidated after the Second World War, and the Eastern Question system, which marked the outer constraints of Turkish state formation until the 1920s, was replaced by the bipolarity of the international system. From 1945 onwards, the international framework of the Cold War gave Turkey a chance to convert its geo-strategic location into financial and institutional opportunities, leading to its full integration into the Western bloc and the world market.

Nevertheless, the need to adjust Turkey's polity to the political structures of the West counterbalanced the opportunities provided by the Cold War. Outside pressure therefore limited, but did not end, the coercive trajectory of Turkish modernisation. The democratisation of Turkish politics gave the previously silent masses of the periphery a voice which wrapped the promotion of their interests in the ideological slogans of a global political culture. As the intellectuals of the Tanzimat had applied the European discourse of nationalism, constitutionalism and scientific reasoning, the workers, students and street fighters of the Second Republic resorted to the socialist, anti-imperialist and egalitarian ideas prevalent among both Western students and national movements in the Third World. Against the Kemalist dream of a unitary society, Turkey's political awakening painted the picture of a deeply fragmented society that was no longer willing to accept the political, economic and cultural domination of the Kemalist state. The power monopolies that the Kemalist institutions had achieved during the single-party era were at stake, since the masses increasingly wanted to participate in and benefit from the resources that Turkish modernisation provided.

In this situation the military detached itself from society and tried to take over the monopolies once held by the Kemalist state. Establishing its autonomous role, the army carried forward the Ottoman ideals of a reforming state elite and the total identification of state apparatus and state elite. Since its first political intervention in 1960, the military has perfectly applied the policies of co-optation and coercion we know from Ottoman and early Republican times. In routinising Atatürk's charismatic authority in ideological (Atatürkism) and institutional (National Security Council) terms, the army partly succeeded in binding newly emerging elites together and subordinating party politics under their guardianship. Based on a cartel of interests, the Turkish military has acquired supremacy over a none the less very fragile hegemonic bloc that is held together by both a tacit agreement over the exclusive distribution of societal resources and a set of attitudes and values that we can label as the Kemalist social habitus.

Regarding our central question of Ottoman–Turkish continuities, the Kemalist habitus perpetuates the Ottoman legacy in two respects. On the one hand, Turkey's Kemalist establishment shares the kind of patriarchal elitism of the Ottoman state elite that goes along with a strictly authoritarian notion of the state. Using it as an entry ticket to the social establishment, the newly rising modern elite adapted to this legacy of military–bureaucratic modernisation that enormously hampers the democratic and pluralistic transformation of Turkish society. On the other hand, the Ottoman experience of external conspiracy and internal betrayal found its way into the world-view of the representatives of the Kemalist elite. Culminating in the 'Sèvres syndrome' – the conviction that there is an international conspiracy to weaken and to divide Turkey – the Kemalist habitus sets up an obstacle to addressing the major domestic and international problems of the country in an adequate way.

The demise of the Soviet Union aggravated the domestic conflicts with which Turkey's state elite is confronted; indeed, since the end of the Cold War international and local developments have increasingly overlapped. The scenario of overlapping spheres applies specifically to the Middle East, whose geo-strategic structure and political landscape is currently undergoing dramatic changes. Basing our view on common variables such as history, ethnicity, Islamic culture, state formation, political systems, armament and conflict structures, we can speak of an evolving 'Greater Middle East', including the Caucasus and Central Asia (Dietl 1999). This new regional framework is developing under the impact of what is hidden behind the catchword 'globalisation' – the increasing political, economic and cultural interdependence of societies and individuals, as well as the weakening of the organisational power of the nation-state. The emergence of a Greater Middle East affects Turkey's future in various ways. Most dramatically, it revives the neglected Ottoman heritage and confronts the state elite with challenges and opportunities for which the Kemalist power bloc does not seem to be equipped.

The political instruments of Kemalism – authoritarian decision making; a narrow territorial and unitary notion of the state; neglect of social, ethnic and religious divisions; viewing national security in strictly military terms – have already remained passive in dealing with domestic social change. In Kurdish nationalism, Islamic internationalism, pan-Turkist revivalism, and the Armenian question being now a matter of bilateral relations, the old political demons of Ottoman times are re-emerging under new conditions and confronting the Kemalist elite with its own neglected legacy. At the beginning of the twenty-first century, the Turkish state elite has to face both the successes and the omissions of two centuries of top-down modernisation in a new regional and international environment. There is no doubt that this situation holds both promises and dangers. The second part of our book will address this new situation and the question of whether Turkey can find an adequate role in the emerging Greater Middle East.

Notes

1   This quotation is taken from the communiqué as cited in Weiker (1963: 20–21).
2   Between 1950 and 1975, the urban share of the total Turkish population grew from 18 to 41 per cent (Sayari and Hoffman 1994: 163).
3   The crucial role of the army does not mean that the officer corps has a unitary character. Broadly, four ideological streams can be distinguished: a conservative wing with a nostalgic attachment to the early Kemalist reform period; the defenders of parliamentary and constitutional rule; younger officer groups with either a nationalist or a socialist inclination to radical reform; and military professionals without political ambitions (Tufan and Vaner 1984: 179–180). However, since the first military intervention in 1960, the high command has been able to establish its hegemony over the different groups, based on a strong sense of seniority and a common understanding of the essentials of Kemalist ideology.
4   The various steps of Turkey's Western integration are described in Chapter 6.
5   The term counter-elites refers to the increased emergence of modern actors in

Turkish society who confront the power monopoly of the Kemalist establishment, see Göle (1997).

6   With regard to the political exclusion of the countryside, it is important to notice that in the 1920s around 90 per cent and in the 1960s still 60 per cent of the population worked in agriculture (Hermann 1999: 45).

7   The overwhelming majority of the DP, who received only fifteen per cent more votes than the RPP, was due to the electoral system created under Republican rule (Ahmad 1993: 109).

8   The DP could raise its total share of the votes to 58.4 per cent, which gave it a majority of 503 seats in the assembly, leaving only 31 seats for the Republican camp (Zürcher 1993: 234).

9   President Bayar was a banker, Prime Minister Menderes a cotton-growing landlord and Foreign Minister Köprülü a historian (Ahmad 1993: 103–4).

10 According to Harris, the first secret political groups within the army were formed just after the 1946 elections (Harris 1965a: 64). Most of the members of the 1960 junta reported that they became engaged in conspiratorial activities around 1954; some even claimed that their concern with the political situation of the country started as early as 1950 (Weiker 1963: 120).

11 For a detailed account of the conflicts among the members of the National Unity Committee and between the junta and the rest of the army, see Özbudun (1966: 30-39) and Weiker (1963: 127–38).

12 Quoted from the 'Constitution of the Turkish Republic' as documented in *Middle East Journal*, 16 (2), 1962, 227–8.

13 From the 1950s until the late 1970s the Turkish population increased by 2.5 per cent to 2.7 per cent annually. In total, the population grew from 21 million in 1950 to 40 million in 1975 (Rustow 1979: 97). At the beginning of the twenty-first century, Turkey's population is still growing at an annual rate of 2.17 per cent and approaching a total of 70 million (Seufert 1999: 26).

14 Istanbul, for example, had around 1.75 million inhabitants in 1965 (Saran 1974: 331). By 1990, its population had risen to 7.3 million, crossing the threshold of 10 million at the end of the century. In Ankara, with more than three million inhabitants, almost 80 per cent live in a *gecekondu* (Wedel 1996: 437).

15 According to the figures given by the junta leader, General Kenan Evren, the armed clashes claimed 5,241 lives and 14,152 casualties during the two years before the military intervention of September 1980 alone (Birand 1987: 193).

16 According to a report in the Turkish daily *Hürriyet*, 650,000 people were detained and more than 23,000 associations were closed down (Sahin 1999: 28–9).

17 In a remarkable speech at the opening of the legal year 1999–2000, Dr Sami Selcuk, the president of the supreme court, said that Turkey should not enter the new century with a constitution acknowledged to have been imposed under massive pressure by the military, and which lacks almost every kind of democratic legitimacy. Cited from the German translation of the speech, published in *Nützliche Nachrichten*, 1999 (3), 15–19.

18 During three years of military rule more than 669 laws, 1,000 regulations and 100 decrees were issued (Türsan 1996: 217).

19 After sitting for a short period between 1973 and 1976, so-called state security courts were re-introduced in 1983. They sit in eight cities and are composed of

two civilian judges, one military judge, and two prosecutors. The state security courts deal with accusations of terrorism, of organised crime and of acts or ideas 'damaging the indivisible unity of the state', as well as 'inciting racial or ethnic enmity'. In June 1999, the Turkish parliament passed a law to demilitarise these courts. Apart from the civil courts, Turkey also has military courts that are responsible for military-related cases (cf. Öztürk 1999: 101 and US State Department 1999).

20   See TÜSIAD 1997, Chapter One: Perspectives on Democratisation in Turkey, Section V: The Issue of Civilianisation, 2) National Security Council (Article 118 of the Constitution).

21   See the theoretical explanations in chapter 2.

22   About the briefings, see Turkish Daily News, 1 April 1998. According to formal protocol, the chief of the general staff ranks fifth after the president, the head of the constitutional court, the speaker of parliament and the prime minister (Birand 1991: 184–5).

23   Alparslan Türkes died in April 1997 and received a first class state funeral.

24   See TÜSIAD 1997, Chapter One: Perspectives on Democratisation in Turkey, Section I: Political Parties, 10) Central, Provincial and District Organisations (LPP, Art. 13 to 21).

25   For an interesting account of the high degree of patriarchal and personalised systems of authority in the economic field, especially among the migrant population of the gecekondu, see Dubetsky (1976).

26   An interesting investigation into the impact of modernisation on forms of patronage among the traditional leaders in the eastern Black Sea region is provided in Meeker (1972).

27   According to a survey of the Turkish Social and Economic Studies Foundation, conducted in five representative provinces during 1997, 94 per cent of those questioned expressed confidence in the military, whereas the political parties could gather only 30 per cent. Quoted in Heper (1999).

28   Cf. the article by Par Nur Dolay: 'Les ambiguités d'une press à scandale', Le Monde Diplomatique, July 1997.

29   About the different stages of Turkey's policy of import-substitution, see Balassa (1983: 430–33).

PART II

Turkey in
the Greater
Middle East

Kemalism Challenged

6 Susurluk, Political Islam and Kurdish Nationalism

Economic liberalisation and counter-insurgency: Susurluk and its socio-historical background

On 3 November 1996, a Mercedes limousine ran into a truck close to the west Anatolian town of Susurluk. The driver of the limousine and two of the passengers died on the spot, while a third passenger was severely injured and taken to hospital. Given the enormous death toll on Turkish roads, this accident could have been considered as nothing more than routine, but the composition of its passengers stirred a major state crisis, disclosing the involvement of politicians and security forces in the mafia-like web of Turkey's organised crime.

Behind the steering wheel was a high-ranking police officer who formerly headed a special department to combat terrorism. In the back of the car, a beauty queen died alongside Abdullah Catli, an internationally wanted killer, a prominent figure in Turkey's organised crime and a former leader of the Grey Wolves, the fascist youth group at the spearhead of the right-wing terror during the 1970s. Catli left behind him automatic weapons, some cocaine, two diplomatic passports, and papers that identified him as an officer of the Istanbul police service. Sedat Bucak, a traditional Kurdish leader and a parliamentary representative of the True Path Party, survived on the front seat. More than 3,000 people bore Abdullah Catli to his grave, his coffin wrapped in the Turkish flag, Sedat Bucak found medical treatment in Istanbul's university hospital protected by his private guards.

The 'Susurluk Investigation Committee', which had been charged by the Turkish National Assembly with the investigation into the accident, released its report in April 1997. This gave ample evidence for close ties between state authorities and criminal gangs and specifically for a prominent role for the former interior minister, Mehmet Agar, in this criminal web. Agar, also a member of Tansu Ciller's True Path Party, had to resign in November 1996, after revelations that he personally had signed Catli's passports. Moreover, a report of the Turkish intelligence service (MIT) accused Agar of being a leading member of a mafia-like organisation that was linked to the extreme right and involved in drug-trafficking as well as racketeering and kidnapping in Germany, Holland, Belgium and Azerbaijan.[1]

Susurluk was nothing more than the tip of an iceberg. The disclosed criminal network, including various politicians, members of security forces, banks and enterprises, right-wing terror groups, drug traffickers and money launderers, reflected the disastrous state that Turkey's political institutions had reached in the mid-1990s. Parallel to this inner erosion by rampant corruption and state–mafia ties, the Kemalist state came under the pressure of Islamist and Kurdish nationalist organisations. All three processes – the erosion of state institutions, the rise of Islamist movements and the nationalisation of Kurdish identity – were related to the social repercussions of the 1980 coup. Two points seem to be particularly salient in this respect. First, to a certain extent these processes were social consequences of Turkey's economic adjustment programme, of Turgut Özal's politics of economic liberalisation without liberty. He implemented radical economic reforms from above without any bargaining power in the hands of society. Second, the persistence of guerrilla warfare and counter-insurgency in south-east Anatolia caused a gradual deterioration of Turkey's internal security, corrupted politicians and members of the security forces alike, and finally put the state monopoly of physical force in jeopardy.

The economic reforms, initiated by the junta, executed by Turgut Özal, and financed by structural adjustment loans of the World Bank, aimed at a radical export-oriented transformation of the economy (cf. Kirkpatrick and Önis 1991). And indeed, macro statistics show the success of this transformation. In the years between 1981 and 1998, Turkey had, with an average of 5.2 per cent, the highest annual growth rate among the OECD countries.[2] Turkish private industries achieved rates of productivity that pushed the country up among the forty most competitive economies in the world. However, these impressive figures represent just one side of the coin. While the economic restructuring decisively transformed Turkey's statist economy,[3] the adjustment programme heavily aggravated the social costs of modernisation. The dramatic fall in real incomes, painful cuts in social expenditure, and an extremely high rate of inflation also gave Turkey a lead among the countries with the least equal distribution of wealth and income (Önis 1997: 751). The majority of the population was thus excluded from the economic miracle and experienced the macro-economic success as material hardship at the level of everyday life.[4]

Taking these social costs into account, it was also a purpose of the 1980 coup to secure the implementation of economic reforms against possible public resistance. The political division of labour during the 1980s clearly reflects this aspect. Whereas Prime Minister Özal concentrated on the management of economic affairs, former general chief of staff and then President Kenan Evren presided over foreign policies and internal security (Ahmad 1985: 217). In the absence of political competition, Turgut Özal consolidated his personal position and formed in the Motherland Party an amalgam of mainly inexperienced politicians held together basically by patronage and personal ties. Most of the new politicians owed their positions directly to Özal, and his cabinets reflected this 'absolute control over the party which he rarely consulted before making appointments' (Ahmad 1993: 193). In addition to political patronage, Özal established an uncontrolled fund economy, distributing money to whomever and for whatever he wanted. Comprising almost half the state budget in 1986, this fund economy was legalised by the National Assembly, giving Özal the right to distribute money according to his own directions. Thus, using public resources for political purposes, the economic reformer Turgut Özal established corruption as a legitimate and legal practice (Ahmad 1993: 191). Evidently, the post-1980 creation of a 'new class of politicians' did not abolish but rather radicalised the inherited patronalistic and clientelistic patterns of Turkish politics.

The escalation of the Kurdish question further spurred this moral and institutional deterioration of Turkish politics. In 1984, only shortly after civilian rule was restored, the Kurdistan Workers Party (PKK) began its guerrilla war in the south-eastern provinces of Turkey. Given the combination of suppressed political freedom and economic hardships, the socialist and nationalist rhetoric of the PKK found an ever greater response among Turkey's Kurdish population.[5] Moreover, with its massive military retaliation against both PKK fighters and civilians suspected of being associated with the PKK, the Turkish authorities further alienated the Kurds. The military solution in the south-east created a major predicament for Turkish society. According to official statistics, more than 34,000 people were killed, an estimated 3,000 villages depopulated, and between 350,000 and two million people forcibly evacuated from the war zone (US State Department 1999: 13). Fifteen years of war destroyed vast parts of south-eastern Anatolia, shattered popular confidence in the Turkish state, and aggravated religious and ethnic divisions within the populace.

The strategy of securing the integrity and sovereignty of the Turkish state by military means swung to the other extreme. In distributing arms among an estimated 70,000 village guards (Kilic 1998: 102), Kurdish vigilantes loyal to and enrolled by Turkish authorities, the state partly passed on its monopoly of physical force to tribal leaders and kinship groups. The only survivor of the Susurluk accident, Sedat Bucak, was one of those leaders, with thousands of armed men at his disposal. These irregular forces, the PKK, and special police units (özel tim) – which had been raised to fight Kurdish separatism and fell under the control of the extreme right – entered into a fierce competition over drug profits. The characters involved in the Susurluk incident perfectly reflected this web of organised crime that emerged in Turkey's south-east (cf. Seufert 1998: 390).[6] Additionally, the war not only strained the state budget by more than US$8 billion per year, but it further weakened the economy of the eastern provinces, where the per capita income dropped to a annual low of US$300 in 1992.[7]

It is this complex scenario of authoritarian rule, economic liberalism, guerrilla war, counter-insurgency and organised crime which forms the background for an explanation of Turkey's most pressing domestic problems of the 1990s. In the light of growing popular dissatisfaction with state institutions, economic and political grievances were increasingly articulated in Islamist and Kurdish nationalist terms. Ironically, the re-engineering in the 1980s caused an escalation of those social conflicts it originally claimed to contain. In sharp contrast to these findings, however, the Kemalist state elite has persistently denounced political Islam and Kurdish nationalism as being driven by external forces. In denying the domestic origin of these phenomena, the Kemalist establishment reacted with exclusively authoritarian means and aggravated the conflict-prone nature of Turkey's internal social problems.

It is therefore appropriate to continue our enquiry about the domestic roots of political Islam and Kurdish nationalism with a brief examination of Kemalist perceptions. How does Turkey's current political elite perceive the challenges of Islamist and Kurdish nationalist movements? How, in this perception, are domestic problems associated with foreign intervention? We will then argue that, contrary to the Kemalist perception of threat, both movements are essentially domestic in origin. The seeds of religious and ethnic rebellion against the Kemalist state were sown with the foundation of the Turkish Republic. It is further argued that since its foundational phase, a gradual separation of those two streams of resistance took place. While one part was motivated by religious symbols and brought about the politicisation of Islam, the other part based its resistance ideologically on the construction of a particular Kurdish national identity. Though both movements are ideological opponents of Kemalism, they nevertheless carry major insignia of the Turkish modernisation process. In this way we have to understand political

Islam and Kurdish nationalism as both resistance to and products of the Kemalist project. The chapter concludes with four assumptions about the consequences of the depoliticisation that the military imposed on Turkish society in the 1980s. This final analysis will locate one major obstacle to solving Turkey's domestic problems in the mental and institutional stagnation that the Ottoman–Kemalist legacy has caused.

Domestic problems in the prism of Sèvres: social conflicts and Kemalist perceptions

The theoretical chapter of this book defined the social habitus as a system of cognitive and normative principles that is historically and socially constructed. As a heuristic tool, the habitus concept allows us to understand these generative principles that shape the particular ways which a certain group pursues its interests. Hence, rationally calculated goals are transformed into action in the light of these ideational patterns. As analysed in previous chapters, one essential aspect of the Kemalist habitus is its perpetuation of the Ottoman experience of external conspiracy and internal betrayal. The historical culmination of this experience, as well as its social transmission to the National Movement, was the Treaty of Sèvres. Although never implemented, the clauses of Sèvres, calling for a territorial division of Turkey, became the incarnation of both the Ottoman defeat and the Turkish national resistance. The following section documents how the Sèvres syndrome developed into a cornerstone of the Kemalist world-view, making it essential for an under-standing of Kemalist perceptions of threat.

A good starting-point is the controversy that erupted in May 1999, when Merve Kavakci, a newly elected female member of the Islamist Virtue Party, entered the National Assembly during the swearing-in ceremony wearing a headscarf. The incident triggered a barrage of protests and accusations from Turkey's Kemalist establishment, which perceived Kavakci's act as a challenge to the very foundations of the secular Republic. Turkey's President Süleyman Demirel called the veiled Turkish deputy an 'agent provocateur' working for foreign powers.[8] These remarks were echoed by Turkey's chief prosecutor Vural Savas, who charged Kavakci with being an agent of Islamic parties, which resembled 'vampires feeding only on blood'.[9] At the same time, the mainstream Turkish press published a series of allegations, ranging from claims that she had close links with the Libyan leader, Colonel Qaddafi, and 'Hamas', to reports that she was a US citizen and a CIA agent. Ironically, the only charge that was sub-stantiated, and eventually caused the removal of Kavakci's Turkish citizen-ship, was the concealment of her dual Turkish–American citizenship.

The 'Kavakci affair', as it was called by the Turkish media, highlights well how deeply a sense of encirclement has become an integral part of Turkish political culture. The Kemalist establishment increasingly views international and domestic developments through the lens of the Sèvres syndrome. Concerning the geographical location of the country, the view of Hikmet Cetin, a former foreign minister and speaker of parliament, is revealing: 'Turkey is in the neighbourhood of the most unstable, uncertain and unpredictable region of the world, it has turned into a frontline state faced with multiple fronts.'[10] The sense of being encircled by aggressive and irredentist states is, according to the retired Turkish General Sadi Ergüvenc, 'mainly due to the somewhat painful and unhealthy dissolution of the Ottoman Empire' (Ergüvenc 1998: 32). The dismemberment of the Empire left a legacy of territorial grievances, historic resentments, political tensions and mutual suspicions which neither Turks nor Arabs have so far overcome.

It is not surprising, therefore, that the state elite is generally inclined to bemoan Turkey's location in a 'bad neighbourhood' and depicts the country as 'besieged by a veritable ring of evil'. Based on these historically constructed elements of the Kemalist habitus, the Turkish establishment continues to associate political Islam and Kurdish nationalism with foreign interference. The distinction between domestic and external threats becomes entirely blurred, and the challenge of the Kemalist power monopoly by Turkish counter-elites is translated into a threat by foreign states to Turkey's national security.

General Fevzi Türkeri, the former chief of military intelligence, for example, stated in 1997, that 'political Islam is working closely with Iran and some other Islamic countries to pull Turkey into an endless darkness'.[11] Non-governmental groups inside Saudi Arabia were also, albeit to a lesser extent than Iran, accused of funding Islamic fundamentalist movements that aimed at undermining Turkey's secular regime.[12] In general, large parts of Turkey's Kemalist establishment consider Islam as an irrational force. Ali Karaosmanoglu, for instance, criticised the lack of any sense of *realpolitik* in Arab foreign policy. He explained this deficiency as a result of the merger between nationalism and religion in the Arab world where 'Islam infuses an irrational element in national politics' (Karaosmanoglu 1985: 68).

It is the Kurdish insurrection, led by the PKK, which greatly exacerbated the 'Sèvres phobia' during the 1990s. The extreme right-wing National Action Party, in particular, exploited the Kurdish insurgency by claiming 'that there is a conspiracy of foreign enemies to use the PKK to destroy the unity of the Turkish state' (Arikan 1998: 127). Although it is indisputable that the PKK has been receiving, since its inception, military and logistical backing from external Middle Eastern powers, the Kurdish issue has domestic origins, and its intensification in recent years is essentially linked to Ankara's policy of reducing the Kurdish question to a problem of terrorism to be solved by strictly military means – a flawed approach that left the political initiative to the PKK. Syria, Iran and Iraq have their own reasons for supporting the PKK, but none of these has an interest in carving up Turkey. In short, Ankara is increasingly vulnerable to the pressure posed by its neighbours in exploiting the Kurdish issue for their own ends; nevertheless, the toll from this has yet to assume regime-threatening proportions.

Whilst Turkey's perception of external threats is historically coupled to the countries located on its southern and eastern borders, the prevailing sense of distrust in its most extreme manifestations also involves Ankara's European partners, and Turkey's staunchest ally, the United States. Turkey's inability to confront the Kurdish reality has led Turkish decision-makers to perceive Western pressure for enhanced democratisation and respect for human rights through the lens of Sèvres. The fundamental incompatibility, from Ankara's perspective, between Turkish and Western approaches to the Kurdish question is well highlighted by Ergüvenc: 'while Turkey expects its allies to give the support that it deserves from them in its fight against the PKK terror, it receives an unwarranted embargo on associated weapons sales' (Ergüvenc, 1998: 40).

The West's support for political solutions, such as the official recognition of Kurdish cultural and linguistic rights, is perceived as part of a devious agenda aimed at undermining the integrity and sovereignty of the Turkish state. Confronted with European instructions to settle the Kurdish question peacefully, Turkish President Demirel responded that there is no other political solution than 'to render these people ineffective by force'. He further accused the West of trying 'to involve the Sèvres treaty to set up a Kurdish state in the region ... and that was what they [the Western states] meant by political solutions'.[13] Prime Minister Ecevit confirmed this standpoint in an interview after the capture of PKK leader Abdullah Öcalan in February 1999. Ecevit pointed out that there is no Kurdish problem in the country, only PKK terrorism supported by outsiders seeking to divide Turkey.[14] Both the Kemalist ideal of a unitary society and the Sèvres syndrome are pivotal in the attitude of Turkey's political establishment in denying the numerous social rifts behind the current domestic conflicts in the country. In contrast to this point of view, the following sections will argue not only that the Islamist and Kurdish challenges are deeply rooted in Republican history, but also that their escalation into severe domestic conflicts was a consequence of the uncompromising policies of the Turkish state elite.

Political Islam: the rise of the Welfare Party and the postmodern coup

In December 1995, the results of the general elections came as a shock for both the Kemalist establishment and the country's Western allies. The Islamist Welfare Party gained 21.4 per cent of the votes, and for the first time in Turkey's republican history an avowedly religious party gained a relative majority of the votes in the general elections.[15] This was not their first success. In the March 1994 municipal elections, the Islamist party captured more than 200 mayoralties, including those of Istanbul and Ankara (Akinci 1999: 76). Governing Turkey's two major cities and having the strongest parliamentary group, the Welfare Party was nevertheless first side-stepped in the formation of a new government. After difficult negotiations, the Motherland and True Path parties formed a minority coalition which in parliament had to rely on the external support of the two left-of-centre parties.[16] Given its minority status and the deep hostility between the two party leaders, Prime Minister Mesut Yilmaz and Foreign Minister Tansu Ciller, the collapse of the government only three months later was only to be expected.

The breakdown of the minority government gave the opportunity to Welfare leader Necmettin Erbakan, the veteran politician of the religious right, to conclude a coalition with Ciller's True Path and to become the first Turkish Islamist prime minister ever. Although giving assurances that he had no intention of damaging either Turkey's republican order or its Western relations, Erbakan embarked on some bold symbolic changes in domestic and foreign politics. For instance, he paid his first state visits to a number of Muslim countries, allowed female bureaucrats to wear the headscarf in the office, and agreed to the adjustment of working-hours during *Ramadan*, the holy month of fasting (Salt 1999: 73).

This 'new way' confirmed the suspicions of the military and triggered the so-called '28 February process', the massive campaign against Islamist tendencies that eventually led to the resignation of Erbakan and his coalition government in June 1997. The undemocratic way in which the Islamist experiment came to an end stirred little protest among Turkey's Western allies. On the contrary, reminded of the Islamic Revolution in Iran, the authorities in Europe and the USA silently approved the 'postmodern coup' in order to prevent Turkey from falling into the hands of Muslim 'fundamentalists'.

However, Western anxieties were much exaggerated. In the first place, the real power of the Islamist party was very limited. With slightly more than twenty per cent of the total vote, the Welfare Party was hardly able to bring about the feared transformation of Turkey's society. Secondly, different ideological wings internally fragmented the party, and only a minority of its voters supported fundamentalist policies. Particularly instrumental in its municipal success was not so much the ideological factor, but the role that religious organisations and foundations played among the urban poor. They took over the social functions of a welfare state whose provisions had been sacrificed in the liberalisation programme of the 1980s (Gülalp 1999: 35). The real reason behind Western fears was the fact that many Western observers still believed in the Kemalist smoke-screen of a complete secular revolution. They were not aware of the prominent political and societal role that religion has always played in Turkey.

As previously indicated, the elitist and iconoclastic Kemalist reforms did not penetrate deeply into Turkish society. While public religious life was frozen during the Atatürk era, the Kemalist ice-cap started to melt after the Second World War and gave way to the almost unchanged religious expression of Turks and Kurds alike (Hermann 1996a: 36). The reappearance of Islam in public, therefore accompanied the post-1945 entrance of the periphery into politics. Without questioning the essentials of the Kemalist reforms, the Democratic Party government of Prime Minister Menderes immediately participated in this Islamic revival. One of its first steps was to abandon Atatürk's prohibition of the Arabic call to prayer. During the ten years of Democratic Party rule, innumerable new mosques were built and saint tombs (türbe) reopened. The government founded new schools for the education of preachers and prayer leaders, the so-called imam hatip schools, as well as university faculties of divinity (cf. Heyd 1968; Reed 1954). From the 1950s onwards, the religious orders (tarikat) and communities (cemaat) reappeared in public and played an important role in Turkish politics and society,[17] reviving the popular religious heritage of Ottoman society. Beginning with the abolition of the political monopoly under single-party rule, the Kemalist domination of the symbolic reproduction of Turkish society has been gradually eroded.

The Welfare Party and its leader, Necmettin Erbakan, were political representatives of this Islamic revival. Since the late 1960s, Erbakan had been spearheading the politicisation of Islam, and between 1973 and 1978 he had already served as deputy prime minister under the coalition governments of both Bülent Ecevit and Süleyman Demirel. The latter had previously prevented his potential competitor from joining the Justice Party (JP), and Erbakan founded the National Order Party together with some JP defectors in January 1970. Dissolved in the aftermath of the coup-by-communiqué, the National Order Party was re-founded as the National Salvation Party (NSP) in 1972.

A more radical offspring of the right-of-centre current, the NSP called for a revival of the historic role Islam had played in Turkish society. In strongly criticising the Western attitudes of the Turkish elite, Erbakan launched an alternative political discourse based on the moral values of the family and religion. Ideologically rooted in the classical ideas of late nineteenth-century Islamic modernism, Erbakan none the less adopted Kemalist state-centrism and its notion of the state as development agency. Accordingly, the NSP wanted to modernise and industrialise Turkey under state control but without abandoning the cultural and moral heritage of Islam. In appealing to religious sentiments and propagating an alternative path to modernity, the NSP found its voters among either traditional communities or educated individuals with a marginal socio-economic status (cf. Toprak 1984).

Yet, not only Erbakan and his Islamist wing of the centre-right, but also Menderes, Demirel and Özal had close ties to religious circles and used religious symbols in their political campaigns.[18] In addition to the ideological value that conservative propaganda assigned to Islamic symbols and idioms in fighting communist and socialist competitors, the centre-right parties also used religion as an effective means of social organisation and political mobilisation. In this respect, the religious orders and communities are of the utmost importance. Their extended networks provide a major source of social cohesion in Turkey and their role has been enhanced since the Kemalist abolition of the *ulema*, the official class of state-related religious scholars. Facilitating the economic, professional and social mobility of their members, these powerful religious networks are active in business, politics, education, the media and social services. Based on the traditional principle of direct personal relations, the religious orders contribute much to the persistence of the clientelistic structure of both Turkish society and politics.[19]

An interesting example is Fethullah Gülen, the influential head of the Nurcu movement. Until President Özal's death, Gülen supported the Motherland Party, then moved to the True Path Party (Hermann 1996b: 627). Gülen is a follower of Said Nursi (1873–1960), whose revivalist ideas are documented in an extensive collection of Koranic exegesis, making him the founder of a powerful text-based religious movement (Yavuz 1999b: 586–9). Far from being a traditional religious teacher, Fethullah Gülen presides over a large empire of business networks, educational institutions and private media in Turkey, and over 150 schools in the Balkans, the Caucasus and Central Asia (Hermann 1996b: 637). In his teaching he gives priority to the community over individual rights and propagates a pragmatic merger of Turkish nationalism and Islam. In criticising the explicit political role of Islam in Erbakan's ideology, Fethullah Gülen sounds like a Kemalist who has rediscovered Turkey's Ottoman–Muslim heritage, and he is among the most powerful proponents of a neo-Ottomanist ideology.

This short analysis of the political role of Islam in Turkey proves the indigenous roots of Turkey's Islamic revival and its interrelation with Kemalist modernisation. The example of Fethullah Gülen shows how traditional religious orders and groups have internally modernised and developed into integral parts of the state elite. A further point to be made concerns the role of the army and its politics of social engineering. Contrary to its image of being the incarnation of secularism, the military itself contributed heavily to the rise of the Islamist challenge. First, the depoliticisation of society after the 1980 coup created a political vacuum that was gradually filled by a religious discourse. The ban on socialist and social democratic parties, particularly, gave Islamist movements the opportunity to articulate the grievances of the socially deprived in religious terms. Given the process of radical economic restructuring, the Islamic discourse of social justice found fertile ground. Second, and more salient, the generals applied the ideas of the so-called 'Turkish–Islamic synthesis' as a tactical means in both their fight against leftist movements and their attempts to maintain the Kemalist ideal of a unitary society.

Supported by the business world and centre-right politicians, a group of conservative intellectuals began to think about Islam as a force to counter the rise of leftist ideas during the political turbulence of the 1970s. They developed the Turkish–Islamic synthesis as an ideological concept integrating Islam and Turkish nationalism; it became prominent among right-wing politicians of Süleyman Demirel's National Front governments (1974–77). The National Action Party (NAP) incorporated the concept into its extreme Turkish nationalist ideology, and its leader, Türkes, went on a well-publicised pilgrimage to Mecca (Ahmad 1988: 760). After the 1980 coup, this 'mixture of fierce nationalism and a version of Islam friendly to the state' appealed to the senior officer corps as an ideology to reintegrate Turkish society (Zürcher 1993: 303). The integrative power of Islam was used for two purposes, first to create the desired unitary character of Turkish society, and, second, to counterbalance the spread of nationalist ideologies among Turkey's Kurdish population.[20]

In spite of its ideological affinity to Fethullah Gülen's teaching, the military used the Turkish–Islamic synthesis, and therefore Islam, as an ideological political instrument. The state-centred Kemalist concept incorporated Islam as a moral source to strengthen the national culture and the legitimacy of the authoritarian state alike. Besides the Islamisation of the state discourse, the strongest manifestation of the Turkish–Islamic synthesis took place in the field of education. Ironically, in their campaign against Prime Minister Erbakan the generals demanded the containment of precisely those educational developments which the junta and Turgut Özal once initiated: the increasing religious character of education, the spread of religious *imam hatip* schools, and the growth in students attending Koran courses. To a certain extent, the electoral success of the Welfare Party and the rising power of political Islam was a late outcome of the third attempt to restructure Turkish society under military rule. It was the military itself that played a major part in making the Islamist political discourse socially acceptable.

Kurdish nationalism: identity construction and militarised conflict

On 15 February 1999, the Turkish authorities surprised the world with a video showing PKK leader Abdullah Öcalan on board a plane from Kenya to Turkey. In front of the Turkish flag, the former strong man of Kurdish nationalism was sitting blindfold and handcuffed telling the astonished spectator that he had always loved the Turkish nation. From his abduction by a special unit of Turkey's security forces onwards, Öcalan was exposed to a number of humiliations whose target was not only the individual leader, but also the political body of Kurdish nationalism. The destruction of the leader, according to the rationale behind this process, would destroy the whole movement. While Öcalan was isolated on the prison island of Imrali, the reaction of Turkish society displayed a major split between parts of its Turkish and Kurdish population. Fifteen years of warfare had left unresolved grief, and whereas Turks who lost their sons in the army's struggle against the PKK called for revenge, the humiliation of Öcalan and his possible execution rallied the Kurds behind the national cause more than ever before.

Like political Islam, the Kurdish question is not a recent phenomenon, but has been a major source of domestic conflict in the Turkish Republic from its outset. In the Atatürk era (1923–38), 18 rebellions against the Republican regime were reported, of which 17 took place in eastern Anatolia and 16 involved Kurdish groups (Kirisci 1998: 74). The crucial date for the eruption of this series of revolts was the abolition of the Caliphate in March 1924, a clear indication that at this point there was no sharp distinction between Kurdish and Islamic aspects of east-Anatolian resistance against Republican rule. In this respect, the famous Sheikh Said rebellion is a good example, and a perfect departure point to explain the development of Kurdish nationalism as an ideological platform to legitimise political resistance, distinct from the symbolic world of Islam.

Pre-empting their clandestine preparations, an accidental clash between followers of Sheikh Said and gendarmes triggered the revolt on 13 February 1925. The next day, Sheikh Said issued a *fetva* in which he called his followers to a holy crusade against Ankara, under his command as a leader of the

Naksibendi order and as a representative of the 'Caliph of Islam' (Olson 1989: 108). Led by religious and tribal chiefs, the rebel forces were able to establish temporary control over the mountainous area north of Diyarbakir. However, they were soon pushed back by comparatively well-trained and well-equipped government troops and Kurdish units loyal to Ankara.[21] On 27 April, Sheikh Said was captured in the vicinity of Mus, and after a short trial, in which the Sheikh was accused of instigating the rebellion with the intention of establishing a Kurdish state, he and 47 other leaders of the rebellion were executed on 4 September 1925 (Bruinessen 1992: 291).

In analysing of the motivations behind the revolt it is necessary to differentiate between leadership and rank and file. Indeed, the original initiative for the rebellion developed within a small, clandestine organisation of Kurdish nationalists. Mostly military officers of a tribal background, they were aware that the nationalist cause was unable to rally support among ordinary Kurds. Therefore they approached the Naksibendi Sheikh Said, who, although a religious notable, was sympathetic to Kurdish nationalist aspirations. In denouncing the government for its godless policies and claiming that he would restore religion, Said translated the nationalist interest of the elite into the everyday language of his followers. Thus religiously inspired, the rebels went with green flags and Islamic battle cries into a 'holy war', claiming to fight for the restoration of Islam and the Caliphate (Bruinessen 1992: 291). Despite the religious motivation, many of the local leaders joined the revolt to defend their traditional power positions against the centralising reforms of the government, and the rebellion also became a stage for traditional banditry, tribal feuds and personal vendettas (Olson 1989: 154). To sum up, the Sheikh Said rebellion still had the character of traditional social banditry but was also motivated through both nationalist and religious symbols.

Although the security situation in eastern Anatolia remained tense, both Islamic and Kurdish resistance were frozen under the authoritarian Kemalist regime until they gradually returned to the surface in the wake of Turkey's post-Second World War developments. Under the impact of the dramatic social transformations of the 1950s and 1960s, however, the Kurdish question became increasingly nationalistic in nature. This intrinsic connection between the rise of Kurdish nationalism and the ongoing Kemalist modernisation project is proved by the change in Kurdish leadership. Traditional tribal and religious chiefs led the revolts of the 1920s and 1930s. Although the traditional leadership showed a certain degree of national consciousness, the rank and file participants in these revolts were mobilised almost exclusively by tribal, local and religious solidarity. If there was a force that could transcend the boundaries of the segmented Kurdish society, then this was Islam and not a 'desire for sovereignty on the basis of Kurdish ethnicity' (Bruinessen 1998: 39–40).

From 1945 onwards, the extension of state bureaucracy, the spread of modern education and Turkey's growing integration into the world marked formed the structural background against which a new modern stratum of Kurdish society emerged. Whereas the traditional Kurdish sheikhs and *aghas* associated themselves with the Turkish establishment, and with the centre-right parties in particular (cf. McDowall 1996: 397-410),[22] the rising modern leadership voiced its interests first among the Turkish left (Kilic 1998: 98). Consequently, the internal conflict between modern and traditional Kurdish forces was associated with the conflict between the Turkish counter-elite and the Kemalist establishment. The radicalisation and nationalisation of Turkish politics in the 1970s, then, provided the framework in which nationalist and separatist organisations among Turkey's Kurds evolved. Persons formerly part of rural and provincial cultures became political actors on the national scene, and the Kemalist education system itself provided the breeding ground for both the radicalisation of Turkish politics and the discovery of a Kurdish national identity.

The interplay between Kemalist modernisation and the rise of anti-Kemalist resistance explained above is clearly visible behind the formation of the PKK and the rise of its leader, Abdullah Öcalan.[23] Born around 1948 in a small village in southeastern Anatolia, Öcalan came to Ankara in 1969 as a 'Turkish Muslim' where he enrolled in the department of political science of Ankara University. Under the influence of the political turmoil in the capital and the politicised university environment, Öcalan turned to the revolutionary Marxist–Leninist left before he founded his first specifically Kurdish organisation in 1974. While the leftist camp already had its heroes, the brand new Kurdish struggle was still open for a 'political career', and fitted well the leadership aspirations of Öcalan's exaggerated character. Drawing on the violent concepts of the Turkish left and contemporary liberation movements of the Third World, Öcalan developed his ideology of armed struggle for an independent socialist Kurdistan, and moved back to the south-east where he founded the PKK in 1978 (Gürgenarazili 1998: 363–4).

Like many of the left- and right-wing activists of the Second Republic, Öcalan almost conforms to an ideal type of 'epic hero' who, according to Serif Mardin, characterised the strongmen of Turkey's violent early years. Their authoritarian character was a meeting-point of traditional rural patriarchalism and national heroism. It combined traditional patterns of violent male behaviour with the positive character that waging war enjoyed in Turkish national culture (cf. Mardin 1978). Accordingly, many of Turkey's Kurdish nationalists were strongly integrated in Turkish culture and were once great admirers of Atatürk (Bruinessen 1998: 40–41). A further demonstration of the Kemalist heritage of Kurdish nationalism is the way it has been constructed since the late 1960s. Given the religious, tribal and linguistic fragmentation of the Kurds,[24] the Kurdish nationalists faced similar tasks to those the Kemalists faced in the 1920s. The task of creating of an all-embracing Kurdish identity turned into a comprehensive cultural reconstruction, of Kurdish language, literature, music, folklore and history, to which the Kurdish graduates of Kemalist education devoted themselves (cf. Bruinessen 1989; Mango 1994b).

This short history of the emergence of Kurdish nationalism makes clear that it presents to a certain extent the mirror image of the Kemalist construction of a Turkish nation. We find the forces shaping both the ideology and the proponents of Kurdish nationalism in the centre of the Kemalist project itself. This equally applies to the violent escalation of the Kurdish question in the 1980s and the emergence of the PKK as a political player in the national and international arenas. If it is true that one of the reasons behind the 1980 military intervention was the elimination of Kurdish separatism, the history of the PKK proves the complete failure of this attempt. In the general atmosphere of economic deprivation, social injustice and physical displacement, three aspects of the army's societal reconstruction strengthened the PKK in the long run. First, the suppression of Turkey's left supported the establishment of an independent Kurdish national discourse, making it a major channel for voicing the grievances of the Kurds. Second, the policies of the Islamic–Turkish synthesis contributed not to the reintegration of alienated Kurds but rather to a further polarisation between Turks and Kurds. The close association of Islam with Turkish nationalism weakened the strongest existing means of cohesion between the two groups, their shared religious belief. Third, political supression, economic deprivation and cultural oppression, such as the language law of 1983,[25] caused mass emigration among Kurdish intellectuals to Europe, where they formed an extra-territorial Kurdish opposition beyond the control of the Turkish state.

The European Kurdish diaspora, in particular, counteracted the cultural oppression of the military regime and developed into 'a catalyst on the Kurds' ethnic self-awareness'. With the foundation of Kurdish cultural institutes in Paris (1983), Brussels (1989) and Berlin (1994), Kurdish intellectuals in Europe continued the construction of Kurdish ethno-national identity. In spreading a wide range of Kurdish books, journals, magazines, cassettes and videos, the Kurdish diaspora initiated the revival and formalisation of Kurmanci as a standardised Kurdish umbrella language (Bruinessen 1998: 45–7).

In May 1994, MED TV started broadcasting in Kurdish and Turkish from

London and Brussels to Europe, West Asia and North Africa. The Kurdish TV channel provides a comprehensive programme of entertainment, news and live debates, in which politicians of different Kurdish parties participate. The constant presence of the Kurdish flag and national anthem confirms the nationalist mission of MED TV. Reaching millions of people daily, MED TV not only disseminates Kurdish culture, but also promotes the idea of national self-determination among Kurds (Hassanpour 1998: 53–9).[26]

In addition to this construction of a Kurdish national culture, the European diaspora provides substantial economic and political assistance for the nationalist struggle. The PKK, for instance, built up a network of organisations in Europe that collected money or levied war-taxes to support financially the war against the Turkish state. Moreover, Europe became a field of recruitment, supplying young men as guerrilla fighters, organisers and technicians (Bruinessen 1998: 45). Undoubtedly, the military intervention of 1980 was the departure point for the internationalisation of the Kurdish question, which meanwhile bluntly reveals the contradictions of Kemalist policies. While the Turkish establishment obsessively searched for European affirmation of Turkey's Western character, the exiled generation counteracted this effort from within Western societies. Applying democratic discourses and modern Western means of communication, the Kurdish diaspora was not only instrumental in the nationalisation of Kurdish identity, but also a crucial promoter of the Kurdish case within the European Union. Thus, all the authoritarian and military means that the Turkish authorities applied against Kurdish aspirations bounced back in the form of political accusations from their Western allies.

The establishment of the 'Kurdish Parliament in Exile' may be a final case in point. It was not until 1990 that an explicitly Kurdish party appeared among Turkey's official political parties. Currently represented by the Peoples Democratic Party (HADEP), this new political current and its representatives have been frequently confronted with legal prosecution because of their alleged ties to the PKK. In 1994, Prime Minister Ciller launched a fierce campaign against the Kurdish Democracy Party (DEP), the predecessor of HADEP, and parliament revoked the immunity of the DEP deputies. The party was banned and some of its members ended up in prison, while others were able to escape (Barkey 1998: 130). In April 1995, six former DEP deputies set up the Kurdish Parliament in Exile in the Netherlands, thus forming an extra-territorial political body that promotes and symbolises Kurdish nationalism in Europe (cf. Kirisci and Winrow 1997: 138). The official politics of suppression thus turned into a source of strength for the Kurdish national movement, operating from Europe.

Conclusions: Kemalist political engineering at its limits

The precarious web of politics and organised crime, the wave of Islamic resurgence and the Kurdish insurgency are all essentially of domestic origin. They not only rest on indigenous social foundations, but also developed within the larger context of the Kemalist project. The leadership patterns and state-centred ideologies of both Kurdish nationalists and Islamists clearly disclose the impact that Kemalism had on the development of these movements. The attempt by the Turkish establishment to blame foreign intervention for the rise of political Islam and Kurdish nationalism is symptomatic of the Kemalist denial of historical reflection. Furthermore, it supports the continuity thesis of this book; we might re-call Halide Edib's description of the Kemalist reaction to the Sheikh Said rebellion of 1925 as an attempt to attribute the Kurdish rising to foreign intrigue (Adivar 1930: 220). To sum up, the problems of the 1990s and the challenges with which the Turkish elite has been confronted are indicators that the Kemalist policy of social engineering has met its limits.

The frequent attempts by the military to preserve the Kemalist heritage by military interventions and societal reconstructions escalated rather than contained the social and political conflicts that unavoidably accompany modernisation. The emergence of political Islam and Kurdish nationalism disclose the elusiveness of a project that is intended to modernise a country whilst holding on to a unitary and authoritarian concept of society. Under the impact of the political awakening of Turkey's periphery, the intrinsic contradictions of Kemalism and its Ottoman legacy came out into the open, and constitute a major threat for the political integrity of the Turkish Republic. The very same social groups once spearheading Turkish modernisation increasingly undermine the indisputable achievements of the Kemalist reform process. Four consequences of the depoliticisation of Turkish society, which the military junta launched at the advent of the Third Turkish Republic, may prove this assumption.

1. Under authoritarian reconstruction, Turkey's political parties further degenerated to mere clientelistic power blocs, filling their rank and file with inexperienced followers whose political careers rested on material benefits and unquestioned obedience to leadership. While real political opposition had to take place outside the official arena, the state itself became a contested market for the trade of legal and illegal resources, leading to open corruption and causing a dramatic loss of public confidence in the authority of political institutions (Önis 1997: 752).

2. Political suppression did not destroy all extremist organisations once

based on radical ideologies. The answer to depoliticisation, particularly on the extreme right, was the criminalisation of former political activists. Abdullah Catli provides a good example of this transformation from political extremism to organised crime. Hence, the 1970s infiltration of state institutions and security forces by partisans of the National Action Party facilitated the emergence of state–mafia links.

3. The silencing of the Kurdish opposition supported the militarisation of the Kurdish question. The complete denial of the Kurdish reality necessarily played into the hands of separatist groups. The ensuing spiral of violent terror and reprisal increased the alienation of large parts of Turkey's Kurdish population from the Turkish state, and transformed elitist Kurdish separatism into a national movement, with substantial support particularly among the modern stratum of Kurdish society. Moreover, the move by Turkish authorities to raise armed auxiliaries among traditionally organised Kurds, a measure already applied by Ottoman sultans, and their alleged support of brutal paramilitaries contributed to the erosion of both the factual monopoly of physical force and the legitimacy of state authority.[27]

4. Re-adopting of the Kemalist top-down imposition of a unitary national ideology via the educational system turned the cultural realm into a major battlefield for Turkey's current conflicts. The ill-fated strategy of producing social cohesion by means of an Islamic–Turkish synthesis not only spurred political Islam as an ideology for the counter-elite of Sunni Turkish origin, but set an example for the articulation of economic and political conflicts in cultural terms. The attempt to forge cultural cohesion from above enhanced the actual fragmentation of Turkish society along religious and ethnic lines.

Theoretically speaking, Susurluk, political Islam and Kurdish nationalism are symptoms of the ongoing deterioration of the essential monopolies that the Kemalist state once held. Besides the previously mentioned critical state of the monopoly of physical force, the capability of the Turkish state to extract resources via its monopoly of taxation suffered tremendously under the impact of both economic liberalisation without public control and the Kurdish insurgency. Black markets, criminal economic transactions and a huge shadow economy emasculated the tax authorities and directed economic resources into uncontrolled channels. The devastation caused by the earthquake of 17 August 1999, for example, supplied terrible proof of the deadly interplay between corrupt state authorities and the construction mafia.[28] Moreover, in the south-east of the country the irregular state militias and the PKK established a war economy. They not only appropriated the means of force, but also began to levy taxes in order to finance and maintain the war. Finally, the so-called identity crisis, the fact that the ideologies of Kurdish nationalists, Islamists, members of the Alevi community, and so-called neo-Ottomanists counter the official national history of Turkey, indicates the collapse of the Kemalist monopoly of symbolic reproduction.

Today, the Kemalist establishment in general and the military in particular are faced with the ruins of their desire to form a modern society according to a blueprint designed at the beginning of the twentieth century, which incorporated major patterns of the Ottoman past. While the Kemalist project successfully modernised Turkish society, the reformers failed to modernise themselves. Under the impact of the Ottoman–Kemalist continuities analysed here, the Sèvres syndrome only highlights the structural and mental stagnation of the Turkish state and its ruling elite. It serves the political establishment as an escape from both the realities of Turkish society and the changes of the international system. With regard to the latter, political Islam and Kurdish nationalism are indicators that Turkey's counter-elites are better equipped to voice their interests in the terms of current international discourses and to de-territorialise their struggle against the Kemalist state elite. They are increasingly able to profit from a globalising environment and to draw on material and symbolic resources that are beyond the influence of the Turkish state.

The attempt by the Kemalist elite to disguise the domestic causes of this struggle behind a smoke-screen of foreign interventionism is doomed. Trapped in the confines of its Ottoman legacy, the ruling establishment's fight to maintain the integrity and sovereignty of the Turkish nation-state, as well as to defend its own inherited privileges, reminds us increasingly of the Ottoman decline. Similar to their Ottoman predecessors, the Kemalists conflate the integrity of their own power with the integrity of the state, and try to apply current political and legal norms to an anachronistic authoritarian polity in an instrumental way. Still confined to the outmoded rhetoric of classical nation-state discourse, the Kemalist elite has inevitably lost its voice in the communication of domestic social conflicts, which are meanwhile articulated in terms of individual political, economic and cultural rights. The impact of this speechlessness on Turkish foreign policy is the topic of the next chapter.

Notes

1 Susurluk and its aftermath are described in Erzeren (1997: 12–27) and the annual report *La Géopolitique Mondiale Des Droques*, September 1997, Paris: l'Observatoire Géopolitique des Drogues.
2 The macro-economic figures are taken from the 'Country Report on Economic Policy and Trade Practices' issued by the US State Department (1999).

3 In contrast to the highly competitive private sector, the public sector remained inefficient. Additionally, the state budget is skewed by a high deficit in its balance of payments and by substantial agricultural subsidies. This is linked to the constraints that the clientelistic structures of the political system impose on economic reforms (Hermann 1999: 50).

4 Statistically, the real incomes of salaried people dropped by more than 50 per cent between 1977 and 1989 (Seufert 1999: 27).

5 The liberal reforms eventually destroyed the fragile existences of subsistence farming and, thus, enhanced rural migration, especially from eastern Anatolia. With only ten per cent of state industrial investment and two per cent of all commercial investment, Turkey's east could not offer employment in the modern sector (White 1998: 146–52).

6 According to the 1997 report of the Observatoire Géopolitique des Drogues in Paris, Turkey developed during the 1980s from being a transit land to being a producer, transformer and exporter of drugs. In 1998, more than five tons of hashish and three tons of heroin were seized by Turkish police (Turkish Daily News, 21 December 1998). Official figures of the interior ministry mention 23,000 village guards dismissed for their involvement in criminal actions (Erzeren 1997: 24).

7 The average per capita annual income in Turkey was at that time US$2,032. For these figures, see Bozarslan (1996: 127–30).

8 Turkish Press Review at www.mfa.gov.tr, 10 May 1999.

9 Turkey Update at www.turkeyupdate.com.tr, 17 May 1999.

10 Quoted in Mufti (1998: 33)

11 Quoted in Meyer (1999: 496).

12 Interview by the authors with two senior officials of the Turkish ministry of foreign affairs, Ankara, 7 April 1999.

13 Quoted in Gözen (1997: 119).

14 Interview with Bülent Ecevit in Die Zeit, 25 March 1999.

15 The results of the elections were as follows: Welfare (21.4%), Motherland (19.7%), True Path (19.2%), Democratic Left (14.6%) and Republicans (10.7%). The National Action Party missed the 10 per cent threshold with 8.2 % (Schüler 1996: 241).

16 These were the Republican People's Party (CHP) and the Democratic Left Party (DSP).

17 The Naksibendi and Kadiri orders are the most prominent ones among the Sunni majority of Turkey. The most important religious organisation of Alevi Islam is the Bektasi order. Yet the orders are internally fragmented and have developed various religious currents and cemaat.

18 In the 1970s Turgut Özal was an electoral candidate for Erbakan's NSP.

19 For a more detailed account of the role of religious orders in Turkish society, see Ayata (1990, 1991), Hermann (1996a, 1996b), Mardin (1991) and Meeker (1991).

20 For an intensive discussion of this ideology and its promotion by the state, see Seufert (1997: 182–202).

21 Although the Republicans exiled a large number of Kurdish notables, by exploiting intra-Kurdish conflicts and distributing material benefits, the regime also

secured the support of traditional Kurdish leaders (McDowall 1996: 397).

22 After the general elections of December 1995, there were 21 tribal leaders and fourteen religious sheikhs among the 50 parliamentarians who represented the ten Kurdish core provinces (Wießner 1997: 300).

23 In choosing the PKK example, we do not claim that this organisation represents Kurdish nationalism in general; that the political awareness of Turkey's Kurds found various expressions is beyond doubt.

24 According to McDowall's statistics, the total number of Kurds in the Middle East in the 1990s was between 24 and 27 million, out of which Turkey had the highest share, with an estimated 13 million (McDowall 1996: 3). Robins cites estimates of the proportion of Kurds in Turkey that differ from both the official 7.1 per cent and Kurdish estimates of 24 per cent (Robins 1991: 6). Yet being Kurdish is only one layer of identity and often not the most important one. Religiously, the Kurds are divided between Sunni Muslims, orthodox Shiites, Alevis, Yezidis and the Ahl-i Haqq sect. In Turkey, for example, intermarriage between Turks and Kurds who belong to the same religious group are far more frequent than between Kurds of different sectarian backgrounds. In terms of language, three major linguistic groups divide the Kurdish population: Zaza, Kurmanci and Surani. These 'dialects' are not mutually intelligible, and the formalisation of Kurmanci as a national language is a recent step. Moreover, tribal and local divisions still play an important role in Kurdish society (cf. Bruinessen 1989; Kreyenboek and Allison 1996).

25 Law no. 2932 of November 1983 'prohibited the use of any language other than "first official language of each country which recognizes the Republic of Turkey" for the explanation, the dissemination and the publication of ideas' (Kilic 1998: 99). It therefore implicitly banned Kurdish. The Law was abolished by Turgut Özal in 1991, but the prohibition of Kurdish as a language of education continues (cf. Salih 1999: 22).

26 MED TV was later renamed Medya TV. At the end of the 1990s, five regional and 10 local Kurdish TV channels were receivable in south-east Turkey and northern Iraq (Nützliche Nachrichten, 2000 (2), 18–19) .

27 For relations between village guards, right-wing criminals and organised crime, see McDowall (1996: 421–3). The extreme fundamentalist Hizbullah was founded in close relation to the Islamic revolution in Iran in the late 1970s, aiming at the establishment by armed struggle of an Islamic state in Turkey's south-east. On the one hand, Hizbullah was used by the Turkish state against the PKK; on the other hand, Hizbullah activists supported Iranian intelligence officers against the Iranian opposition in Turkey (Hermann 1996a: 52–6). In January 2000, a country-wide police campaign was started against Hizbullah, disclosing that this organisation was behind hundreds of unsolved assassinations of journalists, intellectuals, businessmen and politicians with either Kurdish or moderate Islamist background.

28 On the night of 16–17 August 1999, a massive earthquake hit an area around the Sea of Marmara in western Turkey, killing more than 17,000 people. Many of the apartment blocks that collapsed were fairly new and lacked almost all the technical and legal standards that normally should have been applied.

7 Encircled by Enemies?
Turkey's Foreign Policy and its Middle Eastern Neighbours

Islamist initiatives and Kemalist constraints

In October 1996, Prime Minister Erbakan's initiative of adding an Islamic component to Turkish foreign policy came to an end with humiliation and embarrassment. What was intended as a bold symbolic step against Western policies of isolation turned out to be a nightmare for its initiator. Paying a visit to the internationally outlawed regime of Muammar al-Qaddafi, Erbakan suffered a terrible blow from the erratic Libyan leader. At a joint press conference, Qaddafi accused Turkey of conducting an entirely wrong foreign policy, which linked itself to Israel at the expense of the Arab world. But most awkwardly for the Turkish prime minister, who was standing at his side, Colonel Qaddafi insisted in his speech on the establishment of an independent Kurdish nation. On his return to Ankara, the sheepish-looking Turkish prime minister was confronted by a wave of mockery and loud calls to resign. He survived a subsequent no-confidence vote in parliament only by a tight margin (cf. White 1997: 28).

Erbakan's Libyan debacle epitomised a rather rhetorical attempt to give Turkish foreign policy a new, religiously inspired posture. Besides his symbolic visits to a number of Islamic countries and the inauguration of the 'Developing Eight' (D8),[1] the economic bloc of Muslim states that was never really workable, Erbakan's new Islamist posture was far from the revolutionary anti-Western slogans of the Welfare Party's election campaign. Bold promises, such as those to withdraw from NATO and to revoke the Customs Union with the EU, turned out to be hollow. Erbakan not only renewed existing agreements on USA military bases in Turkey, but once in power the Welfare Party also backed the renewal of the provision for allied aircraft to use Turkish facilities for 'Operation Provide Comfort' in northern Iraq.[2] The conclusion of the Turkish–Israeli agreements underlined the almost grotesque flexibility that the Welfare Party showed in power. Coming back from Tehran, his first official visit abroad, Erbakan signed the military agreement on defence industry between Turkey and Israel on 26 August 1996. 'Merely a business deal',[3] was Erbakan's justification for this act, which clearly indicated his de facto acceptance of the new relationship with Israel.

The setbacks and inconsistencies of Prime Minister Erbakan's political performance illuminate two important aspects for the analysis of Turkish foreign policy. First of all, there is the coincidence in timing between his new Islamist approach and the initiative by the military to negotiate a comprehensive alignment with Israel. This simultaneity perfectly reflects the remarkable inroad that the domestic struggle between Islamists and Secularists had made into Turkish foreign policy. It is a good example of the growing conflation of internal and external conflicts that characterised Turkish politics in the 1990s. Secondly, the awkward situation with which Muammar al-Qaddafi confronted the Turkish prime minister emphasised the insufficiency of a new ideological drive alone in bringing about a shift in historically rooted foreign policy practices. Not only did Erbakan's activities meet with strong resistance from the Turkish state apparatus, but he also had to face the persistent legacy of Kemalist foreign policy, which detaches Turkey from the Arab world.

Theoretically speaking, Erbakan's case reminds us of the complex interplay of agency and structures in foreign policy, and of the constraints that they mutually impose on each other. With regard to structural transformations, it has become commonplace to claim a profound change in Turkish foreign policy in the 1990s. In the post-Cold War period, so the assumption runs, the decisive structural change in the international system caused a visible deviation from the cautious and pragmatic foreign policy that Turkey had previously displayed. In particular concerning the Middle East, it has been argued, a new activist pattern replaced a policy that for decades was largely reactive and politically non-interventionist in style.[4]

In light of the historical development of Turkish foreign policy, we must question these assumptions. Does this new pattern of activism truly signal a clear deviation from deep-rooted traditions? Did Turkey really abolish its classical approach on Middle Eastern relations, always viewing them as nothing more than an appendix to its Western-oriented policies? To put these questions into a historical framework, the following section presents four subsequent phases of republican foreign policy: neutrality, Westernisation, rapprochement, and activism. We will argue that transformations of the structural context have had a strong impact on Turkish foreign-policy behaviour, but have never decisively changed its normatively motivated general direction.

The third section then gives an overview of the conflict scenarios that characterise Turkey's relations with its immediate Arab and Iranian neighbours. In this case, the overlap of internal and external conflicts engenders a paradoxical situation in which the country gets more and more embroiled in Middle Eastern affairs. A brief analysis of the complex structures of conflict indicates the severe pressure under which the maintenance of some principles of Turkish Middle Eastern foreign policy have come. We will not conclude that this situation is a result of irreconcilable conflicts or determined by conditioning structural constraints; rather, the observed contradiction of principles and actions is a consequence of the Kemalist habitus and the extremely high degree of 'securitisation' it causes in Turkish politics.[5]

Four phases of Turkish foreign policy: from neutrality to activism

First phase: territorial consolidation and neutrality

During the first two decades of the Turkish Republic, the Kemalist regime was preoccupied with the internal and external consolidation of the new, territorially defined Turkish nation-state. In this consolidation process, Atatürk concluded a series of treaties aimed to secure the territorial and political integrity of the Republic. As early as March 1921, the Ankara government signed a treaty with the Soviet Union in which both sides agreed to abstain from any interference in the internal affairs of the other. In this treaty, made during the War of Independence, Ankara basically rejected the pan-Turkist aspirations of the former unionist regime and thus assured for its nationalist struggle the political and material support of Bolshevik Russia. On 17 December 1925, a treaty of non-aggression and neutrality extended this agreement (Karpat 1975b: 81). While this treaty of friendship with the Soviet Union guaranteed the north-eastern boundaries of the Republic, the national borders in the south-east had to be negotiated with Britain. Here, the major dispute was the future of the oil-rich province of Mosul. British troops had occupied Mosul shortly after the armistice of Mudros (1918), but the Republican government still considered the area as a part of its national territory. However, Britain rejected all Turkish claims, and Ankara eventually had to accept the integration of the province into Iraqi territory (Zürcher 1993: 209–10).

In February 1934, Turkey, Yugoslavia, Romania and Greece signed the so-called Balkan Pact. Containing agreements on, for example, non-aggression, mutual friendship and assistance, judicial and arbitrated settlement of conflicts, and the protection of minorities, the Balkan Pact was directed mainly against the territorial ambitions of Italy and Bulgaria. It provided the signatories, all of them former Ottoman provinces, with an anti-revisionist arrangement that aimed at the defence of the territorial status quo. Several Turkish–Greek agreements on property and border disputes had preceded the Balkan Pact. These treaties of the early 1930s had two basic purposes: on the one hand, Ankara aimed at a legal guarantee for its last European province, eastern Thrace; on the other hand, they served as a protection shield against potential military threats to the demilitarised zones of Thrace and the Straits (cf. Türkes 1994).

While the conclusion of the Balkan Pact marks the normalisation of Turkey's relations with the successor states of the former European provinces of the Ottoman Empire, modern Turkish–Iranian relations began with an official visit of Reza Shah to Ankara in 1934. The founder of the Pahlavi dynasty and Atatürk both were dedicated to modernising their countries according to Western standards. This common goal, as well as mutually perceived threats by communist and traditional forces, eclipsed the legacy of tension and imperial competition that had marred Ottoman–Iranian relations. Parallel to its treaties with the Balkan states, Turkey signed a number of agreements with Iran on tariffs and trade, border demarcation and security issues. In 1937, the two countries, together with Afghanistan and Iraq, concluded a non-aggression pact at the Saadabad Palace in Tehran. Looking almost like a predecessor to the Baghdad Pact (1955), the Saadabad Pact was meant to ensure peace and security among its members, but its stipulations proved ineffective during the Second World War (Pahlavan 1996: 71).

Only a few months after the death of Mustafa Kemal Atatürk, the final step in Turkey's territorial consolidation was taken. In July 1939, the independent Republic of Hatay, the former Sanjak of Alexandretta, situated at the north-east corner of the eastern Mediterranean, voted to become a part of the Turkish state. The decision was based on the Franco-Turkish agreement of 1921, in which France acknowledged the existence of a relative Turkish majority in the Sanjak, which was inhabited by both Turks and Arabs. Although Turkey had approved Syrian claims at Lausanne, Ankara began in the 1930s to demand the integration of Hatay on demographic grounds. After an initiative by the League of Nations in 1937, Hatay was supposed to become an independent territory, represented in foreign affairs by Syria. In July 1938, elections that were conducted in a violent atmosphere resulted in a narrow Turkish parliamentary majority, which instantly declared independence. One year later, the same parliament announced the unification of Hatay with Turkey (Steinbach 1996: 149–50). Syria has never accepted the loss of the

Sanjak under French mandate and this territorial dispute has strained Turkish–Syrian relations since then.

Although Atatürk was following a clear policy of Westernisation in domestic affairs, his foreign policy remained rather indifferent in terms of political integration. In the context of a still multi-polar system of states, the normalisation of Turkish foreign relations was based on the determination to keep the country neutral. Hence, the series of treaties concluded under Atatürk's presidency established principles of non-interference rather than alliances. The immediate successor of Kemal Atatürk, Ismet Inönü, was basically following this cautious line and 'insisted on balanced budgets in order not to be dependent on foreign aid' (Heper and Keyman 1998: 260). The Ottoman experience of the disastrous interplay between the Empire's political power struggle and its financial dependence on foreign loans left a strong imprint on his foreign policy. Inönü also tried to keep Turkey neutral during the Second World War. Under strong pressure from the Allies, he eventually declared war against Germany in February 1945.

On the basis of the previously described social habitus of the republican elite, Atatürk and Inönü were apparently suspicious towards the intentions both of the European powers and of the emerging Arab states. To the leaders of a state with very limited power, the still fresh experience of Sèvres called for a very cautious approach. Early Kemalist foreign policy was therefore guided by detente without engagement, by a deliberate neutrality without being isolated. [6]

Second phase: party politics and Western integration

The second phase of Turkish foreign policy ran parallel to the implementation of multi-party politics and saw Turkey's full integration into the Western system. In 1945 and 1946, the Soviet Union demanded, in a series of notes, the revision of the Montreux convention and the establishment of Soviet bases for a joint defence of the Straits (Karpat 1975b: 83). Previously, the Straits Commission had been abolished, and at the Conference of Montreux (1936) Turkey regained full control over the Bosphorus and the Dardanelles. The post-1945 abrogation of the Turkish–Soviet friendship pact and Stalin's territorial demands to cede the north-eastern Turkish provinces of Kars and Ardahan prompted Turkey to seek full affiliation with the West (Mufti 1998: 41). In an emerging bipolar international system, neutrality could no longer guarantee the security and integrity of the Turkish state. Taking the new geo-strategic context into account, the deep-rooted suspicions against the West had to be overcome. That the emerging Western superpower, the United States, was free of colonial and imperial legacies in the region facilitated this step. In the early 1950s, Turkey shifted from its previous neutrality to nearly the other extreme, now 'acting as if she was a cold war warrior' (Gözen 1995: 74).

Turkey's new alliance with the West developed to a large extent in the form of relations with the United States (Karpat 1975a: 3). The decisions to recognise Israel in 1949, to send troops to Korea in 1950, and to join NATO in 1952 are cases in point. The Cold War pushed the Turkish Republic back into a role comparable to that which the Ottoman Empire had played in the nineteenth century. The Turkish Republic thus inherited the Ottoman task, to counterbalance Russia's power in the eastern Mediterranean. Under Democratic Party rule (1950–60), the Turkish Republic assumed a key role in the US policy of containment of the USSR. However, the structural change in the international system also opened a European avenue for Turkey. Since the beginning of the East–West confrontation, the historical and political integration of Turkey with Europe has been realised in a number of institutional relations. Turkey was a founding member of the Organisation of European Economic Cooperation in 1948 (now OECD), and has been a member of the Council of Europe since 1949. In 1963, Turkey and the European Community concluded the Ankara association agreement, and since then Turkey has pursued full integration into the European Union.[7] Hence, the internal Westernisation of Turkey has been completed with the Westernisation of its foreign relations.

During the 1950s, Turkey also began to play a new role in Middle Eastern politics. In this period, American strategic thinking gradually replaced the hitherto paramount British interest, which focused on the Suez Canal zone. With the USA promoting its concept of the 'northern tier' – the containment of Soviet influence in the Middle East through an alliance between Turkey, Iran, Afghanistan and Pakistan – the centre of gravity of Western Middle Eastern policy moved from its Arab core region to its northern periphery. Two abortive initiatives to forge a Middle Eastern defence pact preceded this shift from centre to periphery. In October 1951, immediately after Turkey's admittance to NATO, Britain proposed the so-called Middle East Command (MEC) together with the USA, France and Turkey. Based on a renewal of the old Anglo-Egyptian treaty, the colonial connotations of this initiative were too strong to find support from Egypt and other Arab states. The Arab League responded with an indigenous proposal to establish an Arab collective security pact. Later, this idea served the Arab states as a basis for the rejection of the second Western defence scheme, the Middle Eastern Defence Organisation (MEDO), which Britain and the USA proposed in June 1952 (cf. Spain 1954; Yesilbursa 1999).

After supporting both the MEC and MEDO, Turkey became the leading regional force in the implementation of the American northern tier concept, and Prime Minister Menderes played a prominent role in negotiating the so-called Baghdad Pact between Iran, Iraq, Pakistan and Turkey. This alliance was finally formed with the Iranian signature in November 1955. Britain joined the Baghdad Pact directly, whilst the USA acted as an observer and concluded bilateral agreements with its member states. Following Iraqi withdrawal in 1959, the Baghdad Pact disintegrated and was renamed the Central Treaty Organisation (CENTO), but its importance as a barrier against the Soviet Union receded steadily (Steinbach 1996: 227–9).

The Menderes government was not only pushing for the Baghdad Pact, but became in general a convinced promoter of Western foreign-policy goals. At the Conference of Bandung (1955), for example, Turkey joined the small group of states that rejected the idea of non-alignment strongly promoted by India's Prime Minister Nehru, Egypt's President Nasser and Yugoslavia's President Tito. In the same year, Turkey embarrassed the entire Third World with its vote at the United Nations against the independence of Algeria. Moreover, in both the Syrian crisis (1957) and the overthrow of the Hashemite monarchy in Iraq (1958), the West had to discourage the Turkish government from taking unilateral military action against its neighbours (cf. Anderson 1995; Sever 1998). The politics of neutrality seemed entirely abolished and for the first time a sign of activism appeared in Turkish foreign policy, although subordinated to and restricted by Western interests.

Under the impact of the Cold War, Turkey sided with the USA and with the former colonial powers. The Menderes government viewed its Middle Eastern relations as the continuation of a policy in which Turkey dealt with the problems of the region through Western powers (Karpat 1975c: 115). The ten years of Democratic Party rule saw an almost complete identification of Turkey's foreign policy with Western interests. This Westernisation brought Turkey back into Middle Eastern affairs, but as a staunch ally of the West and therefore at a cost of almost total isolation from its Arab neighbours. So the second phase of Turkish foreign policy brought about Turkey's institutional integration into the Western world, at the same time causing its increasing isolation in the Middle East.

However, the new course of Western integration was not due to a change in the world-view of Turkey's elite, but was rather triggered by security threats from outside. In addition, Turkey's increasing economic dependence on the West turned the country into a political rent-seeker of the Cold War. Given Turkey's geopolitical importance to the West, 'Menderes and his colleagues apparently expected that the US government would bail them out of their economic difficulties' (Harris 1972: 73). In spite of this economic deviation from Inönü's regime, the foreign policy of the Democratic Party nevertheless focused on the same core issues as under their Republican predecessors: first, on the maintenance of the integrity and sovereignty of the Turkish state; second, on foreign policy as a means of Western integration.

Third phase: Western disappointment and Arab rapprochement
The third phase of republican foreign policy starts in the early 1960s and can be described as a move towards a rapprochement with the Arab world. From the Turkish perspective, a decreasing Soviet threat and rising tensions with Greece characterised the political environment in which this process took place (Karaosmanoglu 1983: 158). In terms of political psychology, the Turkish–Arab rapprochement accompanied the reappearance of the deep-rooted suspicions against the West, which were strongly reconfirmed in the developments of the 1960s and 1970s. The Jupiter missile crisis of 1962–63, the 1964 and 1967 Cyprus crises, the Turkish invasion of northern Cyprus in 1974, and the subsequent arms embargo, which the US Congress imposed on Turkey in February 1975, formed a chain of events during which the Sèvres syndrome re-emerged and the Turkish suspicion of conspiracy was extended to the United States.

An early step in a series of Turkish disappointments with US policies was the withdrawal of the US Jupiter nuclear armed missiles from Turkish soil in the aftermath of the Cuban missile crisis. Although President Kennedy had asked to negotiate the removal of the ageing Jupiters as early as 1961, the Turkish side considered their final withdrawal as a trade-off between the US and the USSR at the expense of Turkey (Harris 1972: 91–5). While the Jupiter missiles caused the first overt Turkish–US dissension, the conflict about Cyprus marks the clear turning-point in Turkish–US relations and stirred anti-American and neutralist sentiments among Turkey's population. As a response to the intensification of communal violence between Greek and Turkish Cypriots in spring 1964, Ankara sought a consensus among its allies for Turkish military intervention. The United States strongly rejected this initiative. In a letter to the Prime Minister, President Johnson went as far as to caution Inönü 'that if Turkish action on the island would invite a Soviet attack, then NATO was not obliged to defend Turkey' (Criss 1997: 119). Against the almost total identification with Western policies that Turkey had previously displayed, the Johnson letter came as a shock. From now on, disagreements about the Cyprus conflict stirred strong sentiments of betrayal among the Turks, who believed more and more that the United States had exploited Turkey's political loyalty (Ahmad 1984: 172).

The Turkish move to normalise its relations with the Arab world was, in the first place, a response to these disappointments with Western policies. In the second place, it was an attempt to overcome the now painful isolation to which the foreign policy of Menderes had brought the country. Whereas its Western allies and Israel did not support the Turkish position concerning Cyprus, the Arab countries openly sided with the Greek Cypriots. Furthermore, in the UN debates about Cyprus, Turkey had to realise a 'nearly total lack of support' by Third World countries in general.

In light of this isolation, Turkish foreign policy makers tried to improve relations with Arab and Islamic countries in order to seek support for their Cyprus policy. In the second half of the 1960s, full diplomatic ties with several Arab countries were (re-)established and a series of mutual high-level visits with Arab leaders took place (Karpat 1975c: 123–7). Additionally, Turkey displayed a certain willingness to act against Western interests in the Middle East. One case in point was the Turkish decision not to allow the US to use their military base in Incirlik during the Arab–Israeli wars in 1967 and 1973. A further illustration was the recognition of the Palestine Liberation Organisation (PLO) in 1976 and the opening in 1979 of the PLO's representative office in Ankara (Gözen 1995: 74–5).

Although rooted in political problems, Turkey's rapprochement with its Middle Eastern neighbours also stemmed from economic strains and the fact that, with the liberal constitution of 1961, foreign policy became for the first time a matter of public discussion. The 1973–74 oil crisis, Turkish supplies of manpower to Arab states,[8] the opening of the country for Arab capital, and later the search for new markets in the Middle East were some of the economic aspects of Turkey's reorientation in foreign policy. Moreover, the oil crisis coincided with the decision of European states to freeze the recruitment of foreign workers. In this situation Saudi Arabia, Libya, Iraq and the Gulf states provided not only an alternative for labour migration, but also a huge market for Turkish contractors. Since the early 1970s, the remittances of Turkish contractors and workers from Arab countries had formed a major source of foreign currency influx, whose annual amount was estimated to be more than US$1 billion in the late 1980s (Unbehaun 1996: 90).

Finally, with the arrival of and public support for left-wing parties on the political stage, Turkey's close alliance with the West came under public pressure. In the historical context of the Cyprus conflict and the internationalisation of the Palestinian question, Turkey's political establishment was increasingly exposed to criticism from socialist as well as from radical nationalist and Islamist groups. Necmettin Erbakan, for instance, was even able, as a member and deputy prime minister of several coalition governments during the 1970s, to voice his demands for a withdrawal from the 'Western Club'. The shift in Turkish foreign policy was still reactive, however, and by no means a change of its general Western direction. The attempt to improve Turkish–Arab relations was a necessary adjustment to rapidly changing international, regional and domestic environments, yet an adjustment that did not imply the abandonment of the dominant principles of the Kemalist worldview.

Fourth phase: activism
The adoption of a new pattern of activism in Turkish foreign policy evolved in the aftermath of the 1980 military coup. This fourth phase was to a large extent initiated by the political decisions of an increasingly high-handed Prime Minister (1983–89) and later President (1989–93) Turgut Özal. He combined his domestic policies of economic liberalisation and moderate Islamisation with an active export strategy, especially with regard to Middle Eastern countries. Between 1980 and 1985, Turkish exports to the Middle East increased fivefold. In 1985, 64 per cent of Turkey's total exports went to its then warring neighbours, Iran and Iraq (Dalacoura 1990: 210). Turkish exports to Iran rose from US$12 million in 1979 to a peak of more than US$1 billion in 1985 (Eralp 1996: 101). Besides these official figures, the Iran–Iraq War of 1980–88, the Kurdish insurgency and the Gulf War of 1991 contributed heavily to the establishment of a cross-border economy, which in the 1990s connected the Kurdish provinces in Iraq and Turkey. Both border regions became increasingly dependent on the commercial transactions, legal and illegal, of a specific kind of 'war economy' (cf. Bozarslan 1996).

Saudi Arabia and the Gulf States are another area in which Turkey intensified its economic co-operation with the Middle East. In addition to the above-mentioned construction industry, Özal also opened Turkey's market to Saudi capital, and several Turkish–Saudi joint ventures were launched. In 1985, the Banks of Bahrain and Kuwait opened branches in Istanbul, and a joint Turkish–Saudi investment holding and the 'Andadolu–Saudi Arabian Co-operation in Industry and Commerce' were founded (Bagis 1985: 87). While economic ties with the Arab world and Iran thus steadily improved, official relations with Israel deteriorated. Only three months after the coup of September 1980, Ankara withdrew its diplomatic personnel from Tel Aviv and Turkish–Israeli relations were not restored to ambassadorial level until December 1991 (Yavuz 1997: 24).

In the 1980s, Özal's activism had a clear economic target and largely followed the established pattern of rapprochement with the Arab and Islamic world. A radical turning point in this rather careful political activism was marked by the Iraqi invasion of Kuwait in August 1990. At that point, Turkey's economic boom with its neighbours had proved to be a passing fancy. Turkey's export rate to Arab countries was falling, reaching a marginal 12 per cent of its total exports in 1994 (Yavuz 1997: 27). The official export boom to Iraq and Iran in the 1980s was due not to the establishment of solid trade relations, but rather to the war, in which Turkey took a neutral position and was therefore able to trade with both sides. Although the Middle East is still Turkey's principal source of oil and a major market for its construction businesses, Turkish regional trade declined steadily between 1985 and 1995 (Önis 1995: 61).

In contrast to the decreasing importance of trade with the Middle East, relations with the USA improved considerably and the US foreign assistance programme for Turkey was restored in 1985 (Makovsky 1999b). Coinciding with the end of the Cold War, the Iraqi occupation of Kuwait gave Turgut Özal a chance to show that Turkey could still play the role of a geo-strategic heavyweight in US foreign policy. Demonstrating Turkey's continuing importance for Western interests in the region, Özal redirected Turkish foreign policy and 'simply brushed aside Ankara's longstanding policy of non-interference in Middle East disputes' (Makovsky 1999a: 92). While diplomats and the army advocated a more neutral policy, he was eager to play a major role in the US-led coalition against Iraq. Özal's decision to close the Iraqi oil pipelines and his pressure to adopt a more active military stance were just some cases in point which were also behind the resignation of Chief of the General Staff Necip Torumtay in December 1990 (Mufti 1998: 44).[9]

The activism and boldness of Turkish foreign policy adopted by Turgut Özal has remained visible since his death in 1993. The new Turkish–Israeli axis, re-emerging pan-Turkist dreams, Turkish military operations in Iraq and the threat of using military force against Syria (October 1998) are some examples that we will deal with in more detail in the coming parts of the book. Yet this more active role in Middle Eastern politics hardly marks a clear departure from long-established traditions. Although his 'single-handed conduct of foreign policy' met strong criticism (Sayari 1992: 20), Özal's new boldness did not deviate in substance from the line drawn by his predecessors. The structural change of the 1990s rather initiated a shift that reminds us of the Democratic Party era. Like Menderes, Özal combined modest domestic Islamisation with the staunch support of Western foreign policies. Under new geopolitical conditions, Özal's primary goal was still to guarantee Turkey's political integrity and to strengthen its Western partnership, thereby emphasising Turkish–American relations in particular.

At first critical of Özal's decisions according to the memoirs of General

Torumtay, Özal simply 'disregarded any source of power in policy making other than his own' (Cizre-Sakallioglu 1997: 158) – the army and large parts of the Kemalist establishment did not escape his impact. On the contrary, without abandoning the basic principles of Kemalism, they are themselves today convinced proponents of this new pattern of activism in Turkish foreign policy (Makovsky 1999a: 106). How both this sense of activism and the Kemalist legacy influence Turkey's foreign policy with its Arab neighbours and Iran is the topic of the following section.

Principles and realities: Turkey's foreign policy towards its Arab neighbours and Iran

In addition to Turkey's fixation on state security and its Western orientation, our periodisation of Turkey's foreign policy in four phases discloses a rather paradoxical tendency. Since the end of the Second World War, Turkey has been dragged more and more into regional politics, without conceiving of itself as a part of the Middle East. The powerless, threatened state of Atatürk's time has grown into a regional power, ready to use its economic and military capabilities in a more active and independent way.[10] This development weakened Turkey's ability to remain aloof from a region whose security complex had indeed became more and more interwoven with the Turkish one. Earlier guiding principles, such as non-interference in local disputes, sensitivity to Arab security interests, non-interference in internal affairs and a preference to handle Middle Eastern affairs on a bilateral basis, tended to be less sustainable (Karaosmanoglu 1983: 166). A glance at the major areas of conflict between Turkey and its neighbours reveals some apparent paradoxes facing Turkish foreign policy in the Middle East.

As indicated in the last chapter, the Kemalist establishment is inclined to attribute the Kurdish insurgency and the rise of religious parties to con-spiracies from outside. Domestic conflicts caused by social change are thus associated with alleged foreign political interference. This tendency is clearly visible in Turkey's relationship with its immediate neighbours, in which fields of possible co-operation tend to become battlefields of confrontation. Turkish–Syrian relations are the most telling example. Territorial questions, the Kurdish insurgency and the distribution of water resources have complicated a relationship that was uneasy from its very beginning, and came under heavy strain from the ideological impact of Cold War politics. The territorial question of Hatay assumed a rather ideological nature, while the water issue overlapped with the Kurdish problem and developed into a dangerous conflict that brought the countries to the brink of war.[11]

The first time water gave rise to conflict between Turkey and Syria was in 1956, when Syria decided to build the Asi Dam. This irrigation project dammed the Orontes (Asi) river, which flows from Syria through Hatay into the Mediterranean. Turkish officials reacted with concern that the Syrian dam could deprive Turkish farmers in Hatay of necessary water resources. In the then tense political atmosphere, Syria rejected Turkish initiatives to negotiate the water issue in a more comprehensive way, which included the flow of both the Orontes and the Euphrates rivers (Schulz 1992: 96). Meanwhile, positions have changed, and Syria now demands from Turkey a guarantee of its share of the waters from the Tigris and Euphrates basins.

Syrian concerns result mainly from the gigantic South-eastern Anatolia Development Project (GAP), which Turkey initiated in the late 1960s. The GAP project aims at a fundamental socio-economic transformation of Turkey's south-eastern provinces, and comprises the erection of 22 dams and 19 hydro-electric plants on the Tigris and Euphrates (Mutlu 1996: 69). Turkey's downstream neighbours, Syria and Iraq, fear that this massive development will cause severe water shortages and thus hamper their own irrigation and energy projects. Because water is also a major issue in Syrian–Iraqi relations, Turkey has frequently rejected Arab demands for a multilateral arrangement on the grounds that this would embroil the country in intra-Arab politics (Robins 1991: 89). Whereas Syria and Iraq suspect Turkey of being 'in possession of a powerful water weapon' (Hoffmann 1998: 255), the Turkish side conceives GAP as an economic answer to the Kurdish question (Beschorner 1992: 30). The GAP project is designed as a strategy of 'agro-industial development' (Mutlu 1996: 69), whose principal objectives are to boost the agricultural production of the region, to develop water and energy resources, and to increase regional employment and infrastructure.

Regarding the socio-economic target of the GAP project, its effects so far could not have been worse. In 1996, Servet Mutlu concluded that, owing to the lack of investment in irrigation the impact on the regional economy had been almost nil (Mutlu 1996: 72). Although more positive economic results should not be ruled out for the future, the GAP project throughout the 1990s contributed politically to rising tensions with Turkey's neighbours rather than to a de-escalation of the Kurdish question. Arab suspicions that Turkey could use its geographical position as upper riparian of the Tigris and Euphrates as a means of political extortion were countered by Turgut Özal with the so-called 'Peace Pipeline Project'. This proposal suggested the building of two pipelines to supply drinking water from the Turkish rivers Ceyhan and Seyhan to the Arab peninsula, Syria and Jordan (Manisali 1996: 166). However, the commercially minded idea has not yet met with a positive response from the Arab side. On the contrary, in the prevailing air of mistrust and suspicion, the Peace Pipeline proposal rather deepened Arab anxieties of increased dependence upon Turkey (Robins 1991: 98). Inevitably, the lack of co-operation turned into open conflict. Damascus used the PKK as a foreign policy tool in the water conflict. The Syrian regime hosted PKK leader Öcalan for more than a decade and provided his guerrilla a safe-haven and training ground in Lebanon. Turkey responded with accusations that Syria was waging an 'undeclared war' and threatened Damascus with military consequences (Makovsky 1999a: 99). The foreign policy dimension of the GAP project therefore contradicted its domestic political purpose and further aggravated the Kurdish question. Contrary to Kurdish separatism's potentially uniting challenge for both Turkish and Syrian security interests, the PKK was able severely to damage the relationship between the two states. A similar constellation, though more complex, can be observed in Turkish–Iraqi relations.

According to official Turkish accounts, the Turkish army intervened in northern Iraq no less than 57 times since the PKK began its war against the Turkish state in 1984 (Gunter 1998: 40). After the 1991 Gulf War and the Kurdish refugee crisis in April and May of that year, northern Iraq became the theatre for major Turkish military operations. In August 1991, almost 5,000 Turkish troops entered northern Iraq to create a buffer zone along the border. More than 20,000 troops backed by tanks and the Turkish airforce crossed the border area to Iran and Iraq in October 1992. In the aftermath of a military operation in March 1995, in which 35,000 Turkish troops went 40 km over a 220-km front into Iraqi territory, Turkey's president Süleyman Demirel spoke publicly about a revision of the Turkish–Iraqi border in favour of Turkey.[12] This statement, together with operation 'Murad', during which more than 50,000 Turkish soldiers entered northern Iraq in May 1997, confirmed old suspicions in the Arab world that Turkey still has territorial claims and might want to revoke the Mosul decision of 1926 (Gözen 1997: 110 and Gunter 1998: 36–8).

The Gulf War and the subsequent Operation Provide Comfort, which created a Kurdish sanctuary in northern Iraq, brought Turkey into a paradoxical position. On the one hand, Turkish officials denied the existence of a Kurdish issue at home, and declared the integrity of the Iraqi state as a major goal of Turkish foreign policy. Turkey in fact wanted to avoid the creation of a Kurdish 'buffer state' in northern Iraq and thus a likely base for Kurdish self-determination. On the other hand, the country's armed forces became fully embroiled in the Kurdish struggle in northern Iraq and participated in the maintenance of the buffer state's *de facto* border. In March 1991, Turgut Özal even invited representatives of Barzani's Kurdish Democratic Party (KDP) and of its adversary, Talabani's Patriotic Union of Kurdistan (PUK), to visit Ankara, a U-turn from the previous policy of not contacting Kurdish groups in northern Iraq (Aykan 1996a: 347). In its war against the PKK, Turkey allied itself with the KDP – an organisation that has been for decades a major force in the Kurdish struggle for independence from Baghdad (Marr 1996: 54–6) – and provided it with facilities for official representation in Ankara.[13]

Looking at the Middle Eastern scene, the results of the 1991 Gulf War and Özal's reorientation turned out to be less of a new opportunity, and more of a new predicament for Turkey's foreign policy. Turkey's military interventions in northern Iraq evoked new suspicions in Baghdad and the Arab world about Turkish irredentist claims to the Mosul province. Both issues were confused with the water problem and the question of reopening the two oil pipelines between Iraq and Turkey. In addition to this climate of mistrust and suspicion, Turkey has officially been confronted with enormous economic losses owing to the embargo against Iraq. According to senior officials in the Turkish ministry of foreign affairs, the Turkish economy had to bear a loss of around US$40 billion in eight years since the end of the Gulf War.[14] This negative economic situation has been further aggravated by the US containment policy against another Turkish neighbour, the Islamic Republic of Iran.

In contrast to Iraq, whose current problems are partly linked to its lack of any tradition of statehood, both Turkey and Iran have a strong historical heritage of patrimonial and imperial rule. Their current frontiers were established by the Treaty of Zohab in 1639, and although the history of Iranian–Ottoman relations can hardly be characterised as friendly neighbourliness, territorial claims between Iran and the Turkish Republic have never existed. In spite of their co-operation in the Baghdad and CENTO pacts, a mutual mistrust in the reliability of the other side has always prevailed.

Since the Islamic revolution in 1979, the ideological difference between Ankara's secularism and Tehran's revolutionary Islamism has aggravated Turkish–Iranian tension over such issues as the Kurdish question, Turkey's alliance with the West, and competing interests in the post-Soviet republics. While Ankara viewed Armenia and Iran as 'physical obstacles' to Turkey's entry into the Caucasus and Central Asia (Eralp 1996: 88), Turkish nationalist agitation in Azerbaijan posed a threat to the national integrity of Iran, pproximately 20 per cent of whose population is of Azeri origin. The nationalist component of Turkish–Iranian friction was particularly apparent during the early 1990s. In a first wave of pan-Turkist agitation, the then Azeri President, Elchibey, used strongly nationalist Azeri rhetoric, and nationalistic political claims to unite 'northern and southern Azerbaijan' were voiced (Eralp 1996: 106).

Whereas the pan-Turkic wave has almost faded away (cf. Bal 1998b), the Kurdish question is still a major source of tension. For a short period from 1992 to 1995, Turkey, Iran and Syria tried to co-ordinate their policies towards northern Iraq in order to prevent the rise of a Kurdish state (Gunter 1998: 35). But the common ground of those tripartite conferences was dissolved with the outbreak of war in northern Iraq between the KDP and PUK in 1996. Since then the three states have again supported their Kurdish clients: Turkey the KDP, Iran the PUK and Syria the PKK.[15] Besides Iranian support for Talabani's PUK, there was rather unsubstantiated support for the PKK from Iran. Turkish sources talked about an estimated 35 PKK camps on Iranian territory.[16] Moreover, Iran was suspected of supporting religious organisations operating in Turkey and aiming at the establishment of an Islamic state in the Kurdish areas.[17] These Turkish accusations were countered by Iranian allegations that among Turkey's large community of Iranian emigres the country hosted radical opponents to the regime in Tehran. Furthermore, Tehran blamed Ankara of supporting the Iranian guerrilla organisation Mujaheddin-e Khalq (Calabrese 1998: 76).

While Pan-Turkism and Kurdish nationalism have always been possible sources of tension in Turkish–Iranian relations, the ideological gap between Ankara's secularist establishment and Iran's religious regime has exacerbated it. Immediately after the Iranian revolution, Ayatollah Khomeini condemned Kemalism, and Iranian representatives have frequently refused to visit the mausoleum of Atatürk while on official visits to Ankara. Furthermore, the Iranian regime has produced anti-secular propaganda material that has been smuggled into Turkey (Dalacoura 1990: 211–18). As a consequence, Turkish officials and journalists attribute the rise of political Islam in Turkey to foreign intervention. How this situation affects the bilateral relationship between Turkey and Iran was clearly visible in the so-called 'Jerusalem incident' in Sincan, a small town near Ankara. On 1 February 1997, the mayor of Sincan, who was a member of the Islamist Welfare Party, organised a rally to protest against the Israeli occupation of East Jerusalem. During the event, placards supporting Hizbullah and Hamas were displayed, and the Israeli–Turkish agreements were denounced in the presence of the Iranian ambassador. Three days later, tanks turned up in Sincan, the mayor was arrested, and the ambassadors were mutually withdrawn from Ankara and Tehran (Yavuz 1997: 22).

Undoubtedly, foreign support for Islamist groups in Turkey was attributed mainly to Iran. But Saudi money, rather than political influence, nevertheless played an additional role. With the economic opening for Saudi capital in the 1980s, Turkey also attracted an influx of 'ideological money' from non-governmental organisations in Saudi Arabia. In this respect an organisation named 'Union of the World of Islam' (Rabitatül Alemül Islam) became most prominent. Based in Saudi Arabia, the Union could draw on the abundance of petro-dollars to finance various kinds of Islamist organisations. Even the military junta under General Evren used the 'Islamic money' of this organisation to finance Turkish institutions of religious education in Europe. This religious teaching was conducted by officially appointed Turkish employees who were on the payroll and subject to the control of the Diyanet in Ankara (Ahmad 1988: 762).

Although Saudi Arabia certainly had no interest in destabilising Turkey, it is apparent that, together with the domestic strategy of the Turkish Islamic Synthesis, Saudi money contributed to the Islamisation of Turkish society. In addition, Turkish–Saudi relations share the historically rooted mistrust and suspicion between Turks and Arabs whose negative impact on regional security has not yet diminished. A good example of the prevailing Arab distrust of Turkey's Middle Eastern ambitions was Saudi Arabia's official reaction to the Turkish offer to send troops during the Gulf War. While accepting military assistance from countries such as the United States, Britain, France, Pakistan, Egypt and Syria, the Saudis refused a Turkish military presence (Birand 1996: 172).

Conclusions: Turkish politics of securitisation

From a historical perspective, the assumptions of Turkey's clear deviation from its previous foreign policy directions are hardly tenable. From the outset, the foreign policy of the Turkish Republic was directed towards the West, and Turgut Özal strengthened this general feature of Western integration, albeit with an emphasis on Turkish–American relations. A further point to be made is that the adoption of an activist pattern in Turkish foreign policy was not without precedence. If this new activism indicated a change at all, then it was a change in degree rather than substance. The conclusion of the Baghdad Pact, Menderes' military intimidation against Syria and Iraq, and the armed intervention in Cyprus are cases in point to support the argument that, given certain conditions, Turkey has always been willing to play a more active and even, in some instances, a more independent role in the region. Hence, it seems to be a sound claim that the general directions of Turkish foreign policy did not change throughout the 1990s. Yet some of its former principles came under severe pressure.

Turkey's military and political involvement in northern Iraq makes this most explicit. In order to hunt down the PKK, the Turkish state threw aside not only its principles of non-interference, but also its claimed sensitivity for Arab security concerns. The frequent military incursions into Iraq and the Turkish alliance with Barzani's KDP made Turkey a participant in the major local dispute within Iraq and deepened the sense of mistrust with which Turkish Middle Eastern policy has been received in the Arab world. Additionally, Turkish interference in Iraqi affairs escalated the water issue to a point where the regimes in Baghdad and Damascus set aside their deep mutual hostilities and resumed negotiations to form a single front against Turkey. By triggering this Iraqi–Syrian rapprochement, Turkey decisively undermined its own preference to handle the water issue on a bilateral basis.

This paradoxical situation between the activities and principles of Turkish foreign policy is undoubtedly linked to the fact that in the Middle Eastern security complex Turkey's major domestic problems, political Islam and Kurdish nationalism, became de-territorialised and intertwined with regional inter-state disputes. At first glance, this finding seems to confirm the conspiracy theories of Turkey's Kemalist elite, and indeed both the PKK and Turkish Islamist organisations found political and material support from Turkey's neighbours. However, the explanation offered through the prism of the Sèvres syndrome confuses cause with effect. The historically guided analysis of the development of both Turkey's domestic conflicts and its foreign policy makes it apparent that the Ottoman–Kemalist heritage of encirclement has meanwhile turned into a self-fulfilling prophecy. Not only is the 'hydro paranoia', viewing the water issue as an inevitable source of conflict, a myth (cf. Hoffmann 1998), but also other matters of conflict could equally be seen as potential fields of co-operation. Turkey and the secular Arab states of Iraq and Syria are rather natural allies than foes, particularly against threats posed by Islamist and Kurdish nationalist movements. In order to understand these paradoxes of Turkey's Middle Eastern policies it is again necessary to shed light on the political world-view of the Turkish establishment. It is the Kemalist policy of securitisation that explains how perceived threats develop into real ones and fields of co-operation turn into areas of conflict.

Previous chapters discussed the fact that the Kemalist concept of security is at the same time both narrow and wide. It is narrow in its strict concentration on the notion of national security as the defence of the integrity of the state, and wide in the sense that internal and external conflicts in a variety of fields are immediately viewed as a matter of national security. With regard to the latter, the Kemalist establishment displays a marked propensity to securitise nearly every single issue that challenges its power position or its world-view.

Theoretically, securitisation is an extreme version of politicisation, and it presents an issue as an existential threat. To securitise an issue is to require emergency measures and the application of extraordinary means (Buzan et al. 1998: 23–6). In the Turkish case, the National Security Council is the institutionalised form, and the rhetoric of Sèvres the cognitive expression of this process of securitisation that gripped Turkish politics. Given the strong military flavour of the Kemalist security concept, it comes as no surprise that it is the army that has the 'mission' and the means (force) to apply these emergency measures.

Accordingly, the observed linkage of domestic and regional conflicts is not so much a result of the nature of the issues in conflict, but of the way the Kemalist establishment perceives them. The problems between Turkey and its neighbours do not have an insoluble zero-sum character, but become, under the historical legacy of mutual distrust, securitised from both sides.[18] As a well-known Turkish journalist put it, 'Turkey's seventy-year history has not been long enough to erase the memories of being backstabbed by the Arabs as the Ottoman Empire was nearing its end' (Birand 1996: 171). On the contrary, although the historical accuracy of the Turkish–Arab narrative of mutual suspicion seems highly questionable,[19] this perspective was even reinforced by the political experiences of the post-Second World War period. Regarding the Turkish application of this discourse of conspiracy and betrayal, it is hard to tell conviction and instrumentalisation apart. Most likely it is both: on the one hand, the instrumental usage of historically grounded perceptions of threat to defend the endangered position of the privileged Kemalist elite; on the other hand, the expression of a relatively stable social habitus that had meanwhile become utterly anachronistic to the changing social and political environment.

Under the conditions of a Greater Middle East, Turkish foreign policy has to undergo a revision, although not a complete change. An appropriate Turkish role in the Middle East does not contradict the country's Western orientation. Foreign policy objectives such as striving to 'set an example in terms of economic performance, secularization, and democracy' (Öniş 1995: 48) are best based on both a continuation of Turkey's Western integration and a new rapprochement with its Middle Eastern neighbours. Yet this foreign policy has to start at home. The Turkish state elite should take Atatürk's 'peace at home, peace in the world' seriously. It is not Turkey that resembles an 'outsider on the margins of both Europe and the Middle East' (Robins 1991: 16), but its Kemalist establishment. Presided over by the armed forces, the Kemalist elite has isolated itself from both Turkey's neighbours and its own society. While cultural, economic, political and personal ties increasingly connect and integrate Turkish society with its European and Middle Eastern counterparts, the politics of securitisation has led to a self-exclusion of Turkey's state elite.

Notes

1 On an initiative of Erbakan, Turkey, Iran, Egypt, Nigeria, Pakistan, Bangladesh, Indonesia and Malaysia formed the 'D8'.

2 In December 1996, Operation Provide Comfort was renamed 'Operation Northern Watch'.

3 As quoted by Olson (1997: 179).

4 Regarding this argumentation, see Karpat (1996), Makovsky (1999a, 1999b), Mufti (1998), Önis (1995), Robins (1991), Sayari (1992).

5 The precise meaning of the concept of 'securitisation' will be explained in the conclusions.

6 Although Turkish nationalists could have had an affinity with Arab nationalists, there was hardly any link between them and the Turkish republican movement, see: Eppel (1992) and Tauber (1994).

7 A Customs Union with the European Union was signed in 1996. Since the EU summit in Helsinki 1999, Turkey is a candidate for full membership of the EU.

8 In 1975, for example, Turkey and Libya agreed about 600,000 Turkish workers being supplied to Libya (Aykan 1993: 98).

9 For an account of these events from Torumtay's memoirs, see: Heper and Günay (1996: 626–9).

10 During the Cold War Turkey developed the second biggest army in NATO. The permanent force of 514,000 men includes 72,000 professionals, while more than 900,000 men serve as reserve. With a large tank force (4,300 combat tanks, including 400 Leopard I), and an air force of 750 combat aircraft (240 F-16), the Turkish armed forces are technologically and in manpower certainly one of the strongest military powers in this volatile region. Furthermore, in an ambitious modernisation programme, Turkey is going to invest US$150 billion during the next three decades, chiefly to enhance the combat power of the air force and the navy. Data from Korkisch (1999: 140) and Sadlowski (1998).

11 It is not possible to present here the complexities of water conflicts in the Middle East, of which the Turkish–Syrian–Iraqi triangle constitutes one crux. For further reading, see Beschorner (1992), Kliot (1994), Lowi (1995), Murakami (1995), Ohlsson (1992), Rogers and Lydon (1994).

12 Former President Özal and the founder of the extreme right-wing MHP, Alparslan Türkes, are also known for loudly contemplating the 'Mosul question'.

13 Since 1945 the Kurdish organisations in Iraq have fought in six wars against the regime in Baghdad (Jung 1997: 340-42). During the 1970s, Mustafa Barzani waged war against the Baathist regime, supported by Iran and the CIA. Meanwhile his son is Turkey's main ally in fighting the PKK in northern Iraq, receiving massive Turkish military and logistical support. For an analysis of the shifting alliance in the Kurdish movements in Iraq, see Freij (1998).

14   This is the figure mentioned by representatives of the Turkish Foreign Policy Institute in Ankara, interviewed by the authors on 7 April 1999.

15   For a good account of the intra-Kurdish fighting, see Gunter (1996a, 1996b).

16   Interview with the Foreign Policy Institute, 7 April 1999.

17   According to an interview with senior officials of the ministry of foreign affairs in Ankara conducted by the authors on 8 April 1999.

18   There is no doubt that the Turkish government is not solely to blame for the conflict-prone atmosphere in the region. Yet as we are focusing on Turkey, Arab responsibilities are only touched upon.

19   For a critical account of Turkish–Arab relations during the last decade of the Ottoman Empire, see Kayali (1997).

8 The Uneasy Alignment
Turkey and Israel

Political activism and Ottoman–Jewish legacies

In late April 1997, the Turkish Minister of Defence, Turhan Tayan, publicly acknowledged that the Turks had had no problems with Israel and the Jewish nation throughout their history, something that he would not and could not honestly say about the Arabs (Pipes 1997/98: 35). Being on an official visit to Israel, Tayan thus referred to Turkey's decision to embark on a bold alignment with Israel, which officially began with a military co-operation agreement in February 1996. Since then, the speed and scale of the development of ties   military, intelligence, economic and civilian   between Turkey and Israel have suggested a decisive departure from Turkey's hitherto low-key approach to the Middle East. Moreover, the Turkish–Israeli alignment stirred a profound unease among Turkey's Middle Eastern neighbours and embroiled the country in the imponderabilities of the Arab–Israeli conflict. It comes as no surprise, therefore, that representatives of both sides were at pains to present the intensification of Turkish–Israeli relations in the 1990s and their emerging strategic axis as nothing more than a matter of historical continuity.

In line with this new stress on the positive heritage of Turkish–Jewish relations, the former Israeli President, Ezer Weizman, declared upon his arrival in the Turkish Republic in 1994 that 'Israel will never forget that the Jews were accepted by the Ottoman Empire when they were expelled from various European countries some 500 years ago'.[1] Two years earlier, various groups in Turkey, Israel and the United States lavishly celebrated the Ottoman past on the occasion of the 500th anniversary of Sultan Bayezid's (1481–1512) decision to welcome to his domains the Jews expelled from the Iberian peninsula. Both Turkey and Israel enthusiastically endorsed these celebrations, and

153

Ottoman–Jewish relations re-emerged as an apparent Ottoman legacy, on which Turkey's Kemalist establishment wished to draw in justifying its new partnership with the Israeli state.[2]

Yet the prevalence of a friendly relationship does not alone explain the sudden emergence of a bold alignment between two states. The positive historical background probably indeed facilitated the development of Turkish–Israeli relations, but it did not necessarily lead to close co-operation between Ankara and Tel Aviv. As analysed in the previous chapter, Turkey's political, cultural, military and economic alignment with the West has undoubtedly been the chief factor in conditioning its regional foreign policies. The ultimate aim of Turkey's foreign policy towards Middle Eastern states has been to minimise any danger to its security and independence and to contribute to its Western-focused agenda. As a consequence, Turkey has not been so far able to build a solid and reliable working relationship with any of its southern or eastern neighbours. Rather, Ankara's relations with Middle Eastern countries have been characterised by open hostility, with respect to Syria and to a lesser extent Iraq; permanent distrust, with respect to Iran and Saudi Arabia; and a clear lack of substance with respect to Egypt and Jordan.

Against this background, the essential correctness that has distinguished Turkish–Israeli relations stands in sharp contrast. This is partly a result of the cultural and political affinities that Turkey and Israel share, together with a 'common sense of otherness' in a region dominated by Arab culture and undemocratic political regimes (Makovsky 1996: 169). Due to their common attachment to the West and Western values, which is otherwise unknown in the Middle East, Turkey and Israel find themselves having to exist in a region where 'they feel profoundly ill at ease' (Robins 1991: 82). Yet despite these commonalities – pro-Western foreign policy orientation, formal commitments to democratic rule and similar economic interests – relations between Turkey and Israel nevertheless fluctuated during the Cold War, between intense co-operation and almost imperceptible interaction. Neither the Ottoman heritage nor cultural and political affinities had been strong enough to build lasting patterns of co-operation between the two states. This ambivalence in Turkey's relationship with Israel was best highlighted by Israel's founding politician and first prime minister, David Ben-Gurion, who in 1958 reportedly complained that 'the Turks have always treated us as mistress, and not as a partner in an openly avowed marriage' (Nachmani 1987: 75).

Given this ambivalence in Turkish–Israeli relations, this chapter investigates the driving forces motivating Turkey to engage into this 'openly avowed marriage' with Israel in the 1990s. More precisely, we pose the question of why the Kemalist elite was willing at this particular juncture to deviate from

THE UNEASY ALIGNMENT: TURKEY AND ISRAEL

Turkey's traditionally cautious policy of non-involvement in Middle Eastern affairs. In answering this question, we first take a brief glance at the history of Turkish–Jewish relations. Then we analyse the fluctuation in Turkish–Israeli relations during the Cold War. We argue that this fluctuation reflects the different phases through which Turkish foreign policy has moved since the end of the Second World War. After a description of Turkish–Israeli agreements in the fields of military, security and civilian co-operation, we examine the factors and goals behind the Turkish initiative to seek a close alignment with Israel. This examination brings us to the conclusion that, on the one hand, Turkey's decision has to be understood in the broader structural context of the strategic, political and economic changes linked to both the end of the Cold War and the emergence of a Greater Middle East. On the other hand, we will show that the interests behind Ankara's initiative are nevertheless in line with its traditional foreign policy, that is, to perceive its Middle Eastern relations as an extension of the country's Western orientation.

Historical legacies: the Ottoman and early Kemalist experiences

In a remarkable contrast to the European experiences of religiously inspired anti-Judaism and political anti-Semitism, the Jewish community enjoyed, as 'people of the book', legal protection and a comparatively high level of freedom in the Ottoman state. Recognised as the third millet, along with the Armenians and Orthodox Christians the Ottoman authorities permitted them to preserve and develop their own culture. Behind Sultan Bayezid's decision to provide Jewish refugees with a safe haven were nevertheless several pragmatic considerations. The linguistic and scientific knowledge of European Jews, as well as their skills and experiences in commerce, banking and crafting, were all well suited to the needs of the rising Empire, and indeed the Iberian Jews took a leading role in the development of Ottoman domestic and international commerce (Levy 1994: 37). Some Jews also attained high positions in the political and economic administration of the Empire, the most famous being Joseph Nasi (c. 1524–79), the trusted confident of Selim II (1566–74). The Ottoman–Jewish symbiosis was well reflected by Nasi, who, although an 'infidel', was able to reach the highest peaks of success and political influence, thereby serving the interests of both the Ottoman state and his own community (Levy 1994: 33).

The Turkish–Jewish mutuality of interests came to the surface once again during the era of Ottoman modernisation, in which the nature of the Ottoman polity had been gradually redefined on the basis of pluralism. Facing the dangers posed by the nationalist revolts in the nineteenth century, the

Sublime Porte in 1835 granted formal recognition to Ottoman Jewry as one of the official communities constituting the Ottoman institutional system. The Ottoman state also favoured Jewish participation in government services and in the civil bureaucracy, particularly during the final period of the Empire following the Young Turk revolution (1908). In contrast to Christians, Jews never became ministers, but as under-secretaries and technocrats in key ministries they played a role that was probably more significant than that of the ministers themselves (Ahmad 1992: 428). Despite the strong opposition of the Ottoman government to Zionism, this stance did not have an explicit anti-Jewish motivation. In fact, the bulk of the Jewish community in the country was unaffected by the measures adopted against the Zionists (Ortaylı 1994: 527–37). One can therefore agree with Levy's assessment that 'the record of the Jewish experience in the Ottoman Empire was exceptionally good and long-lasting' (Levy 1994: 124).

While the Kemalists' position vis-à-vis the Jewish community (and other minorities) was somewhat unclear during the War of Independence, it soon became evident that the early Turkish Republic was strongly opposed to any manifestation of racism or anti-Semitism and was treating its Jews on an equal footing with other citizens. Mustafa Kemal's fierce and determined reaction against an anti-Semitic group, which in summer 1934 attempted to force the Jews out of several places in Thrace, was acknowledged with praise by the Turkish Jewish community (Shaw 1993: 14–20). Turkey also welcomed hundreds of Jews and non-Jewish victims of political persecution fleeing Nazi Germany during the 1930s. This group of German émigrés included leading physicians, artists, and professors who contributed greatly to Turkish academic and intellectual life by resuming their work at Turkish universities and research centres.[3] The positive attitudes and perceptions of the Jewish community in Palestine towards Mustafa Kemal Atatürk were well captured in the articles published in the Hebrew press the day after his death on 10 November 1938. The newspaper Davar (World), for instance, wrote that 'Turkey has lost her founder and builder who restored her national youth, and humanity has lost one of the foremost and enlightened reformers of the modern age'. Similarly, Ha'aretz (The Land) underlined that Atatürk was deservedly seen by many as the greatest reformer of his time, and it was expected that his name would be eternally preserved in the history of the Turks and of the world.[4]

During the Second World War, neutral Turkey defended its Jews and rejected Nazi Germany's demands for them to be deported for extermination in the death camps (Shaw 1993: 35). On the contrary, because of its strategic position and the government's intention to co-operate in the effort to rescue

European Jewry, Istanbul became a true 'Bridge to Palestine', a transit centre to Palestine for Jewish immigrants persecuted in their European homelands (Shaw 1993: 256–64). In 1941, 4,400 Jewish refugees passed through Turkey on their way to Palestine, and even greater numbers in the subsequent years, reaching an estimated 100,000 by the end of the war.[5]

Later on, the Istanbul offices of the Jewish Agency were allowed to organise the emigration to Palestine – whether of the local community or of people in transit from Iran, Syria, Iraq and Bulgaria. In 1958, while Iraqi Jews were being persecuted by the revolutionary regime in Baghdad, Turkey facilitated Jewish emigration to Israel (Nachmani 1987: 10). As a result of different waves of Jewish emigration from Turkey, a community of an estimated 120,000 Turkish Jews is now living in Israel, whose main location is to be found in the coastal city of Bat Yam.[6] According to Robins, this community is very active as a lobby on Turkey's behalf because their sense of Turkish identity remains very important to them (Robins 1991: 85). The current number of Jews in Turkey, predominantly in Istanbul, is around 24,000. Thanks to its wealth and the historically prominent position it has played in commercial life, this Jewish community is still very influential in Turkish society. Summing up this brief history of Turkish–Jewish relations, it is important to note 'that historically speaking friendly relations between Turks and Jews prevailed, that as communities and as states they never confronted each other' (Karpat 1975c: 113). However, the prevalence of a friendly relationship in the history of the two communities did not automatically translate into open co-operation between the Turkish Republic and the Israeli state.

Hesitation and ambivalence: Turkish–Israeli relations in the Cold War era

It was mainly due to US pressure (Robins 1991: 75) that Ankara granted de facto recognition to the Jewish State of Israel in March 1949. Twelve months later diplomatic relations were established.[7] The Turkish government officially explained its decision to recognise Israel from a strictly legalist perspective, arguing that the recognition of a state which had already been admitted to the United Nations was a requirement of international law. Yet it is possible to discern that this decision was partly based on the fact that the Turkish elite perceived Israel as an example of a modern Western state. Furthermore, admiration for the military strength that Israel demonstrated during the 1948 war presumably influenced Ankara's move (Yavuz 1991: 45). In the general historical context, Turkish policy-makers saw the decision as a further step towards full affiliation with the West, and in clear opposition to the ostensibly neutralist position that the Arab states had adopted in the East–West conflict.

As a part of a more widely conceived 'periphery strategy', Israel immediately showed its eagerness to develop its ties with Turkey further and to establish friendly relationships beyond the 'Arab fence' (Nachmani 1987: 48). However, these Israeli advances were met throughout most of the 1950s by substantial hesitations from Ankara. Any judgement of Turkey's ambivalent position toward Israel must reflect the general strategic developments in the Middle East. Looked at from this general perspective, Tel Aviv's early advances clashed with Turkey's new role promoting Western defence schemes in the region. In particular, the Turkish assignment given by Great Britain and the US to induce Arab countries to adhere to regional defence pacts against the Soviet Union (Karpat 1975c: 116) inevitably undermined attempts to establish more friendly Turkish–Israeli ties. Instead, relations with Israel suffered under Turkey's role as regional broker on behalf of the West. In facilitating the establishment of a Western-oriented defence system, Ankara even included in the Baghdad Pact a passage stressing that the articles relating to military assistance in times of crisis were valid for, and specifically linked to, the Palestinian problem. Moreover, in seeking other Arab states to join in the pro-Western defence treaties, Turkey repeatedly pointed to the limited nature of its ties with Israel and to its refusal to issue a declaration of support for Israel's territorial integrity and sovereignty (Nachmani 1987: 67).

However, with the disintegration of the Baghdad Pact, Turkey's hesitations towards improving its ties with Israel were suddenly swept away. In the late 1950s, new domestic, regional and international circumstances pushed the two countries towards more genuine co-operation. The threats of Soviet-backed Communist and Nasserist subversion, the Syrian crisis (1957), the fall of the pro-Western Hashemite regime in Iraq (1958) and the penetration of the region by the United States were some important political aspects behind Turkey's decision to join Israel in a secret 'peripheral alliance' (Karaosmanoglu 1988: 158–9). The summer of 1958 found Israel and Turkey concluding agreements for co-operation in the diplomatic, military and intelligence spheres, as well as in commerce and scientific exchanges.

From a Turkish perspective, the failure to establish a regional defence system confirmed the traditional mistrust with which Ankara viewed the Arab world and justified the new Turkish–Israeli accord, which marked a high point of political co-operation with Israel. Moreover, the growing strength of US–Israeli ties now made Israel a vehicle to further develop Turkish–US relations. As Nachmani argues, 'in the 1958 agreement, the Turks appeared to have adopted the notion of "complementary nations"' (Nachmani 1987:

75). The co-operation between the two countries took place in a number of fields: Israel provided know-how for the construction of an oil pipeline from Iran to Turkey, expertise in the development of Turkish industry and agriculture, and military equipment for the Turkish armed forces. In return, it was agreed that Israel would enjoy the support of Turkey's massive army (Nachmani 1987: 75), and Turkey replaced Cyprus as Israel's chief listening-post for monitoring the Arab states. At secret meetings in Geneva, the two countries worked on scientific co-operation in highly sensitive spheres, and frequent consultations were held between diplomats of the two countries.

Ankara's motives in siding with Israel were principally linked to changed regional circumstances, to Moscow's war of nerves against Turkey and, to a lesser extent, to the economic crisis that hit the country in the second half of the 1950s. Under the changing regional and international conditions, Turkey's predominant rationale for this move was to improve its standing in the eyes of the US administration. In this respect the Turks were convinced that Israel could act as an advocate for Turkish interests in Washington (Nachmani 1987: 75). As such, further strengthening relations with the United States was simply imperative for a country bordering the Soviet Union and facing increasing isolation in the Middle East.

Moreover, as discussed in previous chapters, the domestic tide had begun to turn against the Democratic Party regime of Prime Minister Adnan Menderes. The US criticised Menderes' resort to authoritarian political means, as well as the mismanagement and irresponsible spending of economic assistance. Washington therefore replied negatively to the continual requests for additional economic assistance that the Turkish authorities advanced in the second half of the 1950s. In this situation, Ankara was convinced that Turkey's prospects of receiving US financial aid would improve greatly if this request was backed by American Jewry, whose hearts it hoped to soften by way of closer relations with Israel (Nachmani 1987: 52).

Yet most of the 1958 agreements never fully materialised. The confluence of domestic, regional and international developments that acted as a catalyst for the Turkish–Israeli agreements soon disappeared and gave way to a new political constellation, which shaped the third phase of Turkish foreign policy, the period of Western disappointment and Arab rapprochement. Consequently, Turkish–Israeli relations came under stress and deteriorated during this phase in an unprecedented way. In the early 1980s, commercial relations with Israel were negligible and diplomatic relations downgraded to a historic low.

The country's worsening economic condition and the need for diplomatic support following the military operation in Cyprus (1974) pushed Turkey to try to improve its political and economic relations with the Arab states. In the 1970s, Turkey shifted to a general support for Arab resolutions at the UN General Assembly, including the 1975 resolution labelling Zionism as a form of racism. In 1980, Turkey reacted sharply to the decision of the Israeli Knesset to enact a law declaring that 'Jerusalem is the united and permanent capital of Israel'. Under intense domestic pressure to break off its relations with Israel, the coalition government of Süleyman Demirel condemned the 'Israeli annexation of Jerusalem' and declared the closure of the Turkish consulate general in Jerusalem in August 1980. With this move, the Turkish government adopted the minimum measures necessary to alleviate domestic criticism and maintain friendly relations with the Arab world (Aykan 1993: 101–2).

Finally, in December 1980, the military regime that had replaced the civilian government in September 1980 formally downgraded diplomatic relations with Israel to the second secretary level. According to the spokesman of the ministry of foreign affairs, this decision was adopted because 'Israel would not retreat from its intransigent policy toward the Middle East conflict and the *fait accompli* that it wishes to create in connection with the legal status of Jerusalem'.[8] Despite this official explanation, it seems that the decision to downgrade relations with Israel was, on the one hand, an attempt by the military rulers to gain internal and external Islamic credibility;[9] on the other hand, it was also determined by mere budgetary needs. In 1980, the total value of Turkish exports was about US$2.2 billion, while oil import expenditure alone reached the figure of US$2.6 billion (Yavuz 1991: 43). Because of the severe economic crisis, and in order to obtain the necessary oil for the coming winter, the Turkish authorities were forced to seek the assistance of the Arab oil-producing countries. According to George Gruen, a Saudi cheque for about US$250 million was delivered to Turkey on 2 December, the very day that Turkey announced the downgrading of its relations with Israel (Gruen 1993: 38).

However, this pro-Arab leaning proved to be only temporary, closely tied to transitory circumstances and Turkey's deep disappointment with the West. It could also be argued that in the phase of Turkey's Arab rapprochement Ankara deliberately underplayed its relations to Israel (cf. Evriviades 1998). A first sign that the pendulum was swinging back in favour of Israel was Turkey's abstention from the UN voting on a resolution condemning Israel's annexation of the Syrian Golan Heights (resolution ES 9/1, 1982). This shift – not by chance – coincided with the decline of the Middle Eastern markets in Turkey's trade profile and the oil price falls of the mid-1980s, both developments significantly eroding the economic and political leverage of the Arab states vis-à-vis Turkey.

Moreover, Turkish Prime Minister Özal's desire to improve Turkey's relations with the US, and especially with the US Congress, added further reasons for the swing back to Israel. Özal openly relied on the sympathy of the influential Jewish lobby to reach his aim. In an interview given to the newspaper *Günes* (Sun), Özal declared that 'if the Arab countries ask for it [severing ties with Israel] we will always place emphasis on the cost-benefit issue. We know the role of the Israeli lobby in the US'.[10] Three years later, Özal's words were confirmed by events: in August 1987, thanks to the support of the Jewish lobby, the resolution aimed at declaring 24 April the 'day of commemoration of the Armenian genocide' was rejected by the US House of Representatives.[11] In the light of the fact that Ankara continues to deny any historical responsibility for the Armenian massacres in 1915–16, passing the resolution would have been a major diplomatic slap in the face for the Turkish government.

The vicissitudes in Turkish–Israeli relations during the Cold War prove that neither positive historical legacies nor political and cultural communalities were decisive forces in shaping Turkish foreign policy behaviour. Turkey's ties to Israel were always subordinated to pressing short-term goals and to Turkey's general relationship with the West. Turkish–Israeli relations have been following precisely the classic pattern of relations with the Middle East being an appendix to Turkey's Western policies; they present thereby a mirror image of Turkish–Arab relations. Thus Turkey's Arab rapprochement was reflected in its detachment from Israel.

The new Turkish–Israeli axis

The military and security dimensions of the Turkish–Israeli agreements
On 23 February 1996, Israel and Turkey signed a military co-operation agreement providing for the exchange of military information, experience and personnel.[12] It called, for *inter alia*, joint training exercises, the exchange of military observers at each other's exercises, reciprocal port access for naval vessels and for each country's planes to exercise in the other's airspace for one week four times a year. Since April 1996, the training exercises of the two air forces have occurred regularly. Such visits are mutually beneficial. They enable the Israeli pilots to gain experience flying long-range missions (a skill that would be necessary for missions over Iran) and over mountainous areas, where visually identifying an enemy aircraft is more difficult than during flights over sea. In exchange, Turkish pilots have the opportunity to benefit from Israel's systems of training in advanced technological warfare. In particular, they have access to the air combat manoeuvring instrumentation

range in the Israeli Negev desert. Since such exercises also enable both air forces to become familiar with the procedures and tactics used by their counterparts, this could greatly facilitate co-operation in wartime.

A higher stage in Turkish–Israeli military co-operation was reached in January 1998, when the navies of Israel, Turkey and the US held joint naval search and rescue (SAR) exercises – named 'Reliant Mermaid' – in the eastern Mediterranean, which involved five vessels and helicopters. Despite their official 'humanitarian purpose', the SAR manoeuvres were, according to the experts, similar to naval operations aimed at localising and intercepting an enemy vessel.[13]

The military agreement is also believed to have strengthened the long-standing intelligence ties between Turkey and Israel. In April 1996, in his address to the Washington Research Institute, the Turkish Deputy Chief of Staff, Cevik Bir, revealed that Israel had requested Turkey's assistance in collecting intelligence information. Israel's first priority target was Syria, while Iran was the second, the Turkish general said. Ankara's positive reply was taken for granted. In exchange, Turkey benefited from Israel's experience in the 'security zone' of Lebanon in monitoring its borders with Iraq and Syria, as well as preventing cross-border infiltration by PKK guerrillas. During his visit to Israel in May 1997, the Turkish defence minister visited the Golan Heights in order to see whether the methods employed by the Israelis to prevent cross-border infiltration were applicable on the Turkish–Iraqi border. It also seems likely that – despite denials from the Turkish and Israeli authorities – Israeli military advisers were involved in planning Turkish military offensives in northern Iraq and in laying mines and trip-wire sensors along the Turkish–Iraqi border (Olson 1997: 189–90).

A more controversial point in terms of strategic co-operation concerns the issue of terrorism. During a visit to Israel in February 1997, Turkey's then Chief of the General Staff, General Ismail Karadayi, stated that the struggle against international terrorism should be the priority of this co-operation (Leitmann and Erdem 1997). However, despite the fact that the two countries share a similar approach to fighting international terrorism, Israel has always played down Ankara's invitation to join a campaign against the PKK. Indeed, the Turkish thesis, put forward by Foreign Minister Hikmet Cetin during his 1993 visit to Israel, that several terrorist factions protected and sponsored by Syria threatened Ankara and Jerusalem equally did not entirely convince the Israelis. Significantly, the Israeli authorities pointed out that the PKK had never targeted Israel. Cetin's call for a joint Turkish–Israeli effort against the PKK failed; the Israelis quickly rejected the Turkish request by replying that 'Israel did not wish to have new enemies'.[14]

Nevertheless, Israel did not exclude the possibility of co-operation against international terrorism, but refused to join in a campaign specifically against the PKK. An arrangement was reached in November 1994 that relegated anti-terrorist efforts to a mere bilateral police agreement. Israel's policy of steering clear of Turkey's dispute with the PKK, which had been carefully implemented by the governments of Rabin and Peres, came to an end with Binyamin Netanyahu's election as Israeli prime minister in May 1996. The Likud premier did not hesitate in condemning Syrian support for the PKK, as well as the latter's terrorist campaign, and he vigorously supported the idea of a joint Turkish–Israeli struggle against terrorism aimed at isolating countries sponsoring terrorist groups.[15]

Finally, a joint forum for strategic research and assessment, which meets every six months, has been institutionalised. By establishing a network of institutional and personal relationships amongst the military and political hierarchies of the two countries to provide the necessary basis for a solid relationship, this security forum may be the most significant aspect of the Turkish–Israeli alignment. As Efraim Inbar, director of the Begin–Sadat research centre, argues, 'this is probably the heart of the relationship' (Inbar 1998).

Besides strategic co-operation, the military agreement on the defence industry, signed on 26 August 1996, has established the legal framework for the transfer of military technology and know-how between the two countries. This allows the Turkish army – with the Pentagon's blessing – to obtain weapons and technology that Turkey would not be able to get in Europe or in the US because of its human rights record and its dispute with Greece. The technology, the reliability, and the capacity to cover almost all defence needs has made the Israeli military industry a unique partner for the Turkish armed forces, which are engaged in a giant programme of investment: a plan for rearmament and modernisation costing in the order of US$150 billion in twenty-five years.[16]

The transfer of Israeli technology is also functional to Ankara's goal of developing its own national defence industry, which in the late 1990s could cover only 21 per cent of the Turkish armed forces' requirements. The agreement on defence industry co-operation has led to an extraordinary range of possible and actual arms sales, overwhelmingly from Israel to Turkey, characterised by a significant amount of work given to Turkish firms.[17]

The giant defence investment programme undertaken by Turkey constitutes a gold mine for Israeli defence industries. As the then Israeli Minister of Defence, Yitzhak Mordechai, said, 'we have opened the way to Israeli firms in order to increase the volume of sales and activities in Turkey ... we are just at the beginning'.[18] The defence contracts concluded with Turkey constitute an invaluable opportunity for the Israeli defence industries striving to maintain their technological advantage over neighbouring countries and, contemporaneously, suffering because of Israel's decreasing defence budget and the crisis in the world arms market.

The potential inherent in Turkey's defence needs were clearly stated by General (retired) Sitki Orun, a technical adviser of the Turkish Armed Force Foundation, who declared that the suspensions in arms export adopted ever more frequently by the US and European countries give a great advantage to Israeli firms.[19] Since both Israeli and Turkish military inventories are based on US equipment, Turkey saw Israel, on the one hand, as an alternative and at times cheaper source of supply. On the other hand, purchases from Israel may enable Turkey to circumvent US conditions on arms sales, a fact stressed by a Turkish scholar who argues that the Israeli approach to Turkey is free from concerns such as Turkey's domestic performance on human rights, its stand on the Kurdish issue and improving its standards of democracy, factors which characterise the US approach to Turkey (Aykan 1999: 14). Additionally, Israel's state-of-the-art military technology and its well-documented specialisation in modernising ageing and obsolete equipment make it an invaluable partner for Ankara.

The civilian dimensions of the Turkish–Israeli agreements

Yet what Israel offers Turkey is not limited to security and military concerns. The civilian side of the Turkish–Israeli axis thrives as well. The total volume of non-military trade between the two countries quadrupled between 1992 and 1996 to about US$450 million a year. In March 1996, during Turkish President Süleyman Demirel's visit to Israel, the two governments signed a Free Trade Agreement (FTA), which came into force in July 1997, when the coalition government headed by Mesut Yilmaz approved the relevant decree.[20] The decree opened new possibilities for economic relations between the two countries, not only in the commercial sphere but also in investments and industrial and agricultural co-operation. The aim of both sides was to reach a bilateral trade volume of US$2 billion by the end of 2000, an ambitious target but not unrealisable, taking into account the robust growth that Turkish–Israeli trade has shown since the FTA came into effect.

Moreover, this figure does not include the receipts generated by the thousands of Israeli tourists that have been visiting Turkey annually since the early 1990s. The tourist industry, with its annual turnover of about US$400 million has become one of the main components of the bilateral economic relations, as well as an indication of the friendly atmosphere prevailing between Turkey and Israel.[21] A further point to be made is that Israel has opened the US market to Turkish products: Turks sell textiles and other commodities duty-free to Israel, which adds its labour to the products and then re-exports them to the United States duty-free.[22] In addition, Israeli firms have shown a considerable interest in the GAP region, where Israeli companies participate in irrigation and agricultural projects. Several textile firms attracted by the lower labour costs moved from Israel to Turkey's south-east. Many opportunities to use Israeli technology for the transportation and distribution of water are also foreseen. The co-operation includes training activities: Turkish officials involved in the GAP project regularly attend training courses at the International Training Centre for Agricultural Development and Co-operation (CINADCO), Israel's large agricultural research and training centre.[23]

Since 1990, Turkey has also been showing a marked interest in selling water to Israel. Water was a major topic of discussion during both the March 1996 and the July 1999 visits of President Demirel to Israel. Turkey's offer to sell 180 million cubic metres of water per year to Israel, which in the past had met with repeated refusal seemed to attract the interest of Ehud Barak's administration, as confirmed by the decision to set up a joint committee to discuss the feasibility and commercial aspects of the project.[24]

The importance of the economic relations cannot be underestimated, especially if we take into account the existing opportunities for further developments both within the two countries and in the neighbouring regions of Central Asia and the Transcaucasus, where a Turkish 'entrance card' may facilitate Israel's desire to expand exchanges.[25] During Turkish Foreign Minister Hikmet Cetin's visit in November 1993, the Israeli Trade Minister Micha Harish indicated that Ankara was an essential partner in the Israeli plan to increase its commercial ties with the countries of Central Asia and the Transcaucasus. The Israeli minister openly stated that 'Turkey can play an essential role as an intermediary between Israel and the Muslim Republics of the former Soviet Union'.[26]

Israeli Foreign Minister Shimon Peres attracted the interest of the Turks when he proposed – during his visit in April 1994 – the possibility of a collective partnership between the US, Israel and Turkey aimed at launching economic projects in the Central Asian republics of the former Soviet Union. Following Washington's approach, Peres declared that 'any person of common sense should pray for the success of the secular and democratic Turkish model over the Iranian in the competition to achieve influence over the Central Asian Muslim Republics'.[27] A few months later, an agreement was signed between the Turkish International Co-operation Agency (TIKA), Israel and the US to launch a common agricultural program in Uzbekistan and

Turkmenistan (Winrow 1995: 40). More recently, Israel has shown interest in gaining access to oil and gas from Turkey if Turkish ambitions to become a major pipeline route for energy resources from the Caucasus and Central Asia should be realised.[28] According to the Turkish press, Israeli businessmen are also seeking funds and loans to help finance important infrastructure projects in Turkey (a number of highways, a third bridge over the Bosphorus and projects related to the GAP) and in Central Asia, in exchange for Israeli participation in these projects.[29] In this regard, it is important to point out that Israeli companies had by the 1950s played a key role in the construction of Turkish airports and roads.

Indeed, Turkish–Israeli relations have developed in an unprecedented way. The extraordinary flurry of high-level visits between the two countries since 1993 has resulted in various agreements embracing virtually all sectors. These include interactions in the domains of culture, education and science; environmental protection; mail and telecommunications; efforts to stop the smuggling of drugs and narcotic substances; health and agriculture; free trade regulations and customs duties; encouragement and protection of financial investments; avoidance of dual taxation; and technical and economic co-operation (Nachmani 1998: 26). In short, alongside close military ties, there is extensive non-military co-operation between Turkey and Israel, with great potential for further expansion. From an Israeli perspective, in the 1990s the attempt to develop friendly relations beyond the Arab fence gathered new momentum.[30]

Factors and goals behind the Turkish–Israeli axis

The Turkish–Israeli agreements, both military and civilian, obviously have a wide range of benefits for both sides. In view of the short-term interests of Turkish foreign-policy-makers the alignment seems to be a pragmatic and rationally calculated move. Closer ties to Israel enhanced Turkey's ability to handle some of the political and economic problems caused by the geo-political changes of the 1990s. Moreover, the Middle East peace process provided a political environment in which Turkey could expect a less hostile reaction from the Arab world to its co-operation with Israel in such sensitive fields as military strategy and defence industry. With regard to the peace process, it was telling that on 13 November 1993, exactly two months after the handshake between Yitzak Rabin and Yasir Arafat at the White House, Hikmet Cetin became the first-ever Turkish foreign minister to visit Israel.

In fact, Ankara's new activism in the international arena had nowhere been more evident in the post-Cold War era than in its opening of a bold diplomatic, economic and military relationship with Israel. But contrary to what is commonly perceived in the Arab world, in 1996 the impetus for the military alignment between the two countries came not from Israel, but from the Turkish side, and more precisely from the Turkish armed forces. While in the late 1950s it was Israel looking at Turkey as a suitable partner for its 'peripheral pact' strategy, in the early 1990s the initiative was largely undertaken by Ankara's powerful generals. As Henri Barkey suggested, 'the old courtship game has been reversed' (Barkey 1996b: 38).

The major factors that pushed Turkey to embark on a bold alignment with Israel are closely linked to the end of the Cold War and the subsequent reorientation of the foreign policy of Turkey's partners in the West. The political developments of the 1990s weakened Turkey's bargaining position vis-à-vis the European Union and the US. In addition, the realities of Cold War politics provided for decades the framework for Turkey's low key approach to the Middle East (Sayari 1992: 9). Ironically, despite the disappearance of the Soviet threat, the importance attached to NATO by the Turks became even more pronounced: the end of the Cold war threatened to undermine Turkey's 'most important institutional and functional link to Europe and the US' (Karaosmanoglu 1999: 215).

As Duygu Sezer asserts, 'the end of the Cold War and the Gulf crisis have brought Turkey's grand strategy to an impasse' (Sezer 1992: 21). Turkey's post-Second World War grand strategy had been almost fully based on NATO, which provided the security for the defence of Turkey's territorial integrity and sovereignty. Moreover, during most of the Cold War period, Turkey's alliance with the Western bloc guaranteed the economic and political support from the West which Ankara considered essential for its goal of becoming an equally modern and industrialised state within the Western world. The end of the East–West conflict and the demise of the Soviet Union raised fundamental questions about Turkey's role in NATO and relations with the West.

In addition to that, the 1991 Gulf War confirmed what the Turks had long suspected: in the post-Cold War era, aggression against Turkey by one of its Arab neighbours would not be considered by some NATO members as aggression against all NATO members. The debate that took place within each European country about the necessity, wisdom and merits of getting involved in protecting Turkey left a bitter taste with the Turks; the Western partners showed that they were far from being reliable allies (Sezer 1992: 29). As the veteran Turkish diplomat Sükrü Elekdag pointed out: 'With the dissolution of the Soviet Union, NATO has totally lost its function of providing support for Turkey's defence' (Elekdag 1996: 54) The 'Central European oriented' approach implicit in NATO's enlargement to encompass some former Warsaw Pact members created further suspicions. From a Turkish perspective, the Alliance's primary strategic goal has shifted to the enhancement of security in Central Europe.

The degree of anxiety that characterised Turkey's relations with its Western allies in the early 1990s is reflected in Hasan Köni's conclusion that 'Western European and US policies have given rise to the isolation of Turkey on the international scene'.[31] This sense of isolation has been significantly fuelled by the attitude of Ankara's European partners toward its efforts to gain full membership of the EU and the Western European Union (WEU). Beginning with Turkey's application for full membership in the European Community (1987), Turkish–EU relations have shown a series of grave set-backs for Turkey. The Maastricht Treaty (1991) and the Copenhagen Summit (1993) strengthened the political aspects of democracy and human rights as decisive criteria for full membership, and further aggravated Turkey's problems in meeting the required standards for future candidates. This became apparent during the final negotiations of the Customs Union between Turkey and the EU in 1995. In emphasising Turkey's poor human rights record, the European Parliament blocked the ratification process for months. The rejection of the Turkish candidacy at the Luxembourg summit in December 1997 came as no surprise, therefore, although it was received in Turkey as a humiliating disappointment.

While the explanations for Turkey's rejections were based firmly on economic and political criteria, Ankara perceived them as an excuse to exclude Turkey because it is a Muslim country. This perception was reinforced by the European inability or lack of determination to put a stop to the slaughter of Muslims in Bosnia and then in Kosovo, and by various incautious statements made by leading European politicians. The European criticisms of Turkey's human rights practices, particularly regarding the Kurdish issue, and the temporary weapons embargo declared by European countries such as Germany, Norway, Denmark and Holland further aggravated tensions. The result was a widespread impression in Turkey that Europe is at best unsympathetic and unreliable, at worst racist and a promoter of terrorism in Turkey.[32]

If the European pillar of Turkey's foreign relations was increasingly showing cracks, the other pillar, relations with the US, showed growing strains. While it is clear that the US is, of all the Western countries, the most sympathetic to Turkey's interests, it is also evident that domestic politics, and not only American strategic considerations, are gaining an increasing influence on Washington's foreign policy. This is intimately linked to the demise of the Soviet threat and the growing assertiveness of human rights groups and NGOs within the US Congress. This development has further worsened Turkey's standing vis-à-vis the Congress, in which Turkey has historically met the joint opposition of the powerful Armenian- and Greek-American lobbies, and suffered from the absence of an effective pro-Turkish lobby. As a consequence, the US administration has found it more and more difficult to defend Ankara indefinitely before members of Congress who are worried about the growing dimensions of the Kurdish conflict and its potential threat to the stability of the region – leaving aside its implications for human rights.

In the light of repeated Congressional criticism and of tendencies to limit aid levels because of Turkey's unfavourable human rights record, and, most seriously, the setbacks suffered in procuring US weapons, Ankara duly realised that enhanced efforts to gain the support of the pro-Israeli lobby were of increased importance in order to balance the strength of the anti-Turkish lobbies. As early as 1994, Elekdag argued:

> The Israeli lobby in the US is far superior to all other ethnic lobbies put together. Whenever this lobby has worked for us [the Turks], Turkey's interests have been perfectly protected against the fools in the US. The development of relations between Turkey and Israel and the formalisation of their de-facto alliance will place this lobby permanently on our side.[33]

As in the previous example of the late 1950s, Ankara deeply believed that an alignment with Israel would ease its way to gaining the ear of the US legislature and 'conquering' Congress on its behalf (Inbar 1998), a belief further reinforced by the Israelis' open acknowledgement that they fully understand and support Ankara's goal of strengthening its ties with the US.[34] Former Israeli Defence Minister Yitzhak Mordechai, for example, confirmed that Israel is assisting Turkey on the American political scene and is encouraging Jewish organisations to follow its example.[35] Against this background, Zvi Bar'el, one of the leading editorialists of the Israeli newspaper Ha'aretz, came to the conclusion that 'the strategic alliance [Turkey] really wants, then, is not with a regional power, even if its name is Israel, but with the US'.[36]

Undoubtedly, the alignment with Israel has grown out of valid strategic concerns – mainly linked to Turkey's ties with the West – but not as a response to any serious external threats posed by its Middle Eastern neighbours. If there was a merely regional concern behind Turkey's initiative, then this was ironically linked to the same peace process that somehow facilitated closer relations between Turkey and Israel. To a certain extent, Ankara was worried about a possible deal between Israel and Syria, which could have freed Damascus to pursue long-standing grievances with Turkey. First,

Ankara was concerned that a possible redeployment of Syrian troops from the Golan Heights might result in a Syrian military build-up along the Turkish border, which would have altered in Syria's favour the military balance in Turkey's south-east.

In 1996, Elekdag rang the alarm bell in Ankara by saying: 'When peace is struck between Syria and Israel, Damascus can be expected to pursue her objectives concerning Syrian demands over Hatay and the waters of the Euphrates much more actively' (Elekdag 1996: 52). Second, the Turks feared that after an agreement between Israel and Syria, there might have been concerted pressure put on Turkey, this time possibly involving Israel and the US, to take a more conciliatory approach towards the water disputes with its southern neighbours. By embarking on a bold alignment with Israel, Ankara could hope to have at least a say on the evolution of the relations between Israel and Syria and, especially, pre-empt any agreement that may affect its interests. In this regard, the timing of Turkey's offer to Israel of a comprehensive military agreement and the following leak of most details to the press was telling. It came exactly when the peace negotiations between Syria and Israel seemed to move towards an agreement in the early months of 1996.

Finally, in the early 1990s it became evident that Turkey had derived neither the economic nor the diplomatic benefits it expected from improved ties with the Arab and Islamic worlds. Turkish policies of rapprochement with the Middle Eastern states did not obtain the desired results as far as Turkish foreign policy was concerned (DPE 1993: 9). This disaffection with a pro-Arab policy that failed to pay anticipated diplomatic dividends was well expressed by the Turkish journalist Semih Idiz:

> Looking at recent history one sees nothing but negative examples ranging from nonexistent 'Islamo-Arab solidarity' for the Turkish cause in Cyprus, to Arab countries actually claiming chunks of Turkey, as Syria does, to the dangerous meddling in Turkey's internal affairs, again as Syria does, through support for a group that every civilised nation sees as a terrorist organisation.[37]

Consequently, there is deep resentment, both at governmental level and among the public, about the lack of understanding and support shown by the Arab world towards Turkey's security issues in the eastern Mediterranean (Cyprus). Turkish foreign-policy-makers have therefore concluded that religious brotherhood with the Arab world could not be a crucial criterion for developing policies related to the national security of Turkey whenever an Arab nation or its interests are involved. Moreover, the economic factor that had functioned as a catalyst in Turkey's rapprochement with its Arab neighbours in the 1970s and 1980s had lost relevance in the mid-1990s (Bolukbasi 1999: 30).

Conclusions: 'pragmatic escapism'

In the light of the previous analysis, the new strategic relationship between Turkey and Israel appears to be a rather pragmatic step by Turkey's decision-makers. Although the new alignment with Israel drags Turkey more into the Middle Eastern scene, the interests behind the Turkish initiative are totally in line with its traditional foreign policy, which perceives its Middle Eastern relations as an extension of its Western orientation. If any kind of fear was involved, then it was not due to the containable threats that Turkey's neighbours pose, but rather a result of the growing uneases between Turkey and its Western allies. Four driving forces are discernible behind Turkey's intensified co-operation with Israel:

1. Israel played the role of a new and reliable source of military technology and hardware at a time when Turkey's Western allies were increasingly more reluctant to do so. The new axis enables the Kemalist regime to pursue its ambitious rearmament programme and to build up of a national defence industry less inhibited by Western political constraints.

2. Turkey expected that the Israeli government and the American Jewish lobby would work on its behalf in Washington. The new alignment was therefore also an attempt to counterbalance anti-Turkish forces within the United States.

3. Albeit to a lesser extent, the economic co-operation with Israel compensated for losses that the Turkish economy faced in its trade with the Middle East and North Africa after the 1991 Gulf War (cf. Önis 1995: 61).

4. The enhanced co-operation in civilian domains served well the interest of Turkey's Kemalist elite in demonstrating Ankara's continued orientation towards the West and its commitment to secularism. As pragmatic as the alignment with Israel seems to be, on the domestic scene it was apparently a function of the Kemalists' increasing sense of siege. This explains also why Ankara, in a clear departure from common practice, gave the new axis great publicity (Bengio and Özcan 2000: 140).

While it is at best uncertain whether friendship with Israel may indeed translate into successful support in the US Congress or not, it is certain that Turkey's alignment with Israel fundamentally had a Western rather than a Middle Eastern 'target'. Specifically, the synergy of co-operation between Turkey and Israel has the potential to increase their mutual importance in the eyes of the US. This is most likely to happen because Turkish and Israeli roles within a US-oriented regional security system can be advocated on the basis of both their strategic importance, especially in the case of Turkey, and their ideological similarity to the US.

If there was a purely Middle Eastern aspect of the alignment, then it was the Turkish interest in putting pressure on regional states accused of supporting Islamist groups and the PKK. In this respect, co-operation between the region's two strongest military powers can indeed have an intimidating effect. The mere fact that the major part of the alignment concerns co-operation in the military field, together with the more assertive posture of Ankara's policy towards the region, have, inevitably, stirred the suspicions of Turkey's neighbours. The rhetorical revival of the Ottoman–Jewish heritage further aggravated this sense of mistrust in the Arab world, where the closing years – at least – of the Ottoman Empire are viewed as a period of harsh political suppression.

As pragmatic as the alignment with Israel seems to be, it was far from being the only response Turkey's foreign-policy-makers could have made to cope with the political turbulence of the 1990s. Furthermore, in the light of strong Arab resentment, it is surprising that the architects of the alignment accepted the subordination of Turkey's regional policies to the imponderabilities of the peace process, while Ankara fiercely rejecting any European interference in Turkish affairs. Against the background of the Sèvres syndrome, the pragmatism can also be interpreted as an attempt to avoid any deviation from firmly established dogmas of Turkish politics. Not only is the continuing emphasis on viewing national security in strict military terms highly questionable, but so also is the fact that in the face of Western demands to democratise the political system, to improve the human rights record and to find a peaceful solution for the Kurdish question, the Kemalist establishment escaped to an ally who has undoubtedly kept a low profile in this respect.

It is this kind of 'pragmatic escapism' that is to be understood within the broader framework of the cognitive structures of Turkey's encirclement syndrome. The avoidance of addressing such problems as the Kurdish issue, political Islam and the water dispute in a new political framework indicates that the Kemalist establishment is either unwilling or unable to pursue regional policies that take into account the emerging geopolitical structures of a Greater Middle East.

Notes

1   Summary of World Broadcast (SWB), EE/1907 B/6, 28 January 1994.
2   A Quincentennial Foundation was established in 1989 to co-ordinate world-wide activities, with offices in Turkey and the major Western countries. Academic

and cultural activities were organised and the gala dinner of the foundation in Istanbul saw the participation of Israeli President Chaim Herzog, and Turkish President Özal and Prime Minister Demirel.

3 An interesting account of these émigrés from Germany is given in the autobiographical book by Fritz Neumark (1980).

4 *Davar*, 'Ataturk Met' (Atatürk is Dead), and *Ha'aretz*, 'Ataturk', 11 November 1938, both reported by Kushner (1985/86: 101–2).

5 Figures indicated by Slutsky (1971: 171) and reported by Shaw (1993: 268).

6 For a detailed study, see Weiker (1988).

7 Turkey recognised the State of Israel on 28 March 1949 and established diplomatic relations on 9 March 1950 by posting a plenipotentiary to Tel Aviv. Then, in 1952, ambassadors were exchanged.

8 *The Middle East*, February 1981, p. 30.

9 Regarding this point, compare the role that the Turkish Islamic Synthesis played in the political strategy of the military regime.

10 Quoted from Yavuz (1991: 49).

11 The same happened in February 1990 in the Senate.

12 The original memorandum that constituted the basis for the military co-operation agreement reached in February 1996 was signed in the previous September. Regarding the exact place and date of the latter signature substantial confusion still prevails. The data indicated were given by General Cevik Bir to the Turkish newspapers *Yeni Safak* and *Cumhuriyet*. See SWB, ME/2634 MED/8, 10 June 1996.

13 *Jane's Defence Weekly*, 17 December 1997, p. 6.

14 Cetin, in an interview given to the *Jerusalem Post*, openly accused Syria of protecting and guaranteeing a safe haven to the terrorists of the PKK, Islamic Jihad and Hizbullah, and added that 'Turkey and Israel should fight together against Damascus' sponsored terrorism'. The Israeli position appears in the same article: *Jerusalem Post*, 16 November 1993.

15 *Ha'aretz*, 27 May 1997; *Jerusalem Post*, 2 May 1997.

16 *Turkish Daily News*, 7 February 1998.

17 The largest contract that Israel has won so far is a US$630 million agreement to upgrade 54 Turkish F–4 fighters; then an Israeli–Singaporean consortium won a US$75 million contract to do the same to 48 F–5s. Turkey agreed to buy 100 Popeye I air-to-ground missiles, larger fuel tanks for its F–16s and to co-produce 200 Popeye II for the same aircraft. Israel has proposed to upgrade Turkey's aging M–60 tanks and to sell unmanned aerial vehicles (UAVs) and early warning aircraft (AEWC). In 1998, Israel and Turkey reportedly agreed to co-operate on the production of a new medium-range anti-ballistic missile called 'Delilah'.

18 *Reuters*, 'Israel eyes "gold mine" in Turkish arms deals', 9 December 1997.

19 Steve Rodan, 'Turkey wants more arms deals with Israel', *Jerusalem Post*, 27 January 1997.

20 The Free Trade Agreement provides for the mutual elimination of customs duties for more than 90 per cent of goods.

21 Figures indicated by Ekrem Güvendiren, president of the joint Turkish–Israeli Council for Economic Co-operation, reported by the *Turkish Daily News*, 7 February 1998.

22 See Saadet Oruc, 'Turkish trade via Israel to the US expected to boost export

volume' Turkish Daily News, 5 January 1999.

23 Turkish Daily News, 'Turkish–Israeli ties on the eve of the 21st century', 3 December 1997.

24 Turkish Daily News, 'Turkey, Israel to establish a Water Commission', 16 July 1999.

25 Laurent Mallet, 'Nell'ex Asia Sovietica sionismo fa rima con capitalismo', LiMes 4 (1995), p. 255. However, it should be pointed out that the Israeli–Turkish relationship on the politics of Central Asia has been so far less successful than expected for both participants. See Lochery (1998: 57).

26 Jerusalem Post, 15 November 1993.

27 SWB, EE/1972 B/6-7, 15 April 1994.

28 See Saadet Oruc, 'Turkey wants to become a transit country for Turkmen gas to Israel', Turkish Daily News, 11 March 1998; and by the same author, 'Turkey, Israel to enhance strategic ties with Caucasus', Turkish Daily News, 16 March 1998.

29 Turkish Daily News, 'Israel offers to find funds for joint projects in Central Asia', 25 May 1999.

30 In this regard, Turkish–Israeli relations seem important, because the peace treaties with Egypt (1979), the PLO (1993) and Jordan (1994) have not so far materialised in friendly relations beyond government level, see Khouri (1998).

31 Quoted in Barkey and Fuller (1998: 163).

32 See the interview given by Turkish Minister of Foreign Affairs Ismail Cem to the Turkish Daily News, 23 January 1998.

33 Milliyet, 14 December 1994.

34 Yediot Aharonot, 3 April 1997, translation carried by Foreign Broadcast Information Service (FBIS), 4 April 1997, and Ha'aretz, 17 December 1997.

35 Ron Ben-Yishav, Yediot Aharonot, 3 April 1997, translation carried by FBIS, 4 April 1997.

36 Ha'aretz, 14 December 1997.

37 Semih Idiz, 'So what does Turkey owe the Arabs?', Turkish Probe, 14 June 1996.

9 The Revival of Pan-Turkism
Turkish Policies in Central Asia and the Transcaucasus

Enver Pasha's return

On 4 August 1996, seventy-eight years after the 'Unionist triumvirate' escaped from Turkey in great secrecy on the German torpedo submarine U–67, the remains of Enver Pasha were laid to rest at Istanbul's Eternal Freedom Hill. The remains of the former Ottoman minister of war arrived from the plains of Central Asia, where he died in 1922, while pursuing his pan-Turkist ideals at the head of an indigenous movement (the Basmachis) that was fighting the Bolsheviks' oppressive policies. Many prominent figures in Turkey's political and military establishment attended the funeral ceremonies of the former unionist leader, who was reburied with full military honours. Moreover, hundreds of members of Turkish ultra-right groups marched behind Enver Pasha's hearse, waving flags and chanting the slogan: 'Turkey will become the great Turan', thus referring to the imaginary union linking all ethnic Turks in the vast area stretching from the Adriatic to China.

The official reburial of Enver Pasha indicated a marked break with the historical dogma of Kemalism, which had discarded Enver's pan-Turkist activities as mere 'adventurism'. This departure became most evident in President Süleyman Demirel's ceremonial speech, in which he stated that Enver Pasha was 'a nationalist, an idealist and an honest soldier who loved his country'. Demirel further declared the strong man of the unionist regime a 'hero in the eyes of the Turkish nation whose exile has ended'.[1] Given the fact that Enver Pasha's remains arrived at 'Kemal Atatürk' airport in Istanbul on board a Turkish Air Force C–130 from Tajikistan, his exile ended in a historical irony. It was the unionist leader who had strongly opposed Mustafa Kemal Atatürk in the last years of the Empire and during the War of Independence. Precisely this rivalry between the two men later led to the condemnation

175

and demonisation of Enver's memory by official Kemalist historiography.[2]

Taking this Kemalist denigration of Enver Pasha into account, his funeral ceremony marked the rehabilitation of one of the most controversial figures in Turkish history. In the 1990s, Enver Pasha's record in the Transcaucasus and Central Asia, as well as his pan-Turkist ideas, appealed to Turkey's newly emerged ambitions to extend its influence over the Turkic republics of the former Soviet periphery. In the new geo-strategic setting of a Greater Middle East, the contradictions of Kemalist nation-building and the unsettled questions of the late Ottoman Empire again came to the fore. The development of new relations between the Turkish Republic and the five Turkic states – Azerbaijan, Kazakhstan, Kyrgyzstan, Turkmenistan and Uzbekistan – therefore elucidates best the challenges and opportunities with which Turkey has been confronted since the Cold War.

On the occasion of the second Turkic summit in Istanbul (1994), President Süleyman Demirel interpreted this new geo-strategic situation as follows: 'Our history, which was divided by various events, has overcome the obstacles in its path and has returned to its natural course. The inevitable was realized in 1991 and these five brotherly republics have re-emerged as independent and sovereign states. We welcome this rebirth with great enthusiasm.'[3] This chapter sets out to inquire into this 'natural course' of Turkish history and will question the ideological assessments made by Süleyman Demirel and Turkey's former President Turgut Özal, who claimed that with the end of the Cold War 'the shrinking process that began at the walls of Vienna' had been reversed.[4] In order to understand the ideological dimension of Turkey's relationship with the newly independent states of Central Asia and the Transcaucasus, we will first give a brief account of the origin and development of Pan-Turkism. The political euphoria and subsequent disappointments of Turkish initiatives will be analysed. This analysis leads us to an assessment of the economic and cultural ties that have been established between Turkey and the five Turkic states. The chapter will conclude by putting the revival of Pan-Turkism in Turkey into a historical and theoretical perspective.

Islamic modernism, pan-Turkism and Turkish nationalism: historical ideas and their political legacies

The dissolution of the Soviet Union and the emergence of Azerbaijan in the Transcaucasus and the four Central Asian Turkic republics as independent states brought the dream of the 'Grey Wolf' (Bozkurt) – the union of all people of Turkic origin – back into the centre of Turkey's public debate.[5] Originally, the idea of a union of Turkic people evolved in the late nineteenth century among the Turkic-speaking communities in the 'soft underbelly' of the Russian Empire. In the revolutionary atmosphere of that time, some Tatar intellectuals responded to the pressures of pan-Slavism with the development of pan-Turkist ideologies (Landau 1995: 8).

One of the founding fathers of this national awakening of Russia's Muslim population was the Crimean Tatar Ismail Gasprinsky (1851–1914).[6] Educated in Odessa, Moscow, Paris and Istanbul, Gasprinky shared a social and intellectual background comparable to the Young Ottomans, and his thoughts were part of the same general stream of Islamic modernism. He published articles in Russian and in the Crimean dialect pertaining to Muslims in general and to the Tatar communities in particular. In 1883, Gasprinky founded the newspaper *Tercüman* (Interpreter), whose purpose was to disseminate the ideas of Western civilisation among the Muslims of the Russian Empire. Its central message combined the imperative of a cultural revitalisation of the Islamic community with a cautious advocacy of a secular nationalism that had distinct pan-Turkist nuances. Owing to its double-language format, being published in Russian alongside a simplified Turkic translation, the *Tercüman* found a wide circulation, reaching not only southern Russia but also Central Asia and eastern Turkestan.[7]

In addition to his publications, Gasprinsky devised, and subsequently established, a 'new system' of education (*usul-i jadid*), reconciling Islam and modernisation, the ultimate aims of which were to enlighten the Muslim population of the Russian Empire and to awaken national self-determination and cultural renaissance. With the establishment of the first *usul-i jadid* school (1883 or 1884), Gasprinsky initiated educational reforms which, through Tatar missionaries who spread his ideas in Central Asia, would eventually affect thousands of Muslim students within the Russian Empire. By the time of the Russian revolution in March 1917, more than 5,000 schools had been established,[8] and Jadidism, the reform movement inspired by Gasprinsky's ideas, became the uniting force of the Central Asian intelligentsia, who were beginning to strive for cultural and social reforms in the major cities of what was Tsarist Turkestan.

Probably the most influential ideologue of pan-Turkism in the Russian Empire was Yusuf Akcura (1876–1935), a Tatar of the Volga region whose reputation in 1913, according to the prestigious Paris-based periodical *Revue du Monde Musulman*, was equal to that of the famous Islamic modernist Jamal al-Din al-Afghani (Landau 1995: 43). In 1904, Akcura published in the periodical *Türk* the article 'Üc ter-i siyaset' (Three Systems of Government), which various scholars define as the key manifesto of pan-Turkism (Landau 1995: 14; Poulton 1997: 72). In this pamphlet, Akcura came out firmly in favour of an ethnically defined Turkish nationalism (Türkcülük). In deviating from Gasprinky's Islamic perspective, he presented his pan-Turkist ideology as a coherent political alternative to Ottomanism and pan-Islamism, and was thus in line with the ideological shift taking place simultaneously among the Ottoman intelligentsia under Hamidian rule.

While the traditional Ottoman elite viewed Akcura's new Turkish nationalism as inappropriate, it was later adopted by the unionist regime. For them pan-Turkism was a 'way to offset the Empire's African and European losses by intense Turkification at home as well as a purposeful orientation towards the Turkic groups in Asia' (Landau 1995: 48). Enver Pasha, in particular, was largely responsible for making pan-Turkism a state policy (Landau 1995: 51) and, specifically, for pursuing pan-Turkist aims on the military field. It was under the inspiration of the idea of liberating and uniting the Turkic peoples of the Caucasus and Central Asia that Enver embarked on ill-fated military schemes such as the late-1914 offensive against the Russians in the Sarikamish region, the invasion of the Transcaucasus in 1918, which led to the temporary take-over of Baku,[9] and his later personal adventures in Central Asia alongside the Basmachis.[10]

In 1923, Ziya Gökalp (1876-1924) published his 'Principles of Turkism', in which he based his version of Turkish nationalism mainly on cultural bonds, thus replacing Akcura's racial and ethnic criteria (cf. Berkes 1959 and Gökalp 1968). Pointing to the unifying force of the nation in education and culture, Gökalp became the champion of a cultural nationalism that was adopted by the founders of the Turkish Republic. Shifting the focus on to the doctrine of the Turkish nation and Turkish nationalism, Atatürk replaced the old ideas of empire, dynasty, and even religion as an ideological basis for the newly established state. The rationale behind Atatürk's nationalism was that of creating national cohesion among Turkish citizens with different ethnic (Turk or Kurd), religious (Muslim or non-Muslim) and sectarian (Sunni or Alawite) backgrounds (Heper 1999). Most relevant, Atatürk defined the Turkish Republic strictly in territorial terms and firmly rejected pan-Turkist assertions: 'I am neither a believer in a league of nations of Islam, nor even in a league of the Turkish peoples. ... Neither sentiment nor illusion must influence our policy. Away with the dreams and shadows! They have cost us dear in the past.'[11] Atatürk's rejection of pan-Turkism entailed a refusal to become involved in any way in the fate of other ethnic Turkic groups living outside the national boundaries of the Republic, and the repudiation of any irredentist aspiration linked to them.

Within the confines of the territorial state, however, the Kemalists incorporated certain elements of cultural Pan-Turkism in order to construct a new, cohesive nationalist ideology. This was most evident in the role of the Turkish Historical Society, whose manipulative writing of Turkish history constituted Central Asia as the motherland of all Turks, and which as part of official schoolbook history has remained very influential to the present day (Alici 1996: 225).[12] Given this romantic attachment to Central Asia, it is not surprising that Turks' perception of their own identity has remained much broader than the territorial boundaries of the Turkish nation-state. In this way, Kemalism itself prepared the ground for the new phase of euphoria that characterised, in late 1991, Turkey's 're-discovery' of more than 50 million Turkic people in the former Soviet republics of Kazakhstan, Turkmenistan, Kyrgyzstan, Uzbekistan and Azerbaijan.

Euphoria and disappointments: a Turkish century?

Approaching a Turkish century: the re-emergence of pan-Turkism
The political independence of the five Turkic republics unleashed a feeling of excitement and euphoria throughout Turkey. At the same time, some circles in the West began to raise expectations about Ankara's future geopolitical role in Central Asia and the Transcaucasus. The general idea was that the independence of the five former Soviet Turcophone states would pave the way to a new union of Turkic states in which Turkey itself was going to occupy the leading role. Addressing the Turkish parliament at the end of the Cold War, President Turgut Özal declared that the disintegration of the Soviet Union offered Turkey 'the historic opportunity to become a regional power'. Özal appealed to the assembly not to 'throw away this chance which presented itself for the first time in 400 years'.[13] In the prevailing euphoria, Turkey's cultural, linguistic, historical and religious bonds with the newly independent states were frequently mentioned as the basis for Ankara's influential future role in the Transcaucasus and Central Asia. Moreover, in the emphatic atmosphere, the talk of a 'Turkish-speaking community of states stretching from the Adriatic to the Great Wall of China' increasingly became part of official discourse.[14]

A number of Western politicians, particularly representatives of the United States, encouraged these exaggerated expectations. They identified Turkey, with its secular democratic system and its commitment to a liberal market economy, as a crucial regional force that could prevent the northern expansion of Iranian influence. Thus various sides presented the Turkish Republic as an acceptable and viable role model for the Turkic republics, which in the early days of their independence were engaged in significant and demanding processes of self-identification and state-building.[15] In February 1992, US President George Bush, for instance, pointed to Turkey 'as the model of a democratic, secular state which could be emulated by Central Asia'. A similar view was later restated by both the British Foreign Secretary, Douglas Hurd, and Catherine Lalumière, secretary-general of the Council of Europe. Furthermore, the 'Turkish model' developed into a favourite topic of important Western media.[16]

Desperately searching for political and economic support, the leaders of the newly independent republics happily took up the idea and lavished extensive praise on Turkey. When visiting Ankara in December 1991, both the Uzbek and Kyrgyz presidents gave emotional speeches and declarations emphasising Turkey's leadership role in the Turkic world. Islam Karimov of Uzbekistan stated that 'our example is Turkey, we will establish our state according to this example'.[17] A few days later, President Askar Akayev of Kyrgyzstan poetically defined Turkey as 'the morning star that shows the Turkic republics the way'.[18] Similar statements could be heard from key statesmen of Azerbaijan, Kazakhstan and Turkmenistan.

Consequently, the beginning of the post-Soviet era was characterised by a feeling of elation in Turkey. Boosted by the exaggerated expectations which officials of Western states and the Turkic republics had raised, Turkish policymakers announced grandiose goals for Ankara in the Transcaucasus and Central Asia. The new Turkic co-operation was supposed to bring about further growth and development in Turkey, to enhance its regional influence and to increase Turkey's international standing in the eyes of its Western allies. At the first Turkic summit in Ankara (30–31 October 1992), Turgut Özal captured well the spirit of the moment. In his inaugural speech, the Turkish president announced that 'if we can exploit this historic opportunity in the best possible way, if we do not make any mistake, the twenty-first century will be the century of the Turks'.[19]

However, in marked contrast to Özal's optimistic scenario, the first Turkic summit ended with a major disappointment for Turkish officials. In fact the summit constituted a turning point, prompting Ankara to realise that it had to re-evaluate and significantly scale back some of its policy objectives toward the former Soviet republics. Turkey entered the summit with rather ambitious expectations, such as the establishment of a common market, the foundation of a Turkic development and investment bank, and firm pledges from Azerbaijan, Kazakhstan and Turkmenistan to build oil and gas pipelines to Europe via Turkey. However, the first multilateral meeting of the presidents of the six Turkic states ended with a vaguely worded declaration that entailed no any specific commitment, but only loose political statements.

Suddenly, Ankara had to discover that the links between the Turkic republics and Russia were far more solid than suspected, and that the Central Asians and Azerbaijanis were willing neither to stray too far from the policies of Moscow nor to bind themselves exclusively to Turkic bodies. Moreover, it became apparent that the Turkic states, by that time aware of Turkey's limited financial and technological means, were not interested in developing a 'privileged partnership' with Ankara. Instead, they were eager to cultivate direct ties with other states in the region and, particularly, with the Western industrialised nations. As a result, Turkish policy toward the Turkic republics shifted from 'fanciful notions of ethnic solidarity' to a more explicit notion of self-interest (Robins 1993: 610), replacing the excessive emphasis on commonalities by a more sober and realistic attitude based on inter-state relations.

Although these early perceptions, assessments and expectations surrounding Turkey's activities in Central Asia and the Transcaucasus were gravely disappointed, the development of closer political co-operation and enhanced economic relations has remained Ankara's long-range goal (Turan and Turan 1998: 202). In order to expand its political, economic and cultural ties with the Turkic republics, Turkey launched a series of initiatives, particularly in promoting a variety of educational and cultural programmes in Central Asia and Azerbaijan. It is possible to argue, therefore, that following the phase of euphoria, Turkey's foreign policy in the region has been characterised by a major emphasis on cultural and economic relations rather than on political ones. In addition, there has been a clear shift in Ankara's policy from the initial multilateral to a more bilateral approach in dealing with the former Soviet republics.

Disappointed dreams: the political realities of pan-Turkism
After the Central Asian republics and Azerbaijan gained their independence, Turkey provided them with considerable diplomatic support in their search for membership of international institutions. Thus Ankara was able successfully to facilitate their entry into the Conference for Security and Co-operation in Europe (CSCE, later re-named OSCE), in the North Atlantic Coordination Council (NACC), the World Bank and the International Monetary Fund (Sayari 1994: 182). Similarly, Turkey was instrumental in getting the five Turkic states (Kazakhstan only as an observer) to join the Economic Co-operation Organization (ECO) in 1992.[20] In this context, Turkey's political support for the participation of the five Turkic republics in international and regional organisations was 'based on a strategy ... to end their isolation and to facilitate economic recovery and political stability in Central Asia and the Caucasus' (Sayari 1994: 182).

Regarding Turkish leadership attempts, Ankara's highest-profile initiative was a series of summits in which the Turkish president met his counterparts from the five republics. Although these Turkic summits, known as T6, have become a regular forum for discussion,[21] they have by far fallen short of Ankara's initial plan significantly to institutionalise the ties between the six states. Their main outcome has been decisions to implement similar periodic gatherings at ministerial level, to support inter-parliamentary co-operation and to create a permanent secretariat of the summit.[22]

Looking at concrete political measures taken, bilateral relations have clearly dominated multilateral approaches (Kramer 1996: 119). By December 1996, Ankara had concluded more than 470 bilateral agreements of various natures with the five republics, whereas the number of multilateral agreements was only forty-three.[23] The grave disappointment at the first Turkic summit was a key experience for Turkish policy-makers, who since then have taken a more hard-headed view of Ankara's interests. The shift from multilateralism to bilateral agreements was further spurred by the growing awareness of Turkish officials that they were dealing not with a homogeneous whole but with five distinct states, each pursuing its own national interests.

Concerning those bilateral relations, Ankara's relationship with Azerbaijan – its closest foreign-policy partners from the former Soviet Union – is a good example to highlight the limits of Turkey's quest for regional influence. The centrality of Azerbaijan for Turkey's expansion into the Trancaucasus and Central Asia has been well summarised by Sezer:

> Among all the Turkic languages, Azeri Turkish comes closest, after Gagauz [a very small Transcaucasian Turkic people and language], to the Turkish spoken in Turkey. The republic's proximity to Turkey; its position as a bridge to the other countries of Central Asia; its abundant oil reserves, and its pro-Turkish orientation until the overthrow of nationalist President Abulfez Elchibey in mid-1993 have all contributed to Turkey's special focus on Azerbaijan in the early post-Soviet period (Sezer 1997: 16)

In spite of this special focus on Azerbaijan, it did not take long until Turkey's relations with Azerbaijan fell victim to the inflated expectations that both sides harboured about the other. In particular, Ankara's clear determination not to become directly involved in the bloody conflict between Armenians and Azeris over Nagorno-Karabakh was a major source of tension with Baku. In April 1993, Ankara turned down President Elchibey's repeated pleas for Turkish helicopters to evacuate trapped Azeri civilians during the Armenians' Kelbejar offensive. According to official statements, this happened because of the technical impossibility of sending helicopters from Turkey to Azerbaijan.[24] In reality, however, 'Prime Minister Demirel refused to help, believing that this could draw Ankara into the conflict, and into confrontation with Russia' (Bolukbasi 1997: 85).

In order to keep the 'delicate balance' in the Nagorno-Karabakh conflict (cf. Cornell 1998), Turkey closed its airspace to Western relief aircraft bound for Yerevan and concentrated a higher number of troops at its border with Armenia.[25] This rather symbolic reaction was neither appropriate for a country portraying itself as a regional power nor a satisfactory response to Azeri requests for help. Instead, Ankara clearly displayed its determination to stay out of a conflict that may have brought it into a confrontation with Russia. Only two months later, the Turkish authorities reconfirmed their reluctance to intervene in times of crisis. On 18 June 1993, renegade military forces, allegedly supported by Moscow, toppled the legitimately elected Azeri President Elchibey.[26] Ankara's failure to condemn unequivocally the ousting of the enthusiastically pro-Turkish Elchibey badly affected Turkey's standing in the eyes of the other Turkic states (Robins 1998: 141).[27] Furthermore, it proved Russia's undiminished ability to intervene in the domestic political affairs of the former Soviet republics.

Besides Turkey's imperative to maintain good relations with Moscow for both political and economic reasons, Ankara has faced historical constraints in the formulation and implementation of its policies towards the Transcaucasus. With the independence of Armenia, the Ottoman legacy of the alleged Armenian genocide of 1915–16 re-emerged. Turkey had to balance its desire to support Azerbaijan militarily and logistically in the Nagorno-Karabakh conflict against the risk of being accused of 'planning new atrocities against the Armenians' (Cornell 1998: 66). More determined action from the Turkish side would inevitably have sparked the reaction of the powerful, anti-Turkish Armenian lobbies in the United States and France, probably causing severe damage to Turkey's international standing. Prime Minister Demirel made this very clear in his rejection of repeated demands from both extreme right and extreme left in Turkey to give active military support to Baku: 'one step too many by Turkey would put the whole world behind Armenia'.[28] At the same time, the dangers of a Turkish intervention were stressed by the CIS Commander-in-Chief Marshall Shaposhnikov, who warned that Russia could not 'remain indifferent' to such an action.[29]

In a way, Turkey's bilateral relations with Azerbaijan fully exemplify Ankara's limits in pursuing a truly independent policy in the Transcaucasus and Central Asia. Turkey's geopolitical location, its insufficient power resources and the still undigested Ottoman past have visibly contradicted the exaggerated pan-Turkist rhetoric of the early 1990s and, moreover, have constrained Turkey to present itself as an able security provider for the region.

To a certain extent, the dismantling of the Soviet Union brought the 400-year old rivalry between the Tsarist and Ottoman Empires once again to the fore. As in the past, the Russian–Turkish rivalry of the 1990s entailed conflicting Christian/Slavic and Muslim/Turkic blocks. As suggested by Baev, in the post-Soviet Russian political establishment the categories of 'eternal hostility' and 'creeping aggression' are often used when dealing with Turkey (Baev 1997: 13).

By the same token, the Turks have not forgotten imperial Russia's ambitions toward the Ottoman Empire and its policies of expelling the Ottomans from the Black Sea, the Balkans, and some parts of the Caucasus (Mufti 1998: 41). This historical memory of constant adversity is at least partly responsible for the reawakening of Russian–Turkish tension following the demise of the Soviet Union. It therefore came as no surprise that Ankara soon got into more routine inter-state relations with the five Turkic states after the initial euphoria had evaporated. Since then, realism has increasingly replaced nationalistic lyricism, and Turkey has been showing greater respect for Russia's sensitivities in relation to the Turkic republics.

Building co-operation: economic and cultural ties between the Turkish Republic and the Turkic states

Economic avenues: aid, construction, telecommunications, transportation and energy
The rapid evaporation of early signs of political adventurism is also linked to the fact that the emergence of new states in the Transcaucasus and Central Asia seemed to offer unprecedented economic opportunities for the Turkish Republic. By forging close economic ties with the Turkic republics, it was hoped to open up new markets and investment areas for Turkey at a time when the country was facing growing foreign trade deficit. The economic ventures between Turkey and the former Soviet republics have so far been concentrated in four major fields: the allocation of developmental assistance, trade and construction, transport and telecommunications, and the energy sector.

Turkey has become one of the leading countries in the allocation of economic and humanitarian aid to the five Turkic states. The extension of humanitarian aid to more than US$78 million, of technical assistance to US$50 million and credit offers to US$1 billion made Turkey one of the chief donors of economic assistance in the region. Aiming at enhanced economic co-operation between Turkey and the Turkic republics, Ankara's programmes have been largely planned and implemented by the Turkish Co-operation and Development Agency (TIKA), established within the ministry of foreign affairs in January 1992. In its first six years of activity, TIKA has carried out 150 bilateral and 60 multilateral projects, mostly of an educational and advisory nature.[30]

Alongside TIKA, Eximbank is another public organisation in charge of promoting economic relations with the new republics, though not exclusively oriented towards them. In particular, Eximbank has opened credits to assist Turkish exports to, and to finance the works of Turkish construction companies in, Central Asia and Azerbaijan. Despite the initial pledge to open a credit line of US$1 billion for the five Turkic states, Turkey could not, for both financial and bureaucratic reasons, raise all the promised funds. As of April 1999, Eximbank had allocated a total of US$850 million, of which more than US$776 million had already been disbursed (Aras 2000: 46).[31]

Between 1992 and 1998, the trade turnover between Turkey and the Turkic states registered a growth of around 472 per cent, moving from just US$275 million to almost US$1.3 billion.[32] However, of Turkey's total trade, the exchange with the five Turkic states is less than two per cent. A major part of Turkey's economic involvement in Central Asia took place in the field of construction, building and restoring hotels, airports, hospitals and small factories. At the end of 1999, the total economic value of construction projects reached US$3 billion. Other Turkish firms operating in the Turkic markets are in the food-processing, textile, automotive and retail sectors. Reliable data about their activities is scarce, and many joint-venture agreements remain on the drawing board. According to TIKA and the Turkish Foreign Economic Board (DEIK), more than 1,400 Turkish firms were operating in the five Turkic states by late 1999, generating a total investment of around US$20 billion. More than 320 Turkish firms are active in Kazakhstan,[33] 450 in Azerbaijan,[34] and 200 firms in each of Turkmenistan,[35] Uzbekistan[36] and Kyrgyzstan.[37]

Aiming to become the geo-economic pivot between the West and the southern region of the former COMECOM, Turkey has devoted a massive economic effort in the field of telecommunications and transport since 1991. Thanks to the prompt donation (to the value of some US$25 million) of digital telecommunication exchanges to each of the five republics, Ankara has been able to 'create a dependent relationship at an early stage, which made the republics reliant upon Turkey for access to international lines' (Robins 1998: 145). Since then, other Turkish companies, notably Netas and Türkcell, have assumed an important profile in the strategic sector providing the infrastructure for telecommunications. In 1999, Netas was operating in Azerbaijan and Kazakhstan through its subsidiaries Ültel and Vesnet, respectively. In the growing sector of mobile telecommunications, Türkcell plays a leading role, running GMS services in Kazakhstan, Azerbaijan and Georgia.[38]

In order to close the geographical gap between Turkey and Central Asia, Turkish Airlines (THY) initiated direct flights to Baku (1991), Tashkent and Almaty (1992). Later, regular flights were added to Ashgabad (1993) and to Bishkek (1996).[39] Land transport, however, could not be improved with similar ease. Turkey has focused its attention on Georgia, which, bordering Azerbaijan, could provide the Anatolian Turks with a land bridge to the Turkic world. To this end, Ankara has adopted a plan laid down by the EU's Transport Corridor Europe–Caucasus–Asia programme (TRACECA) to build a highway along the Black Sea coast joining with the Caucasian corridor Sarp–Supsa–Tblisi–Baku.[40] Additionally, Ankara and Tbilisi signed several agreements for the opening of a third border crossing, and for the restoration and joint use of Georgia's Batumi airport. Even more important is the intended construction of a direct rail link between the Turkish and Georgian cities of Kars and Tbilisi, which, once completed, will be connected to the railway to Baku and, through the provision of train–ferry services, to Central Asia.[41]

The single most critical determinant of the future nature of economic relations between Turkey and the Turkic Republics will be, as suggested by Robins, 'the energy export routes chosen by the main fuel producer states in the latter area [Central Asia]' (Robins 1998: 145).[42] Basically there are three main goals being pursued by Turkey: economic benefits deriving from transit fee income; the reduction of Turkey's dependence on Russian gas and Middle Eastern oil; and employment opportunities that pipeline constructions would create in less developed eastern Turkey.

At least as important as these economic goals are strategic considerations linked to Turkey's involvement in the extraction, transportation and consumption of Central Asian energy. In fact, the exploitation of Caspian oil and gas resources became a grand strategic game, with the United States, Russia, Turkey and Iran as its most important players. From an economic point of view, pipeline projects through Turkey, such as the Baku–Ceyhan or the trans-Caspian pipelines, are determined politically rather than economically. They play a crucial role in US strategies to enhance Western and to match Russian influence in Central Asia, as well as to maintain the US containment policy against Iran. Iran could provide an existing network of pipelines, easily expandable to transport oil and gas from Central Asia to Europe and South Asia. International oil companies are pushing strongly towards this cheaper solution and thus the pipeline issue has developed into a 'case of grand geostrategic designs versus dollars and cents' (Gorvett 2000: 31). It is therefore highly questionable whether the treaty on the distribution of Central Asian oil signed at the Istanbul summit of the OSCE in November 1999 will ever be put into effect. The Caspian oil saga has evidently become another case of showing the limitations of Turkey's role in the Transcaucasus and Central Asia (Altunisik 1998: 157).

Two other economic factors have contributed to limiting Turkey's regional influence. In the first place, there are the economic ties that link the former Soviet republics and Turkey to Moscow. Concerning the Central Asian countries, excessive economic specialisation and geographical isolation are a part of the economic legacy of the Soviet past.[43] None of the former Soviet republics enjoyed any degree of economic and agricultural diversification. This has resulted in an exceptionally high degree of regional interdependence in trade, and in the structural dependency of Central Asian economies on direct links with Moscow. This handicap has been further aggravated by the fact that existing rail and road networks and pipelines are predominantly directed towards Moscow, which has remained for Central Asia the main outlet to potential markets.

The second factor relates to the role that Russia plays in Turkey's economy. It has to be noted that, despite its marked economic interest in the Turkic republics, Ankara has an important economic relationship with the Russian Federation, which it aims to retain and develop (Turan and Turan 1998: 189). Turkish-Russian economic relations in the 1990s were much more profitable than business between Turkey and the Turkic states. In the period between 1992 and 1998, the official trade volume between Russia and Turkey was, on average, at least three times as high as that registered between Ankara and the Turkic republics.[44]

Yet these figures do not include the extensive 'suitcase trade' between the two countries: Russian 'tourists' taking goods home from Turkey and selling them on the Russian market. According to DEIK figures, this suitcase trade had an annual volume of US$5–6 billion between 1992 and 1997.[45] Another important source of income for Turkey is provided by Turkish companies' contracting services in Russia; this rose to record levels, reaching almost US$9 billion in 1997. Between 1992 and 1997, Russia alone accounted for 42 per cent of the total volume of business transactions registered by the companies affiliated to the Turkish International Contractors Union.[46] Well aware that the potential for co-operation with Russia is still greater than that with the Turkic republics, Ankara has been compelled to make sure that its policies in Central Asia and the Transcaucasus do not harm its economic relations with Moscow. As Fuller put it, 'deciding if and when to give priority to Russian concerns in these areas, over Turkey's own interests, will be critical for Ankara' (Fuller 1993: 86).

Finally, Washington's early declarations and initiatives that promoted and supported the 'Turkish model' as an ideal development path for the new republics, and elevated Turkey to the role of a channel for Western economic aid, turned out to be hollow. Ankara received the promised economic and political support neither from the US nor from its European partners. Consequently, virtually no international aid was channelled through Turkey to the new republics (Robins 1998: 142; Pope and Pope 1997: 290–91). It soon became clear that Ankara was not able to act, as promised during the initial euphoric phase, as an engine for the economic development of the Turkic states. Turkey's financial collapse in spring 1994, followed by the imposition of a draconian austerity package, further eroded the already limited Turkish capability to provide loans and credit facilities to the cash-strapped Turkic republics. As suggested by Mayall, 'Turkey increasingly found that it [economic weakness] thwarted attempts to exert regional influence. The appeal of ethnic and religious solidarity in Central Asia could not compete with the financial clout of the Unites States, Japan, South Korea, and Western Europe' (Mayall 1997: 74–5). As it became apparent that Turkey did not have the necessary capital for large-scale investment, the Central Asian Turks increasingly turned their attention towards other partners.

Cultural avenues: language, history, television and education

Given the focus on culture and education of both the pan-Turkist movement and Kemalist modernisation, it is understandable that Turkish initiatives for enhanced co-operation with Central Asia and the Transcaucasus have been numerous in the cultural realm. Most of these initiatives, which Turkish state and non-state actors have launched in the fields of education and the media, have concerned linguistic, literary and historical matters. But as in the political and economic realms, the initially high expectations on the Turkish side have been disappointed. Also, in terms of cultural co-operation, pan-Turkist ideals and the realities of the post-Soviet Turkic societies have been difficult to synchronise. It became apparent that the euphoria felt by Turkish politicians, bureaucrats and intellectuals was based on ideologies and romanticism rather than on knowledge about the 'other Turks'. The efforts to create a common Turkish language demonstrate this lack of realism.

The elevation of Istanbul Turkish to a lingua franca for the new republics has been one of Ankara's main objectives. Since the establishment of relations with the Turkic republics, the official Turkish language policy has promoted the idea of a unified linguistic area within the 'Turkic world'. This bold scheme was based on the alleged linguistic homogeneity that, according to a widespread assumption in Turkey, characterises the entire 'Turkic world' and specifically Turkey and the five Turkophone republics of the former Soviet Union (Bal 1988a: 61). Yet this vision ignored the fact that, though related, the Turkic languages are not all mutually intelligible, and that the historical experiences of the various Turkic peoples have created further differences. Contrary to the enthusiastic declaration of the Turkish authorities, the 'Turkic world' does not share the mutual intelligibility that distinguishes the Hispanic or Anglo-Saxon worlds.[47] The blatant ignorance of the reality of post-Soviet Central Asia and, above all, the ideological bias that initially characterised Ankara's policies, led Turkish diplomats and politicians to underestimate the importance that the elite in the Turkic republics attribute to their own national languages, which flourished as symbols of a national and cultural renaissance even during the last phases of the Soviet regime (Carrère D'Encausse 1979: 195).

This was clearly visible in Ankara's vigorous campaign for the adoption of the Turkish form of the Latin script. A final agreement among the six Turkic states on the so-called 'joint Latin alphabet' (Ortak Latin alfabetesi) could be reached only after much heated discussions. This came to an end in March 1993, with a compromise formula under which five characters were added to the 29 normally used in modern Turkish. The fact that these five letters of the joint Latin alphabet are totally alien to Anatolian Turks occasioned strong criticism from Ankara, whose representatives further deplored the idealist and absolutist negotiating attitudes of their counterparts.[48] Turkey's promotion of the Latin alphabet has achieved only mixed and, from Ankara's perspective, rather disappointing results. Being aware of the sensitivities of their Russian minorities, the governments of Kyrgyzstan and Kazakhstan retain the Cyrillic alphabet. Uzbekistan, Turkmenistan and Azerbaijan have decided to switch to the Latin script, but each country has adopted its own national version of the alphabet, making them distinct from both the endorsed 'joint Latin alphabet' and the modern alphabet of the Turkish Republic.[49]

Language problems also contributed to limiting the success of the Eurasia television network system (TRT Avrasya), which the Turkish state launched in spring 1992. Broadcasting in simplified Turkish, and often with Latin-script subtitles, to Central Asia and Azerbaijan, the programmes were designed to convey a sense of community among Turkic peoples and to promote familiarity with the Latin script (Turan and Turan 1998: 183). In order to ensure that the transmissions could reach a wide Central Asian audience, Turkish technicians from the Directorate of Post, Telegraph and Telephone (PTT) built earth stations in each republic able to receive the signals transmitted from Ankara via satellite. Although initiated with great excitement,

Turkish satellite television has never gained much popularity in Central Asia. It turned out that even the simplified version of Turkish was for many in Central Asia too difficult to understand. Furthermore, the poor quality of the programmes did not match the taste of their audience. Additional problems were created by the aversion of authoritarian governments, such as those in Turkmenistan and Kazakhstan, to allowing neighbouring states to broadcast directly to their citizens without scrutiny (Robins 1998: 144). Similarly, the project of the Turkish ministries of education and culture to introduce standardised history textbooks in schools throughout the Turkic states had to face the firm opposition of the respective governments.

Despite this reluctance of the Turkic states to endorse Turkish cultural policies, Ankara has established a number of institutions promoting its pan-Turkist agenda. In 1993, the Turkish ministry of culture sponsored the founding of the Turkic Cultures and Arts Joint Administration (TÜRKSOY), which brings together cultural officials from the Turkic states (Uzbekistan excluded), the Turkish Republic of Northern Cyprus and the Russian republics of Tatarstan and Bashkortostan. According to its first director, the primary aim of TÜRKSOY is 'to increase cultural relations among the Turkish speaking countries and communities, to do research on Turkish culture, to improve and protect it, make it known in the world and to agitate [blend] it with the world culture' (Bülbüloglu 1996: 45). Yet in spite of its bold agenda, this organisation has so far distinguished itself by its poor management rather than by the quality and quantity of its activities.[50]

Another Turkish state institute with a marked Turkist and nationalist orientation is the Institute for Research of the Culture of the Turks (TKAE). This institute, which reached the peak of its activities and success in the late 1960s,[51] has greatly benefited from the revolution in Turkey's geopolitics following the collapse of the Soviet Union. Being essentially moribund in the late 1980s because of its strong pro-military and official character, TKAE went through a revival in the 1990s thanks to the renewed interest in the Turkic world. The main 'scholarly' work of the institute remains the tome entitled 'Handbook of the World of the Turks' (Türk dunyasi el kitabi), published originally in 1976 and then reprinted in an enlarged version in 1992. As suggested by Landau, the most revealing part of the book is 'The Contemporary World of the Turks', a substantial block of articles committed to the proposition of the essential unity of the Turks (Landau 1995: 162). In addition to the TKAE, there are several other Turkish institutes that have increasingly focused on the 'Turkic world' and are linked either to the ministry of culture or to various universities. Amongst them are such traditional Kemalist bodies as the Turkish Historical Society (TTK) and the Turkish

Linguistic Society (TDK), the research institutes on Turcology at the Universities of Marmara and Istanbul, as well as the recently founded Research Centre on the Turkic World at Ege University.[52]

Providing professional training and developing the human resources of various agencies of the newly independent states has, since early 1992, served as a further channel for cultural interaction and transmission. Since then, the Turkish foreign ministry, for instance, has been providing vocational training courses for diplomats from the Turkic republics.[53] By October 1998, over 1,600 high-ranking officials from various republics of the former Soviet Union had been trained at the Multilateral Training Centre on Taxation in Ankara, thanks to the economic and organisational support of TIKA, the Turkish ministry of finance and the OECD.[54] TIKA, in close co-operation with international bodies such as the United Nations Development Programme (UNDP), the OECD, the World Health Organisation (WHO) and the German Institute for Technical Assistance (GTZ), shared the responsibility for designing and implementing developmental activities in the private and public sectors.[55]

At the heart of Turkey's educational policies has been a scholarship programme at Turkish high schools and universities for a total of 10,000 students, 2,000 from each of the five republics. According to official figures, more than 7,700 of the scholarships offered had been taken by December 1998. Yet problems linked to the chronic overcrowding of Turkish universities, the insufficient value of these government scholarships, and linguistic obstacles have seemingly caused a relatively high drop-out rate.[56] Nevertheless, taking into account the importance of elite links for long-lasting relationships, it is plausible to argue that in the long run the scholarships scheme may turn into an asset for Turkey's relations with the Turkic republics (Behar Ersanli 1996: 9).

Finally, Turkey has financed the opening of a network of elite public high schools, of four universities, and funded the posting to them of teachers and administrators.[57] These schools, modelled on elite public schools in Turkey, offer both English and Turkish classes, thus filling a foreign language gap that the local educational systems are, apparently, unable to close. In addition to these state initiatives, different Turkish non-state actors – associations (dernek), foundations (vakif) and, especially, Muslim brotherhoods (tarikat) – have been most active in the educational field. Among the most impressive non-state activities are more than 70 schools founded and run by the missionaries of Fethullah Gülen, leader of the Nurcu sect.[58] In contrast to the distinct religious orientation of the schools that Fethullah Gülen runs in Turkey, those in the former Soviet republics emphasise the importance of a common language and culture for the Turkic people. The curriculum also appeals to common Turkic ethnic ties and includes the teaching of traditional Anatolian customs and manners.[59]

In the light of the above analysis, it is possible to argue that Turkish activities for enhanced educational contact and language reform in the Turkic republics have been strikingly reminiscent of the initiatives undertaken by Jadidism, the reform movement inspired by Ismail Gasprinsky a century earlier. The activities of Fethullah Gülen in particular, and the importance that his organisation attributes to the dissemination of education, information, rational discourse, Western sciences and modern technologies, are close to a revitalisation of the cultural heritage that the different facets of Islamic modernism had left behind. Even the secular Turkish state seems to have acted in line with this heritage, which, since the time of the Young Ottomans, has been an essential part of the intellectual life of Turkic Muslim peoples. More striking, however, is the fact that the emergence of a Greater Middle East has also brought the hidden pan-Turkist legacy of Kemalism again to the fore.

This revival of pan-Turkism does not mean that Turkish governments have been engaged in irredentist, expansionist or even racist pan-Turkist policies. Contrary to the dreams of some activists on Turkey's extreme right, rekindled upon Enver Pasha's return, Ankara has been pursuing what Landau defined as 'cultural pan-Turkism', a variant of political pan-Turkism purged of its irredentist component (Landau 1988: 179; Winrow 1992: 109). If the Turkish authorities had pursued this cultural policy without a 'big brother attitude', with less missionary zeal and with greater regard for the distinctive national and cultural identities of each country, the outcome of this pan-Turkist revival might have been even more successful.

Conclusions: facing Ottoman and Kemalist legacies in the Transcaucasus and Central Asia

Despite the fact that the Sublime Porte never ruled Central Asia, the legacy of the Ottoman past has exerted a profound and sustained influence on Turkish policies toward the former Soviet republics. This Ottoman legacy has survived in the contradictions of Kemalist nation-building. On the one hand, the Kemalist rulers of the early Turkish Republic resolutely rejected all forms of pan-Turkism and placed prime emphasis on the development of a strictly territorially bound nation-state. On the other hand, they adopted in the 1930s an official history that told romantic narratives about the Turks' historic homeland in Central Asia and their affinities with other Turkic peoples. Indeed, the Kemalists propagated a concept of national identity with a latent tendency to transgress the territorial delimitation of the Turkish state, which was deeply influenced by the Ottoman intellectual debates of the late nineteenth and early twentieth centuries (Dumont 1984: 30).

For example, the Kemalists' linguistic approach to conceptualising Turkish national unity and identity clearly shows the influence of intellectuals such as Ismail Gasprinsky and Ziya Gökalp.[60] The pan-Turkist leanings of Kemalist nationalism have thus led to a retention of a strong sense of 'kin' with Turkic people living outside Anatolia (Poulton 1997: 287). This explains the emotional outburst of sympathy and friendship, as well as the short revival of imperial political attitudes, that characterised the Turkish reaction to the initial establishment of political, economic and cultural relations with Central Asia and Azerbaijan. Yet the 'shrinking process' of the Ottoman Empire had not been reversed, nor could the Turkish Republic long maintain its claim to be the role model for the future development of the newly independent states. The enthusiastic schemes of veteran Turkish politicians such as Süleyman Demirel or Turgut Özal were proven wrong.

Besides the political and economic obstacles, there was another historical legacy that re-emerged with the end of the Cold War, limiting Turkey's role in Central Asia and the Transcaucasus. The demise of the Soviet Union and the reawakening of Russian nationalism marred Turkish–Russian relations with historical passions and legacies of mistrust that both countries had inherited from the imperial competition between the Tsarist and Ottoman Empires. As Sezer suggests, the pan-Turkist activities of Enver Pasha in Turkistan in 1921–22 appear to have instilled among the Russians a lasting mistrust of Turkey's aspirations in the Transcaucasus and Central Asia (Sezer 2000: 62). So it is not surprising that in the 1990s Moscow repeatedly criticised Ankara for pursuing an allegedly pan-Turkist and neo-Ottomanist policy in Central Asia and Azerbaijan. Specifically, radical Russian nationalists viewed Turkey's interests in the region as a 'foreign conspiracy to split Russia along a Turkic line from Kazakhstan to Yakutia and to obstruct the "rebirth" of Russia' (Zviagelskaya 1994: 137–8). Together with the eminent political and economic role that Russia plays in Turkish politics, this historical legacy added further constraints to Turkish ambitions.

There is no doubt that with the emergence of a Greater Middle East several 'demons' of the Ottoman past have been resurrected. In a new historical context, these suppressed Ottoman legacies have challenged the inflexible structures of Kemalist modernisation and call for a redefinition of Turkey's political and cultural identity. Freed from the straitjacket of Cold War politics, Turkey suddenly had to develop new political directions, for which the Kemalist dogmas could no longer serve as guidelines. The short history of relations between Turkey and the Turkic states has proved that these new guidelines need a sober assessment of Turkey's political and economic resources, as well as clear-eyed reflection upon its Ottoman and Kemalist history. In the context of these findings, former President Süleyman Demirel was wrong. Turkey's history has not returned to its 'natural' course; the 1990s have shown that the country needs to rethink some of its historical dogmas and to open a new chapter of its history.

In 1992, Aydin Yalcin wrote that pan-Turkism was an ideology whose time had come, and the collapse of the Soviet Union had 'finally given a public expression and support to Pan-Turkism'.[61] This time lasted for a short, disappointing moment. Turkish decision-makers soon had to adjust their policies to the geopolitical and economic realities of the post-Cold War era. Their approach to Central Asia and the Transcaucasus turned into a policy of economic penetration and cultural diffusion, setting aside outmoded irredentist and hegemonic aspirations that may have embroiled the country in conflicts with its neighbours (Landau 1995: 222). Thereby, Ankara's new strategy of expanding cultural, scientific and economic relations with the Turkic republics has shown an interesting mix of old pan-Turkist schemes and modern transnational interactions. This strategy has not been entirely without success and has so far been able to guarantee Turkey a position as *primus inter pares* among the Turkic states (Dannreuther 1994: 60; Cornell 1998: 69). In the light of Turkey's new geo-strategic position, its traditionally Western-oriented foreign-policy priorities and its crucial interest in maintaining an economically rewarding relationship with Russia, this could be defined as, at least, a fair result.

Notes

1 Quoted from the *Guardian*, 'Reburial Restores Enver Pasha to His True Glory', 5 August 1996.

2 For a short analysis of the personal rivalry between the two Turkish leaders, see Sonyel (1989: 506–15).

3 Foreign Broadcast Information Service (FBIS), DR-WE, 20 October 1994.

4 Interview in *Der Spiegel*, 23 December 1991.

5 The 'Grey Wolf' is the totemic animal of the pre-Islamic Turks of Central Asia, and serves together with the crescent and the star as the distinctive symbols of the pan-Turkist doctrine.

6 For in-depth analyses of Gasprinsky, see the various chapters focused on his life and activities in Allworth (1988).

7 As reported by Landau, the circulation was 'of about 5,000 in the 1880s, and 6,000 some twenty years later, an impressive figure for that time'; see Landau

(1995: 10).

8   Quoted by Abduvakhitov (1994: 69) from Fisher (1988).

9   The Turkish advance in the Caucasus is well analysed in Gökay (1997).

10 For a brief account of Enver's campaign in Central Asia, see Sonyel (1990).

11 Quoted by Poulton (1997: 93)

12 Winrow explains this widely shared romantic attitude of Turks to Central Asia as follows: 'From an early age almost every Turkish schoolchild learns how, many centuries ago, Turks migrated in waves from the depths of Eastern Asia to spread civilization across central Asia, the Middle East and the Indian subcontinent' (Winrow 1995: 5).

13 Minutes of the Turkish Grand National Assembly, term 19-1, vol. 1, no. 3, p. 25.

14 This slogan was used for the first time by the then Turkish Prime Minister Süleyman Demirel and then adopted by both Özal and pan-Turkist organisations.

15 The question of the 'Turkish model' of development is analysed by Bal (1998b: 105–29).

16 Bush's statement is quoted from Rashid (1994: 210) and Hurd's from Robins (1998: 135). The declaration of the then secretary general of the Council of Europe is reported in Mango (1993: 726). For samples of editorials and articles in the Western media supporting the idea of a 'Turkish model', see The Economist, 'Turkey: Star of Islam', 14 December 1991; The Times, 'The Sick Man Recovers', 28 January 1992; Newsweek, 'The Turkish Model on Display', 3 February 1993; Corriere della Sera, 'La Turchia "ombelico del mondo"' (Turkey 'underbelly of the world'), 31 July 1992.

17 Quoted in Bal (1998b: 118).

18 Quoted in Smolansky (1994: 299).

19 Özal's speech is reported in Summary of World Broadcasts (SWB), ME/1527 E/1– 3, 2 November 1992.

20 The potentialities and limits of ECO are well analysed in De Cordier (1996: 47–57).

21 So far summits have taken place in 1992 (Ankara), 1994 (Istanbul), 1995 (Bishkek), 1996 (Tashkent), 1998 (Astana) and 2000 (Baku).

22 The Turkic presidents pledged to create a permanent secretariat during the 1998 summit, see FBIS-WEU-98-161, 10 June 1998.

23 Authors' estimate according to the data provided by Kanbolat (1997: 1103–38).

24 See the statement released by Erdal İnönü, then acting Turkish foreign minister, reported in SWB ME/1657 C/1, 7 April 1993.

25 Turkish Probe, 6 April 1993.

26 The toppling of Elchibey is well described by Goltz (1994: 409–45).

27 In this regard, it is interesting to quote some parts of the debate that took place, on 5 July 1993, during the TV program '32nd day' between the Turkish journalist Mehmet Ali Birand and Turkish Foreign Minister Hikmet Cetin. Birand: 'Turkey does not wield the same influence in Azerbaijan now as it did in the past'. Cetin: 'I believe it would be wrong, however, to tie Turkey's relations with Azerbaijan to a specific individual. Our peoples are relatives and brothers', as reported by SWB ME/1736 C/1-2, 9 July 1993.

28 New York Times, 7 March 1992. See also Pope (1992).

29 Cited in Harris (1995: 17).

30 *Eurasian File*, special issue, October 1998, p. 2.
31 It should be mentioned that a substantial confusion regarding these figures still prevails. Winrow indicates that 'of the US$666 million of credits the Turkish Eximbank had offered to these states, around $500 million had been opened', see Winrow (1998: 102). According to Turan and Turan (1998), the Eximbank had by late 1995 allocated a total of US$936 million, but only 55 per cent of this total had been disbursed.
32 Turkey's exports to the Turkic republics (US$ million).

	1992	1993	1994	1995	1996	1997	1998
Azerbaijan	102.8	68.2	132.1	161.3	216.3	319.7	325.3
Kazakhstan	19.4	67.8	131.7	150.8	164	210.6	213
Kyrgyzstan	1.8	17	16.9	38.2	47.1	49.4	41.5
Turkmenistan	7.3	83.8	84.4	56.3	64.8	117.5	95.6
Uzbekistan	54.4	213.5	64.5	138.5	230.5	210.6	156
TOTAL	185.7	450.3	429.6	545.1	722.7	907.8	831.4

Source: DEIK, 'Türkiye' nin ülkelere göre dis ticareti' available at www.deik.org.tr.

Turkey's Imports from the Turkic Republics (US$ million)

	1992	1993	1994	1995	1996	1997	1998
Azerbaijan	35.1	34	8.9	21.8	39.2	58.3	50.2
Kazakhstan	10.5	43.7	32.3	86.6	100.1	165.3	254
Kyrgyzstan	1.4	3.5	4.3	5.5	5.8	7.6	7
Turkmenistan	21.2	76.8	65.5	111.8	100	74	42
Uzbekistan	21	31.9	78.6	61.5	58.1	95	96
TOTAL	89.2	189.9	189.6	287.2	303.2	400.2	449.2

Source: DEIK, 'Türkiye' nin ülkelere göre dis ticareti' available at www.deik.org.tr.

33 *Eurasian File*, no. 90, January 1998, p. 3.
34 *Eurasian File*, no. 103, July 1998, p. 6.
35 *Eurasian File*, Turkmenistan–special issue, November 1997, p. 5.
36 *Turkish Daily News*, 14 April 1998.
37 *Eurasian File*, Kyrgyzstan–special issue, July 1997, p. 5.
38 *Turkish Probe*, 7 March 1999, p. 7.
39 *Eurasian File*, no. 120, May 1999, pp. 5–6.
40 The TRACECA programme was launched in 1993; for further information see the homepage: www.traceca.org.
41 'Historic Georgian-Turkish Summit', *Monitor*, 4, 51, 16 March 1998.
42 It is beyond the scope of this study to analyse in great detail the questions relating to the energy resources of the Turkic states. These topics are well analysed by Altunisik (1998) and Blank (1999).
43 On this subject, see Kaser and Mehrotra (1992).
44 Turkish–Russian trade volume and Turkish–Turkic Republics trade volume (US$ million)

	Turkey-Russia	Turkey-Turkic Republics
1992	1,479	275
1993	2,041	640
1994	1,865	620

1995	3,320	832
1996	3,394	1,026
1997	4,097	1,308
1998	3,503	1,281

Source: DEIK (1999) 'Rusya ekonomisi ve Türkiye ile iliskileri', Istanbul.

45 Turkish Daily News, 'Istanbul's Suitcase Trade', 30 June 1996.

46 See TÜSIAD (1999: 128).

47 Alongside this erroneous assumption, it is also interesting to note that in Turkey some politicians, journalists and even scholars reserve for the Turkic languages the second-class definition of dialect (the terminology used is Kazak Lehcesi, Özbek Lehcesi, and so on) while Republican Turkish is commonly designated as a language (Türkce). This is a formulation that, wrong as it is from the scientific point of view, reflects well the Turks' general presumption of superiority over the more backward 'outside Turks'.

48 See the statement of Turkish Ambassador Bilam Simsir reported by Turkish Probe, 'Erasing Signs of the Cyrillic Past', 23 March 1993, p. 15; also Öner (1998: 74).

49 This complex issue is well analysed by Tryjarski (1998: 109–17).

50 Interview with an official of TIKA, Ankara, 23 June 1996.

51 The genesis of the TKAE is described by Key (1967).

52 Details on the activities of these institutes are available on the Internet. See www.marun.edu.tr/turkiyat/; www.istanbul.edu.tr/enstituler/turkiyat.htm; http:\\bornova.ege.edu.tr/~orkunt/tdae respectively.

53 For more details, see Eurasian File, no. 107, September 1998/2, p. 8.

54 This figure was indicated by the Chairman of the TIKA in his speech on the occasion of the ceremony marking the sixth anniversary of the agency's establishment, Ankara, 30 September 1998. The speech is reported in Eurasian File, special issue, October 1998.

55 The various projects are described in TIKA's 1995 annual report.

56 These problems were indicated to the authors by Central Asian students in informal discussions in Ankara in March 1999.

57 The four universities are in Simkent and Turkistan (Kazakhstan), in Bishkek (Kyrgyzstan) and Ashgabad (Turkmenistan).

58 Substantial confusion prevails about the number of schools opened by Gülen's followers in the Turkic republics (cf. Hermann 1996b: 637; Winrow 1996: 138; Yavuz 1999: 124). According to the Turkish ministry of education the exact number is 79, as reported by Aras (2000: 50).

59 For a short analysis, see Briefing, 'Hodja's Schools and Model Students', issue 1195, 8 June 1998, p. 6.

60 The language reforms implemented in the early Turkish Republic are well analysed by Lewis (1984: 195–213).

61 Quoted in Hunter (1996 : 138).

10 Conclusions
The Impasse
of Kemalist Modernisation

In April 2000, Kemal Alemdaroglu, the rector of Istanbul University, decided to close down Turkey's only department of the history of science. The staunch Kemalist had had enough of its 'unscientific activities'. The department was investigating the history of science in the Ottoman Empire, a history that, according to Kemalist dogma, simply does not exist. In the official Kemalist reading, the sciences did not enter Turkey until Mustafa Kemal Atatürk established them together with the Turkish Republic. But Rector Alemdaroglu controls not only the various fields of research at Istanbul University, but also the public appearance of his staff members. The rector has thus stipulated the length of skirts and fingernails for female faculty staff, as well as the kind of beard their male colleagues are allowed to have.[1]

The rigid measures of the 'modern' Kemalist rector undoubtedly resemble those of Ottoman sultans. It was soon after the destruction of the Janissaries that Sultan Mahmud II embarked on reforms governing not only the military and Ottoman state structures, but also the attire and appearance of his subordinates in public. In 1829, he released a decree defining in detail what costume and head-gear was to be worn and on which occasion. Furthermore, Mahmud II regulated the precise size and length of beards for his civilian and military staff (Lewis 1961: 102). Almost two hundred years later, the rector of Istanbul University appears to be acting in the manner of his famous Ottoman ancestor, albeit convinced that he represents Turkey's modern elite, which has decisively broken with the traditions of the denigrated theocratic Empire.

Ottoman–Turkish continuities are not always as bold as the example of Kemal Alemdaroglu, which, taken individually, could be labelled as nothing more than just another personified irony of Turkish history. Yet the impact of

198

the unrecognised institutional and habitual legacies of the Ottoman Empire on Turkey's polity is far graver than the rector's grotesque example. From a more general perspective, the awkward potentate of Istanbul University symbolises the depth and solidity of the authoritarian, elitist and patriarchal structures that the Kemalist state and its representatives have unconsciously inherited from the Ottoman past. The republican elite has not been able to shake off this Ottoman legacy, and Kemalist modernisation has largely continued the Ottoman example of defensive modernisation from the top down.

In order to elucidate the impasse of Kemalist modernisation, our conclusions will begin with another glance at different aspects of these Ottoman–Turkish continuities. This re-examination of our historical–sociological argument will be based on the three theoretical concepts introduced in chapter 1: the monopoly mechanism, the imposition of state control over symbolic reproduction (confessionalisation), and the formation of the social habitus of Turkey's state elite. A final reflection on the interrelation of Turkish politics with the new geopolitical space of the emerging Greater Middle East will follow. The book will end with some tentative and speculative thoughts about Turkey's future role.

State monopolies, social habiti and Ottoman–Turkish continuities

From a theoretical point of view, the formation and consolidation of the two key monopolies of the modern state – the legitimate use of physical force, and taxation – are core issues of modern state-building. According to Elias, the formation of these monopolies is inseparably interrelated and takes place in two analytically distinguishable phases. First, there is a competitive contest about elementary resources, whose accumulation in the hands of one actor leads to the build-up of the monopoly. In a second phase, the control over these monopolised resources gradually passes to society as a whole, now becoming institutionalised in a functionally differentiated political system. The particular historical path that this monopoly mechanism follows shapes political institutions and actors, as well as the distinct political culture of a modern nation-state.

Based on these abstract considerations, we will briefly recapitulate the specific historical trajectory that Turkish state-formation has taken. We will argue that both the Ottoman and the Kemalist reforms were largely measures associated with the first phase of the monopoly mechanism, the formation and consolidation of the state monopolies. Turkey's post-Second World War political history, however, has been characterised by the second phase of the monopoly mechanism, the struggle among social forces for the nationalisation of control over the state monopolies; and this continuing struggle is a major force behind the conflict-rich picture of Turkey's domestic politics.

Ottoman reforms, initiated by the palace and implemented by the high ranks of Ottoman bureaucracy, represented a classical example of defensive modernisation. The top-down modernisation of the Empire aimed primarily to strengthen state institutions and to safeguarding the power of its political elite. Following a coercive trajectory, the struggle for acquisition of the monopolies of physical force and taxation was at the heart of the Tanzimat reforms. Basing its efforts on administrative centralisation and the education of a new military–bureaucratic elite, the Ottoman state tried to counterbalance mounting external and internal challenges to its sovereignty. Yet the final consolidation of modern state monopolies was never achieved. Caught up in the complex power structures of the Eastern Question system, the Ottoman elite's attempt to guarantee the integrity and sovereignty of the state by modernising its military, administrative and educational structures failed.

From a different point of view, however, the successful establishment of the Turkish Republic proved that the failure of the Ottoman reform process was only relative. Not only the state-makers of the early Republic – the military–bureaucratic elite that had been educated in the new military and administrative schools of the Ottoman Empire – but also their ideological and organisational resources were a direct outcome of Ottoman modernisation. Whether we look at the more liberal Tanzimat period or at Sultan Abdülhamid's absolutist rule, the social changes during both eras were crucial for the emergence of a modern Turkish nation-state, and the new Kemalist statesmen carried the insignia of the Ottoman reforms. In retrospect, we could therefore read the so-called decline of the Ottoman Empire as the first formative period of the Turkish nation-state. Looked at from this perspective, the Ottoman reforms laid the territorial, administrative, ideological and social foundations of the Turkish Republic.

That this interpretation of late Ottoman history did not become the official history of Turkey is basically due to the particular conditions under which the Turkish Republic was established. In the aftermath of the First World War, the Ottoman state in its theoretical sense, represented by the two key monopolies, was at the brink of collapsing entirely. Moreover, in the crucial years between 1918 and 1923, not only were the key monopolies of the emerging Turkish state re-established against foreign and domestic competitors, but a decisive change within the state elite also took place. The historical simultaneity of elite change and monopoly formation through war enhanced the authoritarian character of the new republican polity that the founders of the Republic had inherited from their Ottoman predecessors.

It was at the end of the Tanzimat period that this new Ottoman–Turkish elite appeared on the political stage for the first time. From a theoretical point of view, the demands for a juridification of state power by the Ottoman constitutional movement marked the advent of the second phase of the monopoly mechanism. Under different historical conditions, it could have led to a transition of power from the palace and the Sublime Porte to a new self-conscious Ottoman middle class. Yet shifting from the Young Ottomans through the Young Turks to the Unionists, this new middle class had been decisively militarised and had adapted themselves to methods of political suppression. In the early 1920s, after decades of autocratic rule and continuous warfare, the Kemalists had been moulded by this decisive shift from liberal civic opposition to militarised nationalist movement. In fighting against foreign intervention, as well as against the traditional Ottoman elite and opposition groups within the ranks of the national movement, the new Kemalist elite had to acquire the monopoly of physical force within a short time, founding the Turkish nation-state almost exclusively by military means.

In this dramatic historical process, the radical and iconoclast character of the Kemalist reforms was a bold expression of the new kind of legitimacy on which the republican elite had to rely. At least for the modernised stratum of Turkish society, the Kemalist reform measures symbolised the new legal character on which Kemalist authority formally had to rest. This aspect of legal authority was further emphasised with the formation of the Republican People's Party, which under single-party rule served the Kemalists as their major instrument of domination and social control. Kemalist modernisation, imposed from above and implemented by force, followed the Ottoman example and concluded the transformation from traditional to legal authority, which had started with the early Tanzimat. Ideologically, however, the republican state elite introduced a new platform of political legitimacy, but one that held within itself the future means for political protest.

Once established on the foundation of legal authority, Kemalism could not escape the challenges that arose from the more general developments towards democracy that legal systems of domination had taken. The introduction of multi-party politics after the Second World War was therefore a logical consequence of the establishment of a legal republican system. Within the limits and constraints of multi-party politics and Turkey's political and institutional association with the West, it was only a matter of time before the Republican People's Party should lose its central function as a means of social control for the Kemalist establishment. Multi-party politics is an institutional setting that clearly marks the dominance of the second phase of the monopoly mechanism. The temporal and representational delegation of political authority through elections is a clear sign that control over the state monopolies is moving into the hands of a broader public.

With the rise of the Turkish military as an autonomous political force above party politics, this crucial second phase of the monopoly mechanism was brought to a halt. Since the military intervention of 1960, the division of power and the monopoly of physical force has been contested between an increasingly politicised society and the Turkish armed forces, which as guardians of the Kemalist reforms have been claiming ultimate control over Turkish state institutions. This hybrid structure of Turkey's political institutions is one of the main causes behind the impasse of Kemalist modernisation, and it has formed a major obstacle to a further democratisation of Turkish society. The social unrest and violence of the 1970s and the military escalation of the Kurdish question are direct expressions of this societal struggle. They exemplify the fact that in the second phase of the monopoly mechanism, its own logical precondition – the state monopolies formed during the first phase – can be put at risk.

Another key element of this historically and socially constructed impasse in Turkey's modernisation process can be found in the Kemalist ideological conception of secularism. In a speech in summer 2000, General Atilla Ates, commander of the land forces, reaffirmed the leading role of the Turkish military in fighting political Islam. The staunch secularist said that 'external powers are encouraging hotbeds of religious extremism in order to destroy Turkey and they find treacherous collaborators amongst our own'.[2] In a wider context, it seems to be rather difficult to find a common definition of the concept of secularism, whose origins, conditions, objects and effects are highly controversial. In the Turkish case, however, secularism has evolved in a particular way, leading from a new profane concept of political legitimacy to an almost re-sacralised dogma of Kemalist ideology. At least in the increasingly polarised struggle between Turkey's Kemalist establishment and political Islam, to declare oneself a secularist has the quality of a 'confession'. During the 1990s in particular, the Turkish notion of secularism came close to indicating a kind of 'civil religion', dividing Turkish society into believers and non-believers.

In structural terms, processes of secularisation are closely associated with the acquisition of the third key monopoly by the modern state, the monopoly of symbolic reproduction. Based on the European example, we discussed this monopolisation of the symbolic reproduction under the concept of confessionalisation. The post-reformation process of confessionalisation in

Europe led to the subordination of the religious realm to political domination. In the Holy Roman Empire particularly, this political domination by territorial principalities found its expression in the territorially and confessionally bounded church. In order to achieve this, the rising modern state appropriated and incorporated religious symbols as a means of legitimising its unprecedented degree of political and social control. This formation of a state monopoly of symbolic reproduction in Turkey gained momentum under Hamidian rule. Although Abdülhamid's politicisation of Islam happened in a quite different historical and religio-institutional context, the subordination and instrumentalisation of Islam by the increasingly absolutist Ottoman state showed clear similarities to European examples.

The historical turning point came with the establishment of the Turkish Republic. In contrast to the politicisation of Islam by Sultan Abdülhamid II, the Kemalists did not appropriate and incorporate religious symbols, but suppressed official Islam and Muslim brotherhoods as a long-term strategy to enhance the political legitimacy of their autocratic regime.[3] Under Kemalist rule, the state successfully acquired the third key monopoly by replacing religious symbols with artefacts of a deliberately constructed national culture. In order to eradicate all previous symbols of Ottoman political legitimacy, the Kemalists banned the public use of religious symbols in the political domain and defined secularism as the ideological cornerstone of their claim to power. It was certainly a bold change, but one which disguised the underlying continuity between Hamidian and Kemalist rule: the attempt of an autocratic state to control the symbolic reproduction of Turkish society.

Meanwhile the dogmatic interpretation of secularism together with the quasi-sacred cult around Mustafa Kemal Atatürk was transformed into an ideological bulwark against social and political change. As the self-appointed worldly priests of secularism, Turkey's powerful generals keep watch over Kemalist principles, thus preserving undemocratic political and societal patterns that emerged under the historical conditions of the 1920s and 1930s. In a time when the liberal democratic state has handed back the means of symbolic reproduction to society, and the realms of politics and religion have become functionally separated, the Turkish state elite still tries to hold on to a concept of secularism that in its essence means not the separation of state from religion, but state domination over religion. It is therefore not surprising that rising counter-elites instrumentalise Islamic symbols in their struggle with Turkey's political establishment. Like the Kemalists in the early 1920s, the Islamists of the 1990s justified their claim to power with a fierce attack on the symbols of their political opponents, and social change again tended to adopt the form of a cultural revolution.

Yet it would be wrong to relate the impasse of Kemalist modernisation to these structural aspects of Ottoman–Turkish continuities alone. The authoritarian state structures also find an equivalent in the thoughts and actions of Turkey's Kemalist establishment. The modernisation and democratisation of a society takes place not only in social and political structures, but also in the minds of its people. Regarding Ottoman–Turkish continuities in the social habitus of the Kemalist elite, the examples of Rector Alemdaroglu and General Ates are equally telling. They show that some traditional norms and values of the Ottoman establishment survived modern elite transformation.

The rector of Istanbul University shows these cognitive aspects of the Ottoman legacy of Kemalism in an almost paradigmatic way. Guided by the norms and values of a patriarchal elitism, Kemal Alemdaroglu rules his university by decree. The elitist attitudes, which characterised the representatives of the hegemonic bloc during the Ottoman reforms, are still visible among leading figures of Turkey's current establishment. Many public institutions, therefore, are undemocratic not necessarily in their formal foundations, but in the hierarchical way in which social action is conducted within them. In many fields of Turkey's social life, the heritage of coercive modernisation from the top down is still visible and constitutes a major obstacle to the unfolding of a pluralist and democratic society. Changing hats, beards and attire is no substitute for the necessary mental change. On the contrary, these bold but superficial measures of Turkish modernisation and the myth of the Kemalist revolution still contribute to hiding Ottoman–Turkish continuities.

A final point has to be made concerning the Ottoman legacy in the Kemalist worldview. In associating political Islam with foreign intervention aiming at the destruction of the Turkish state, General Ates again evoked the atmosphere of external conspiracy and internal betrayal that so deeply moulded the worldview of the Ottoman state elite. Furthermore, a Turkish general views current problems of the Turkish Republic in a similar way to Ottoman statesmen in the late Tanzimat period, in which any demarcation between foreign enemies, separatist movements and internal opposition became blurred. Under the label of the Sèvres syndrome, we analysed how this Ottoman legacy has affected both the ability of the Kemalist elite to handle internal conflicts and Turkey's foreign relations. Understanding this inherited feeling of encirclement is crucial to comprehending the propensity of Turkey's state elite to securitise domestic and inter-state conflicts, and thus to view them through the traditional prism of a rather narrow concept of military security. In the light of modern-day Turkey's military and economic capabilities, as well as the country's integration into Western institutions, the

Sèvres syndrome seems utterly anachronistic. Nevertheless, our analysis has shown that this latest Ottoman legacy in the Kemalist worldview can still limit Turkish policies.

The linkage between the impasse of Kemalist modernisation and Ottoman–Turkish continuities is therefore twofold. On the one hand, the defensive modernisation of both the Ottoman Empire and the Turkish Republic left the institutional setting of Turkey's polity with a legacy of authoritarian structures, which have been maintained and reinforced by different social actors, who prevented the nationalisation of control over the key state monopolies. On the other hand, there is a central corpus of traditional norms and values that has its origin in Ottoman times, which has been able to survive during several stages of elite change. We discussed the macro-sociological and micro-sociological aspects of this Ottoman legacy in the socio-historical reconstruction of Turkish state-formation in the first part of the book. That these Ottoman–Turkish continuities led to an impasse in the Kemalist project in the 1990s, however, is also due to changes in the global political environment. To grasp the regional dimension of these international transformations, we applied the geopolitical framework of an emerging Greater Middle East.

New opportunities and new constraints:
Turkish politics after the Cold War

In its impact on Turkish politics, the post Cold War era reminds us of the important contextual role that the major phases of the international system have played in Turkish state-formation. The Ottoman decision to reform the state structures according to the European nation-state model, Atatürk's abolition of the Empire and construction of a republican Turkish nation-state, and the introduction of multi-party politics are cases in point that demonstrate the interplay of Turkish and international history. In these cases, the shifts from the multi-polar balance-of-power system through the high phase of imperialism to the bipolar Cold War gave the external co-ordinates within which Turkish state-formation developed. Although the modernisation of Turkey has always been propelled by domestic forces, international structures have provided a framework of opportunities and constraints in which this social change took place. In this process, transformations of all three of Elias' elementary functions – the control of physical force, the material and the symbolic reproduction of society – have been a result of interrelated domestic and international developments.

Applying the geopolitical concept of the Greater Middle East, Turkey has been confronted with three general developments since the early 1990s: the 'retreat of the nation-state' (Strange 1996), the globalisation of the economy and the rise of a cultural political discourse. Economic reproduction, which in the past was viewed as production, distribution and consumption confined to particular territories, is now transcending national and political borders. Transnationalised micro-economic links have been creating a non-territorial region in the world economy (Ruggie 1993: 172–4), and the nation-state, defined by its mutually exclusive and fixed territoriality, seems to be being replaced by the 'rise of the virtual state', a state 'that has downsized its territorially based production capability' (Rosecrance 1996: 46). Moreover, modern means of communication facilitate transnational discourses, and migrant communities have established transnational links, articulating religious, ethnic and cultural rights across political borders (cf. Jacobson 1996). Political conceptions no longer coincide with organizational devices of geography, or, as French scholar Bertrand Badie put it, international political theory is confronted with the end of territoriality (Badie 1995).

It is precisely this new stress on global economic competition, ethnic and religious cross-border relations, rising transnational discourses on human rights and democracy, that define the non-geographical aspects of the Greater Middle East.[4] These transnational aspects challenge the poorly consolidated territorial delimitation of the region and re-accentuate the political history of the Middle East before it was carved up into nation-states. Inevitably, this development brings the later history of the Ottoman Empire back into play. In this way, the Greater Middle East not only confronts the Kemalists with their suppressed Ottoman legacy, but it simultaneously challenges their political world-view, which is almost exclusively based on the concept of the territorially defined nation-state. This argument has been the guiding theme throughout the second part of our book.

In analysing Turkey's domestic problems, we have argued that Islamist and Kurdish nationalist movements emerged within the logical course of the political, economic and social changes which Kemalist modernisation has engendered. We traced the roots of both political streams back to the foundation of the Turkish Republic and the transition from empire to nation-state. Forcibly contained during single-party rule, Islamic and Kurdish nationalist symbols have gradually been (re)introduced under the multi-party system. Together with the effects of the political and social engineering in the aftermath of the 1980 coup, it was the changing international environment that contributed heavily to the rise of political Islam and Kurdish nationalism. The 1990s showed that the Kemalist reaction was, in both rhetoric and action, illfated and incapable of coping with the transnational aspects of these phenomena.

Using all kinds of modern communication, Kurdish nationalism has easily extended beyond the boundaries of the Turkish state. Institutionally anchored in the Middle East, Western Europe and the United States, Kurdish nationalism is itself – although it sounds paradoxical – a transnational phenomenon. The same process of transnationalisation applies to political Islam, which is no longer merely a Middle Eastern phenomenon. Like Kurdish nationalists, Islamist organisations rely on economic, political and personal resources of migrant communities in the West, thus using the extra-territorial space and the global discourse of universal political and cultural rights in their struggle with the Kemalist establishment in Ankara (cf. Amiraux 1999 and Bruinessen 2000).

These transnational aspects of Turkey's domestic conflicts have aggravated tensions between Ankara and its Western partners. Moreover, the state-centred arguments with which Ankara has tried to defend its authoritarian course has contradicted its desire to become a candidate for full membership of the European Union. The huge gulf between Kemalist rhetoric of national sovereignty and Turkey's quest to join the supranational EU highlights the dramatic change that the international system has undergone since the establishment of the Turkish Republic. While the Kemalist adoption of the territorially and nationally defined state suited the situation after the First World War, this dogmatic state-centred concept has meanwhile become anachronistic. Turkey's Western orientation is therefore contradicted by the political dogmas the Kemalist movement adopted in the early 1920s.

This anachronism concerning the political categories of the Kemalist world-view is not restricted to Turkey's relations with the West, but has also increasingly affected its relationship with Middle Eastern states. Previously suitable principles, such as non-interference and a pronounced bilateralism, seem to be no longer tenable in the geopolitical environment of a Greater Middle East. Against its will, Turkey has been gradually dragged into the Middle Eastern scene. The 1990s saw a more activist and bold Turkish foreign policy that was in its orientation struggling with the increasingly multilateral character of Middle Eastern and international politics. With the end of the Cold War, Turkey has been pushed into a regional role that demands a multilateral and comprehensive approach to the Middle East. In this approach, foreign policy can no longer be the exclusive domain of an 'enlighted' state elite, but has to take into account the roles of international organisations and regimes, as well as transnationally active non-governmental organisations.

Observing from this angle, we have argued that the new Turkish–Israeli alignment was not a visionary step, but rather a move of pragmatic escapism. It was not the improvement of Turkish–Israeli relations as such, but the strictly bilateral character of the agreements and their emphasis on issues of military security, as well as the way the army pushed them through, that found our criticism. Yet serving several short-term goals of a Kemalist state elite under societal and international pressure, this escape can only be of a temporary nature. In the long run, Turkey will neither find the way to Brussels or Washington via Tel Aviv, nor be able to fulfil its role as a regional power by playing the Israeli card. On the contrary, in concluding agreements that made Ankara Israel's junior partner in the Middle East, Turkey's Israeli initiative reminds us rather of the awkward Middle Eastern policies of the Menderes government. Unfortunately, with the move from Cold War warrior to ally of Israel, Turkish foreign-policy-makers proved that they are still unable or unwilling to pursue an independent Turkish policy towards the Middle East.

This bleak picture becomes a little more differentiated when we add the development of relationships between Turkey and the newly independent Turkic states. With regard to this important dimension of the Greater Middle East, Ankara has been able, after an initial phase of euphoria and exaggerated expectations, to establish sober political, economic and cultural ties to the former Soviet republics without damaging Turkish–Russian relations. Furthermore, Turkey could reinforce its strategic value as a link between the West and Caucasian and Central Asian states. This has been possible because rising pan-Turkist sentiments were contained and Ankara did not engage in any irredentist or expansionist policies. Rather the Turkish authorities have been pursuing a balanced policy of cultural pan-Turkism, expanding the cultural, scientific and economic ties with Central Asia and the Transcaucasus. Indeed, in retrospect one can agree with the position that Turkey's Central Asian policy has got over the teething stage and reached a certain maturity.[5]

Furthermore, it is interesting to note that in this case Turkish foreign-policy-makers have to a certain degree been able to follow the new lines of culturally and economically based international relations. In the beginning, Ankara was trying to found its relationship with the Turkic states on an explicitly multilateral platform. In addition, Turkish activities in Central Asia and the Transcaucasus do not display the rigid state-centred features that we know from other fields of Turkey's foreign policy. In this area the trans-national patterns of post-Cold War politics are clearly visible, and besides the Turkish state, a variety of non-state actors is engaged in economic and cultural fields. Given this new sign of sensitivity to the cultural aspects of politics, sound reflection upon the domestic situation should enable Turkey's political establishment to acknowledge the cultural rights of its own population. If they are prepared to support the cultural and linguistic rights of the Turkic people, they can no longer deny them to their own Kurdish citizens.

Regarding this argument, the emergence of a Greater Middle East may indeed lead to a 'changing Turkey' (Kramer 2000).

Within the geopolitical framework of the Greater Middle East, the second part of the book was dealing with the turbulence in Turkey's domestic and foreign politics during the 1990s. We have been arguing that this turbulence was an expression of the general impasse into which the Kemalist modernisation project has led the country. The legacy of Ottoman–Turkish continuities and the challenges of a Greater Middle East together make major reforms necessary, releasing Turkish society from both the authoritarian political structures and the stifling ideological dogmas of Kemalist modernity. Yet these findings also encompass the need for reform to be of an inclusive character. It must take into account the various institutional aspects of Turkish society, as well as include Turkey's major social forces. It is important to stress that a modern pluralistic and democratic Turkey cannot be built without the participation of Turkey's Kemalist establishment. On the one hand, the Kemalists are still the strongest force within the state apparatus and the military. In finding their appropriate role in an open Turkish society, the armed forces in particular could play the enlightened role that they have claimed to hold for so long. On the other hand, any attempt to exclude Turkey's 'traditional modernisers' would only mean repeating the neglect of the *longue durée* of history and forgetting how deeply Kemalism has shaped both the societal structures and the social *habiti* of modern-day Turkey.

In a recent commentary, Şükrü Elekdag compared Turkey's EU accession process with the era of the Kemalist reforms.[6] Indeed, against the background of our historically guided analysis of Turkish politics, the end of the Cold War and the emergence of a Greater Middle East indicate a major turning point in international history. From the Turkish perspective, the change in the international system is comparable to the situation that the National Movement faced in the closing years of the Ottoman Empire. Yet in our times, it is the Kemalists themselves who, in their insistence on outmoded state-centred and authoritarian political concepts, resemble the Ottoman political establishment trying to salvage a patrimonial empire in a world of nation-states. In this regard, the abandonment of the empire by Mustafa Kemal Atatürk, and his adjustment to the dominant international discourse of his time could provide the direction for a new Turkey.

The Helsinki decision of the EU to offer Turkey candidacy status for full membership could be the external framework within which this new Turkey might be built. Internally, the decision of the PKK to stop its armed struggle against the Turkish state could provide a departure point for the reconciliation and demilitarisation of Turkish society. A positive sign in this direction was the election of the former head of Turkey's constitutional court, Ahmet Necdet Sezer, as president of the Turkish Republic. In his inaugural speech, Turkey's first president with a career outside the military or politics pointed to the country's democratic shortcomings and called for the implementation of the rule of law, a fight against corruption and the establishment of a sound democracy in Turkey.[7] If Turkey's state elite takes both Sezer's programme and the EU option seriously, the future of the country could be much brighter than its recent past. Yet with regard to the past, the recognition of Ottoman–Turkish continuities is an indispensable part of this huge reform programme, and is necessary 'to give Turkey back its memory'.[8]

Notes

1   See the article 'Bücherfeind', by Rainer Hermann in Frankfurter Allgemeine Zeitung, 3 July 2000.

2   Quoted in 'Army warns against Islamic fundamentalism once again', Turkey Update, 18 July 2000, http://www.turkeyupdate.com.

3   It is necessary to reiterate that this process did not begin before the proclamation of the Republic. Particularly during the War of Independence, Islamic symbols played a major role in mobilising that resistance. The point of no return was reached only with the Sheikh Said rebellion in 1925.

4   The geographical aspects are the opening of the Middle East towards the north (Caucasus, Transcaucasus and Central Asia).

5   According to the Turkish Foreign Minister Ismail Cem, in an interview with the Turkish Daily News, 31 July 2000.

6   Milliyet, 24 July 2000.

7   Quoted in 'New President promises to fight corruption and implement rule of law', Turkey Update, 23 May 2000, http://www.turkeyupdate.com.

8   Film director Atif Yilmaz, who produced a critical film about the 1980 coup, describing his task as a Turkish artist, New York Times, 28 May 2000.

Bibliography

Abduvakhitov, A. A. (1994) 'The Jadid movement and its impact on contemporary Central Asia', in Malik, pp. 65–76.

Adivar Edib, H. (1930) *Turkey Faces West: A Turkish View of Recent Changes and Their Origin*, New Haven: Yale University Press.

Ahmad, F. (1982) 'Unionist relations with the Greek, Armenian, and Jewish communities of the Ottoman Empire, 1908–1914', in Braude and Lewis (eds.), pp. 401–34.

—— (1984) 'La politique extérieur turque', *Les Temps Moderne*, 41 (456–7), 156–74.

—— (1985) 'The transition to democracy in Turkey', *Third World Quarterly*, 7 (2), 211–26.

—— (1988) 'Islamic reassertion in Turkey', *Third World Quarterly*, 10 (2), 750–69.

—— (1993) *The Making of Modern Turkey*, London: Routledge (reprint 1996).

Akcam, T. (1996) Armenien und der Völkermord. Die Istanbuler Prozesse und die türkische Nationalbewegung, Hamburg: Hamburger Edition.

Akinci, U. (1999) 'The Welfare Party's municipal track record: evaluating Islamist municipal activism in Turkey', *Middle East Journal*, 53 (1), 75–94.

Alici, D. M. (1996) 'The role of culture, history and language in Turkish national identity building: an overemphasis on Central Asian roots', *Central Asian Survey*, 15 (2), 217–31.

Allworth, E. (ed.) (1988) *Tatars of Crimea: Their Struggle for Survival*, Durham: Duke University Press.

Alpay, S. (1993) 'Journalists: cautious democrats', in Heper *et al.* (eds.), pp. 69–91.

Altunisik, M. (1998) 'Turkey and the changing oil market in Eurasia' in Rittenberg (ed.), pp. 157–75.

Amiraux, V. (1999) 'Transnational en puissance, transnational en acte: le role de l'espace migratoire dans la mobilisation Islamique', *Les Annales de l'Autre Islam*, (6), 97–113.

Anderson, M.S. (1966) *The Eastern Question 1774–1923*, New York: St. Martin's Press.

Anderson, P. (1995) 'Summer madness. The crisis in Syria, August–October 1957', *British Journal of Middle Eastern Studies*, 22 (1–2), 21–42.

Andrews, P.A. (ed.) (1989) *Ethnic Groups in the Republic of Turkey*, Wiesbaden: Harrassowitz.

Antoun, R. and I. Harik (eds.) (1972) *Rural Politics and Social Change in the Middle East*, Bloomington: Indiana University Press.

Aras, B. (2000) 'Turkey's policy in the former Soviet south', *Turkish Studies*, 1 (1), 36–58.

Argun, B.E. (1999) 'Universal citizenship rights and Turkey's Kurdish question', *Journal of Muslim Minority Affairs*, 19 (1), 85–103.

Arikan, E. B. (1998) 'The programme of the Nationalist Action Party: an iron hand in a velvet glove?', *Middle Eastern Studies*, 34 (4), 120–34.

Arjomand, S.A. (ed.) (1984) *From Nationalism to Revolutionary Islam*, London: Macmillan.

Atabaki, T. and J. O'Kane (eds.) (1998) *Post–Soviet Central Asia*, London: I.B. Tauris.

Atatürk, M.K. (1963) *A Speech Delivered by Mustafa Kemal Atatürk 1927*, (Nutuk), Istanbul: Ministry of Education Printing Plant.

211

Ayata, S. (1990) 'Patronage, party, and State: the politicization of Islam in Turkey', Middle East Journal, 50 (1), 40–56.

—— (1991) 'Traditional Sufi Orders on the Periphery: Kadiri and Naksibendi Islam in Konya and Trabizon', in Tapper (ed.), pp. 223–53.

Aykan, M.B. (1993) 'The Palestinian question in Turkish foreign policy from the 1950s to the 1990s', International Journal of Middle East Studies, (25), 91–110.

—— (1996a) 'Turkey's policy in northern Iraq, 1991–1995', Middle Eastern Studies, 32 (4), 342–66.

—— (1996b) 'Turkish perspectives on Turkish–US relations concerning Persian Gulf security in the post-Cold War era: 1989–1995', Middle East Journal, 50 (3), 344–58.

—— (1999) 'The Turkey–US–Israel triangle: continuity, change and implications for Turkey's post-Cold War Middle East policy', Journal of South Asian and Middle Eastern Studies, 22 (4), 1–31.

Badie, B. (1995) La fin des territoires, Paris: Hachette.

Baev, P. K. (1997) Challenges and Options in the Caucasus and Central Asia, Carlisle: Strategic Studies Institute.

Bagis, A.I. (1985) 'The beginning and the development of economic relations between Turkey and Middle Eastern countries', Foreign Policy (Ankara), 12 (1–2), 85–96.

Bak, J.M. and G. Benecke (eds.) (1984) Religion and Rural Revolt, Manchester: Manchester University Press.

Bal, I. (1998a) 'Emergence of the Turkic republics and Turkish reaction', Foreign Policy (Ankara), 22 (1–2), 58–76.

—— (1998b) 'The Turkish model and the Turkic republics', Perceptions, 3 (3), 105–29.

Balassa, B. (1983) 'Outward orientation and exchange rate policy in developing countries: the Turkish experience, Middle Eastern Journal, 37 (3), 429–447.

Banuazizi, A. and M. Weiner (eds.) (1994) The New Geopolitics of Central Asia and its Borderlands, London: I.B. Tauris.

Barkey, H.J. (1993) 'Turkey's Kurdish dilemma', Survival, 35 (4), 51–70.

—— (ed.) (1996a) Reluctant Neighbor. Turkey's Role in the Middle East, Washington, D.C.: United States Institute of Peace Press.

—— (1996b) 'Turkey and the new Middle East. A geopolitical exploration', in H.J. Barkey (ed.) 1996a, pp. 25–44.

—— (1998) 'The People's Democracy Party (HADEP): the travails of a legal Kurdish party in Turkey', Journal of Muslim Minority Affairs, 18 (1), 129–138.

—— and G.E. Fuller (1997) 'Turkey's Kurdish question: critical turning points and missed opportunities', Middle East Journal, 51 (1), 59–79.

—— (1998) Turkey's Kurdish Question, Lanham: Rowman & Littlefield.

Barkey, K. and M. von Hagen (eds.) (1997) After Empire. Multiethnic Societies and Nation–Building. The Soviet Union and the Russian, Ottoman, and Habsburg Empires, Boulder: Westview Press.

Behar Ersanli, B. (1996) 'Turkism in Turkey and Azerbaijan in the 1990s', Eurasian Studies, 3 (3), 2–20.

Benedict, P., E. Tümertekin and F. Mansur (eds.) (1974) Turkey – Geography and Social Perspectives, Leiden: Brill.

Bengio, O. and G. Özcan (2000), 'Changing relations: Turkish–Israeli–Arab triangle', Perceptions, 5 (1), 134–46.

Beriker, N. (1997) 'The Kurdish conflict in Turkey: issues, parties and prospects', Security Dialogue, 28 (4), 439–52.

Berkes, N. (1959) Turkish Nationalism and Western Civilization: Selected Essays of Ziya Gökalp, Westport: Greenwood Press.

—— (1964) The Development of Secularism in Turkey, Montreal: McGill University Press.

Beschorner, N. (1992) Water and Instability in the Middle East, Adelphi Paper 273, Oxford and New York: Oxford University Press, for the International Institute for Strategic Studies, London.

Bielefeldt, H. and W. Heitmeyer (eds.) (1998) Politisierte Religion, Frankfurt am Main: Fischer.

Birand, M.A. (1987) The General's Coup in Turkey. An Inside Story of 12 September 1980, London: Brassey's Defence Publishers.

—— (1991) Shirts of Steel. An Anatomy of the Turkish Armed Forces, London: I.B. Tauris.

—— (1996) 'Is there a new role for Turkey in the Middle East?' in H.J. Barkey (ed.) 1996a, pp. 171–8.

Blank, S. (1999) 'Every shark east of Suez: great power interests, policies and tactics in the Transcaspian energy wars', *Central Asia Survey*, 18 (2), 149–184.

Bloch, E. (1985) *Erbschaft dieser Zeit*, Frankfurt am Main: Suhrkamp.

Bolukbasi, S. (1993) 'The Johnson letter revisited', *Middle Eastern Studies*, 29 (3), 505–25.

—— (1997) 'Ankara's Baku-centered Transcaucasia policy: has it failed?', *Middle East Journal*, 51 (1), 80–94.

—— (1999) 'Behind the Turkish–Israeli alliance: a Turkish view', *Journal of Palestinian Studies*, 29 (1), 21–35.

Bourdieu, P. (1992) *Die verborgenen Mechanismen der Macht*, Hamburg: VSA–Verlag.

Bozarslan, H. (1996) 'Kurdistan: économie de guerre, économie dans la guerre', in: Jean and Rufin (eds.) pp. 105–46.

Braude, B. and B. Lewis (eds.) (1982) *Christians and Jews in the Ottoman Empire. The Functioning of a Plural Society, Volume I: The Central Lands*, New York: Holmes and Meier.

Brown, C. (1984) *International Politics and the Middle East. Old Rules, Dangerous Game*, Princeton: Princeton University Press.

Brown, J. (1989) 'The military and society: the Turkish case', *Middle Eastern Studies*, 25 (3), 387–404.

Bruinessen M. van (1984) 'Popular Islam, Kurdish nationalism and rural revolt: the rebellion of Shaikh Said in Turkey (1925)', in Bak and Benecke (eds.), pp. 281–95.

—— (1989) 'The ethnic identity of the Kurds', in Andrews (ed.), pp. 613–21.

—— (1992) *Agha, Shaikh and State. The Social and Political Structures of Kurdistan*, London: Zed Books.

—— (1998) 'Shifting national and ethnic identities: the Kurds in Turkey and the European diaspora', *Journal of Muslim Minority Affairs*, 18 (1), 39–52.

—— (2000) *Transnational Aspects of the Kurdish Question*, EUI working papers, Robert Schuman Centre for Advanced Studies, RSC No. 2000/22, Florence: European University Institute.

Bülbüloglu, P. (1996) 'Cultural cooperation in the Turkic world', *Eurasian Studies*, 3 (3), 45–7.

Burke, P. (1987) *The Renaissance*, Basingstoke: Macmillan.

Burnouf, D. (1972) 'La situatione en Turquie après les interventions du Haut-Commandement dans les affaires publiques', *Politique Etrangère*, 37 (1), 101–14.

Buzan, B., O. Wæver and J. de Wilde (1998) *Security: A New Framework for Analysis*, Boulder and London: Lynne Rienner.

Calabrese, J. (1998) 'Turkey and Iran: limits of a stable relationship', *British Journal of Middle Eastern Studies*, 25 (1), 75–94.

Candar, C. (1999) 'Redefining Turkey's political center', *Journal of Democracy*, 10 (4), 129–41.

Carrère D'Encausse, H. (1979) *Esplosione di un impero? La rivolta delle nazionalità in URSS*, Roma: E/O.

Chambers, R.L. (1964) 'The civil bureaucracy', in Ward and Rustow (eds.), pp. 301–27.

Cizre–Sakallioglu, Ü. (1997) 'The anatomy of the Turkish military's autonomy', *Comparative Politics*, 29 (4), 151–65.

—— (1998a) 'Rethinking the connections between Turkey's "Western identity" versus Islam', *Critique*, (12), 3–18.

—— (1998b) 'Kurdish nationalism from an Islamist perspective: the discourses of Turkish Islamist writers', *Journal of Muslim Minority Affairs*, 18 (1), 73–89.

—— and E. Yeldan (2000) 'Politics, society and financial liberalization: Turkey in the 1990s', *Development and Change*, 31 (2), 481–508.

Clark, E.C. (1974) 'The Ottoman industrial revolution', *International Journal of Middle East Studies*, 1974 (5), 65–76.

Cornell, S. (1998) 'Turkey and the conflict in Nagorno-Karabakh: a delicate balance', *Middle Eastern Studies*, 34 (1), 51–72.

Cox, R.W. (1987) *Production, Power, and World Order*, New York: Columbia University Press.

Criss, N.B. (1997) 'Strategic nuclear missiles in Turkey: the Jupiter affair, 1959–1963', *Journal of Strategic Studies*, 20 (3), 97–122.

—— (1999) *Istanbul under Allied Occupation 1918–1923*, Leiden: Brill.

Dadrian, V.N. (1991) 'The documentation of the World War I Armenian massacres in the proceedings of the Turkish military tribunal', *International Journal of Middle East Studies*, (23), 549–76.

Dalacoura, K. (1990) 'Turkey and the Middle East in the 1980s', *Millenium*, 19 (2), 207–27.

Dannreuther, R. (1994) Creating New States in Central Asia, Adelphi Paper 288, Oxford and New York: Oxford University Press, for the International Institute of Strategic Studies, London.

Davison, R.H. (1963) Reform in the Ottoman Empire, 1856–1876, Princeton: Princeton University Press.

De Cordier, B. (1996) 'The ECO: towards a new Silk Road on the ruins of the Cold War', Central Asia Survey, 15 (1), 47–57.

DEIK (1999) Rusya ekonomisi ve Türkiye ile iliskileri, Istanbul (available at www.deik.org.tr).

Deringil, S. (1991) 'Legitimacy structures in the Ottoman State: the reign of Abdülhamid II (1876–1909)', International Journal of Middle East Studies, (23), 345–59.

—— (1998) The Well-Protected Domains. Ideology and the Legitimation of Power in the Ottoman Empire 1876–1909, London: I.B. Tauris.

Dietl, G. (1999) Iran in the Emerging Greater Middle East, working paper (6), Copenhagen: Copenhagen Peace Research Institute.

DPE (1993) 'Turkey's foreign policy objectives', Foreign Policy (Ankara), 17 (1–2), 1–19.

Dubetsky, A. (1976) 'Kinship, primordial ties, and factory organization in Turkey: an anthropological view', International Journal of Middle East Studies, (7), 433–51.

Duguid, S. (1973) 'The politics of unity: Hamidian policy in eastern Anatolia', Middle Eastern Studies, 9 (2), 139–55.

Dumont, P. (1983) Mustafa Kemal, invente la Turquie moderne, Bruxelles: Ed. Complexe.

—— (1984) 'The origins of Kemalist ideology', in Landau (ed.), pp. 25–44.

Edib, H. Adivar see Adivar Edib, H.

Eisenstadt, S.N. (1984) 'The Kemalist regime and modernization: some comparative and analytical remarks', in Landau (ed.), pp. 3–15.

—— and R. Lemarchand (eds.) (1981) Political Clientelism, Patronage and Development, London and Beverly Hills: Sage.

Elekdag, S. (1996) '2½ war strategy, Perceptions, 1 (1), 33–57.

Elias, N. (1983) 'Über den Rückzug der Soziologen auf die Gegenwart', Kölner Zeitschrift für Soziologie und Sozialpsychologie, 35 (1), 29–40.

—— (1986) Was ist Soziologie?, Weinheim and Munich: Juventa.

—— (1990) Studien über die Deutschen. Machtkämpfe und Habitusentwicklung im 19. und 20. Jahrhundert, Frankfurt am Main: Suhrkamp.

—— (1991) The Society of Individuals, Oxford: Blackwell.

—— (1994) The Civilizing Process. The History of Manners and State Formation and Civilization, Oxford: Blackwell.

—— (1997) 'Towards a theory of social processes: a translation', British Journal of Sociology, 48 (3), 355–83.

Engin, I. (1996) 'Thesen zur ethnischen und religiösen Standortbestimmung des Alevitentums, türkischsprachige Publikationen der Jahre 1983–1995', Orient 37 (4), 691–706.

Eppel, M. (1992) 'Iraqi politics and regional policies, 1945–49', Middle Eastern Studies, 28 (1), 108–19.

Eralp, A. (1996) 'Facing the challenge. Post–revolutionary relations with Iran', in H.J. Barkey (ed.) 1996a, pp. 93–112.

Ergüvenc, S. (1998) 'Turkey's security perceptions', Perceptions, 3 (2), 32–42.

Erim, N. (1972) 'The Turkish experience in the light of recent developments', Middle East Journal, 26 (3), 245–52.

Erzeren, Ö. (1997) Der lange Abschied von Atatürk. Türkei – ein Land in der Zerreißprobe. Reportagen, Kommentare, Analysen, Berlin: WoZ.

Evin, A. and M. Heper (eds.) (1988) State, Democracy and the Military: Turkey in the 1980s, Berlin and New York: Campus.

Evriviades, M.L. (1998) 'The Turkish–Israeli axis: alliances and alignments in the Middle East', Orient, 39 (4), 565–82.

Findley, C.V. (1972) 'The foundation of the Ottoman foreign ministry', International Journal of Middle East Studies, (3), 388–416.

—— (1980) Bureaucratic Reform in the Ottoman Empire, 1789–1922. The Sublime Porte, 1789–1922, Princeton: Princeton University Press.

—— (1989) Ottoman Officialdom. A Social History, Princeton: Princeton University Press.

Fisher, A. W. (1988) 'Ismail Gaspirali, model leader for Asia', in Allworth (ed.).

Freij, H.Y. (1998) 'Alliance patterns of a secessionist movement: the Kurdish nationalist movement in Iraq', *Journal of Muslim Minority Affairs*, 18 (1), 19–37.

Frey, F.W. (1965) *The Turkish Political Elite*, Cambridge, Mass.: MIT Press.

Fuller, G. E. (1993) 'Turkey's new eastern orientation', in Fuller and Lesser (eds.), pp. 37–97.

—— and I.O. Lesser (1993) *Turkey's New Geopolitics. From the Balkans to Western China*, Boulder, Colo.: Westview Press.

Gellner, E. and J. Waterbury (eds.) (1977) *Patrons and Clients in Mediterranean Societies*, London: Duckworth.

Giddens, A. (1985) *The Nation–State and Violence. Volume Two of A Contemporary Critique of Historical Materialism*, Cambridge: Polity Press, (reprint 1996).

Gillespie, R. (ed.) (1994) *Mediterranean Politics, Volume 1*, London: Pinter.

—— (ed.) (1996) *Mediterranean Politics, Volume 2*, London: Pinter.

Giritli, I. (1962) 'Some aspects of the new Turkish constitution', *Middle East Journal*, 16 (1), 1–17.

Gökalp, Z. (1968) *The Principles of Turkism* (translated from the Turkish and annotated by Robert Devereux), Leiden: Brill.

Gökay, B. (1997) *A Clash of Empires: Turkey Between Russian Bolshevism and British Imperialism 1918–1923*, London: I.B. Tauris.

Göle, N. (1996) *The Forbidden Modern. Civilization and Veiling*, Ann Arbor: University of Michigan Press.

—— (1997) 'Secularism and Islamism in Turkey: the making of elites and counter-elites', *Middle Eastern Journal*, 51 (1), 46–58.

Gözen, R. (1995) 'The Turkish–Iraqi relations: from cooperation to uncertainty', *Foreign Policy* (Ankara), 19 (3–4), 49–98.

—— (1997) 'Two processes in Turkish foreign policy: intergration and isolation', *Foreign Policy* (Ankara), 21 (1–2), 106–28.

Goltz, T. (1994) *Requiem For a Would-Be Republic – The Rise and Demise of the Former Soviet Republic of Azerbaijan*, Istanbul: Isis Press.

Gorvett, J. (2000) 'Pipeline problems plague Turkey', *The Middle East*, April, 31–3.

Gost, Roswitha (1994) *Der Harem*, Cologne: Dumont.

Gould, A.G. (1976) 'Lords or bandits? The derebeys of Cilicia', *International Journal of Middle East Studies*, (7), 485–506.

Gresh, A. (1998) 'Turkish Israeli Syrian relations and their impact on the Middle East', *Middle East Journal*, 52 (2), 188–203.

Gronau, D. (1995) *Mustafa Kemal Atatürk oder die Geburt der Republik*, Frankfurt am Main: Fischer.

Gruen, G. (1993) 'Turkey's potential contribution to Arab–Israel peace', *Turkish Review of Middle Eastern Studies*, (7), 179–214.

Grunebaum, G.E. (ed.) (1971) *Fischer Weltgeschichte, Band 15, Der Islam II: Die islamischen Reiche nach dem Fall von Konstantinopel*, Frankfurt am Main: Fischer.

Gülalp, H. (1999) 'Political Islam in Turkey: the rise and fall of the Refah Party', *Muslim World*, 89 (1), 22–41.

Gürgenarazili, F. (1998) 'Abdullah Öcalan, Führer der PKK', *Orient*, 39 (3), 363–71.

Gunter, M. (1996a) 'Kurdish infighting: the PKK–KDP conflict', in Olson (ed.) 1996a, pp. 50–64.

—— (1996b) 'Civil war in Iraqi Kurdistan: the KDP–PUK conflict', *Middle East Journal*, 50 (2), 225–42.

—— (1998) 'Turkey and Iran face off in Kurdistan', *Middle East Quarterly*, 5 (1), 33–40.

Haarmann, U. (ed.) (1987) *Geschichte der arabischen Welt*, Munich: C.H. Beck.

Hale, W. (1981) *The Political and Economic Development of Modern Turkey*, London: Croom Helm.

—— (1994) *Turkish Politics and the Military*, London: Routledge.

Haley, C.D. (1994a) 'The desperate Ottoman: Enver Pasa and the German Empire – I', *Middle Eastern Studies*, 30 (1), 1–51.

—— (1994b) 'The desperate Ottoman: Enver Pasa and the German Empire – II', *Middle Eastern Studies*, 30 (2), 224–51.

Hall, J. (1985) *Powers and Liberties: the Causes and Consequences of the Rise of the West*, Oxford: Blackwell.

Harik, I. (1990) 'The origins of the Arab state system', in Luciani (ed.), pp. 1–28.

Harris, G.S. (1965a) 'The role of the military in Turkish politics, part 1', *Middle East Journal*, 19 (1), 54–66.

——— (1965b) 'The role of the military in Turkish politics, part 2', Middle East Journal, 19 (2), 169–76.

——— (1970) 'The causes of the 1960 revolution in Turkey', Middle East Journal, 24 (4), 438–54.

——— (1972) Troubled Alliance: Turkish–American Problems in Historical Perspectives, 1945–1971, Stanford: Hoover Institutions Studies 33.

——— (1995) 'The Russian Federation and Turkey' in Rubinstein and Smolansky (eds.), pp. 3–25.

Hassanpour, A. (1998) 'Satellite footprints as national borders: MED-TV and the extraterritoriality of state sovereignty', Journal of Muslim Minority Affairs, 18 (1), 53–72.

Heinemann, K. (1976) Elemente einer Soziologie des Marktes, Kölner Zeitschrift für Soziologie und Sozialpsychologie, (28), 48–69.

Heper, M. (1981) 'Islam, polity and society in Turkey: a Middle Eastern perspective', Middle East Journal, 35 (3), 346–63.

——— (1993) 'Bureaucrats: persistent elitists', in Heper et al. (eds.), pp. 35–68.

——— (1998) Ismet Inönü. The Making of a Turkish Statesman, Leiden: Brill.

——— (1999) 'Islam, Nationalism and the Military. Prospects for the Consolidation of Democracy in Turkey', paper presented at the conference 'At the turn of the century: transitions in Middle East societies', Ben-Gurion University of the Negev, Beer Sheva, 7–8 December.

——— and T. Demirel (1996) 'The press and the consolidation of democracy in Turkey', Middle Eastern Studies, 32 (2), 107–23.

Heper, M. and A. Güney (1996) 'The military and democracy in the Third Turkish Republic', Armed Forces & Society, 22 (4), 619–42.

Heper, M. and F.E. Keyman (1998) 'Double-faced state: political patronage and the consolidation of democracy in Turkey', Middle Eastern Studies, 34 (4), 259–77.

Heper, M. and J.M. Landau (eds.) (1991) Political Parties and Democracy in Turkey, London: I.B. Tauris.

Heper, M., A. Öncü and H. Kramer (eds.) (1993) Turkey and the West. Changing Political and Cultural Identities, London: I.B. Tauris.

Hermann, R. (1996a) 'Die drei Versionen des politischen Islam in der Türkei', Orient, 37 (1), 35–57.

——— (1996b) 'Fethullah Gülen – eine muslimische Alternative zur Refah-Partei?', Orient, 37 (4), 619–45.

——— (1999) 'Die Landwirtschaft – ein Hemmnis für eine EU-Mitgliedschaft der Türkei', Politische Studien, 50, September–October, 44–51.

Herschlag, Z.Y. (1968) Turkey: The Challenge of Growth (second, completely revised edition of Turkey: An Economy in Transition), Leiden: Brill.

——— (1988) The Contemporary Turkish Economy, London: Routledge.

Heyd, U. (1961) 'The Ottoman ulema and westernization in the time of Selim III and Mahmud II', Studies in Islamic History and Civilization, Vol. IX, Jerusalem, 63–96.

——— (1968) Revival of Islam in Modern Turkey, Jerusalem: The Magnes Press.

Hintze, O. (1970) 'Wesen und Verbreitung des Feudalismus' (first published 1929), in Oestreich (ed.), pp. 12–47.

Hoffmann, B. (1998) 'Hydro paranoia and its myths. The issue of water in the Middle East', Orient, 39 (2), 251–69.

Hourani, A. (1981) The Emergence of the Modern Middle East, Berkely and Los Angeles: University of California Press.

Hunter, S. T. (1996) Central Asia Since Independence, London: Praeger.

Hurewitz, J.C. (1956a) Diplomacy in the Near and Middle East, A Documentary Record: 1535–1914, Volume I, Princeton: D. van Nostrand Company, Inc.

——— (1956b) Diplomacy in the Near and Middle East, A Documentary Record: 1914–1956, Volume II, Princeton: D. van Nostrand Company, Inc.

Hyman, A. (1997) 'Turkestan and Pan-Turkism revisited', Central Asia Survey, 16 (3), 339–51.

Ilkin, S. (1993) 'Businessmen: democratic stability', in Heper et al. (eds.), pp. 177–98.

Inalcik, H. (1964) 'Turkey. The nature of the traditional society', in Ward and Rustow (eds.), pp. 42–63.

——— (1977) 'Centralization and decentralization in Ottoman administration', in Naff and Owen (eds.), pp. 27–53.

——— and Donald Quataert (1994) An Economic and Social History of the Ottoman Empire 1300–1914,

Cambridge: Cambridge University Press.

Inbar, E. (1998) *The Turkish–Israeli Strategic Partnership*, Lecture at the Woodrow Wilson Center, Washington D.C., 16 September.

Issawi, C. (1980a) *The Economic History of Turkey 1800–1914*, Chicago: University of Chicago Press.

—— (1980b) 'De-industrialization and re-industrialization in the Middle East', *International Journal of Middle East Studies*, (12), 469–79.

Jacobson, D. (1996) *Rights Across Borders: Immigration and the Decline of Citizenship*, Baltimore and London: Johns Hopkins University Press.

Jean, F. and J.-C. Rufin (eds.) (1996) *Economie des guerres civiles*, Paris: Hachette.

Jensen, P.K. (1979) 'The Greco–Turkish War, 1920–1922', *International Journal of Middle East Studies*, (10), 553–65.

Jorga, N. (1990) *Geschichte des Osmanischen Reiches* (Fünfter Band) (reprint), Darmstadt: Wissenschaftliche Buchgesellschaft.

Jung, D. (1997) 'Die Kriegsregion des Vorderen und Mittleren Orients: 43 Kriege und ein Friedensprozeß', *Orient* (2), 337–52.

Kafadar, C. (1995) *Between Two Worlds. The Construction of the Ottoman State*, Berkeley: University of California Press.

Kanbolat, H. (1997) 'Bagimsizliklarinin besinci yilinda Türkiye Cumhuriyeti ile yeni Türk Cumhuriyetleri aransinda imzalanan anlasmalar', *Yeni Türkiye*, (15), 1103–38.

Karabelias, G. (1999) 'The evolution of civil–military relations in post-war Turkey, 1980–95', *Middle Eastern Studies*, 35 (4), 130–51.

Karal, E.Z. (1981) 'The principles of Kemalism', in Kazancigil and Özbudun (eds.), pp. 11–36.

Karaosmanoglu, A. (1983) 'Turkey's security policy in the Middle East', *Foreign Affairs*, 62 (1), 157–75.

—— (1985) 'Islam and foreign policy: a Turkish perspective', *Foreign Policy* (Ankara), 12 (1–2), 64–78.

—— (1988) 'Turkey's security policy: continuity and change', in Stuart (ed.), pp. 157–80.

—— (1993) 'Officers: westernization and democracy', in Heper et al. (eds.), pp. 19–33.

—— (1999) 'NATO enlargement and the South', *Security Dialogue*, 30 (2), 213–24.

Karpat, K.H. (1964) 'The mass media', in Ward and Rustow (eds.), pp. 255–82.

—— (1972) 'The transformation of the Ottoman State, 1789–1908', *International Journal of Middle East Studies*, (3), 243–81.

—— (ed.) (1973) *Social Change and Politics in Turkey. A Structural–Historical Analysis*, Leiden: Brill.

—— (ed.) (1974) *The Ottoman State and Its Place in World History*, Leiden: Brill.

—— (ed.) (1975a) *Turkey's Foreign Policy in Transition 1950–1974*, Leiden: Brill.

—— (1975b) 'Turkish Soviet relations', in Karpat (ed.) 1975a, pp. 73–107.

—— (1975c) 'Turkish and Arab Israeli relations', in Karpat (ed.) 1975a, pp. 108–34.

—— (ed.) (1996) *Turkish Foreign Policy: Recent Developments*, Madison: University of Wisconsin Press.

Kaser, M. and S. Mehrotra (1992) *The Central Asia Economies after Independence*, London: Royal Institute of International Affairs.

Kayali, H. (1997) *Arabs and Young Turks: Ottomanism, Arabism and Islamism in the Ottoman Empire, 1908–1918*, Berkely and Los Angeles: University of California Press.

Kazancigil, A. (1981) 'The Ottoman–Turkish State and Kemalism', in Kazancigil and Özbudun (eds.), pp. 37–56.

Kazancigil, A. and E. Özbudun (eds.) (1981) *Atatürk: the Founder of a Modern State*, London: C. Hurst.

Kellner-Heinkele, B. (1987) 'Der arabische Osten unter osmanischer Herrschaft 1517–1800', in Haarmann (ed.), pp. 323–64.

Key, K. (1967) 'The publications and activists of the Institute for the Study of Turkish Culture', *Middle East Journal*, 21 (1), 108–9.

Keyder, C. (1979) 'The political economy of Turkish democracy', *New Left Review*, May–June (115), 3–44.

—— (1997) 'The Ottoman Empire', in K. Barkey and Hagen (eds.), pp. 30–44.

Khouri, R.G. (1998) 'The Arab–Israeli peace process: lessons from the five years since Oslo', *Security Dialogue*, 29 (3), 333–44.

Kilic, A. (1998) 'Democratization, human rights and ethnic policies in Turkey', *Journal of Muslim Minority Affairs*, 18 (1), 91–110.

Kinross, L. (1964) Atatürk, The Birth of a Nation, London: Weidenfeld and Nicolson.
Kirisci, K. (1998) 'The Kurdish question and Turkish foreign policy', Private View, Autumn, http://www.tusiad.org/tr/yayin/private.
Kirisci, K. and G.M. Winrow (1997) The Kurdish Question and Turkey: An Example of Trans-State Ethnic Conflict, London: Frank Cass.
Kirkpatrick, C. and Z. Önis (1991) 'Turkey', in Mosley et al., pp. 9–38.
Kliot, N. (1994) Water Resources and Conflicts in the Middle East, London and New York: Routledge.
Kolars, J.F. and W.A. Mitchell (eds.) (1991) The Euphrates River and the Southeast Anatolian Development Project, Carbondale: Southern Illinois University Press.
Korkisch, F. (1999) 'Die amerikanisch–türkischen Beziehungen', Österreichische Militär Zeitung, (2), 131–40.
Kramer, H. (1996) 'Will Central Asia become Turkey's sphere of influence?', Perceptions, 1 (1), 112–28.
—— (2000) A Changing Turkey: The Challenge to Europe and the United States, Washington, D.C.: Brookings Institution Press.
Kreyenbroek, P. and C. Allison (eds.) (1996) Kurdish Culture and Identity, London and New York: Zed Books.
Kushner, D. (1977) The Rise of Turkish Nationalism, London: Frank Cass.
—— (1985/86) 'Mustafa Kemal and his period in the eyes of the Hebrew press and publications in Palestine', International Journal of Turkish Studies, 3 (2), 95–106.
—— (1997) 'Self-perception and identity in contemporary Turkey', Journal of Contemporary History, 32 (2), 219–33.
Landau, J.M. (ed.) (1984) Atatürk and the Modernisation of Turkey, Boulder: Westview Press.
—— (1988) 'The fortunes and misfortunes of Pan-Turkism', Central Asia Survey, 7 (1), 1–5.
—— (1995) Pan-Turkism. From Irredentism to Cooperation, London: Hurst & Co.
Landmann, N. (1997) 'Sustaining Turkish–Islamic loyalties: the Diyanet in Western Europe', Hugh Poulton and Suha Taji–Farouki (eds.), Muslim Identity and the Balkan State, pp. 214–31.
Leder, A. (1979) 'Party competition in rural Turkey: agent of change or defender of traditional rule?', Middle Eastern Studies, 15 (1), 82–105.
Leitmann, J. and C. Erdem (1997) 'Turkey: benefiting from David's army', SFSU IR Journal, available at http:\\psirus.sfsu.edu/intrel/IRJournal.
Lerner, D. and R.D. Robinson (1960) 'Swords and ploughshares. The Turkish army as a modernizing force', World Politics, 13 (1), 19–44.
Levy, A. (1971) 'The Officer corps in Sultan Mahmud II's new Ottoman army, 1826–39', International Journal of Middle East Studies, (2), 21–39.
—— (ed.) (1994) The Jews of the Ottoman Empire, Princeton: The Darwin Press.
Lewis, B. (1961) The Emergence of Modern Turkey, Oxford: Oxford University Press, (reprinted second edition, 1968).
Lewis, G. L. (1984) 'Atatürk's language reform as an aspect of modernization in the Republic of Turkey' in Landau (ed.), pp. 195–214.
Lieven, D. (1999) 'Dilemmas of empire 1850–1918. Power, territory, identity', Journal of Contemporary History, 34 (2), 163–200.
Lochery, N. (1998) 'Israel and Turkey: deepening ties and strategic implications, 1995–98', Israel Affairs, 5 (1), 45–62.
Lowi, M.R. (1995) Water and Power. The Politics of a Scarce Resource in the Jordan River Basin, Cambridge: Cambridge University Press.
Luciani, G. (ed.) (1990) The Arab State, Berkeley: University of California Press.
Macfie, A.L. (1979) 'The Straits question: the conference of Lausanne (November 1922–July 1923)', Middle Eastern Studies, 15 (2), 211–38.
—— (1994) Atatürk, London and New York: Longman.
Makovsky, A. (1996) 'Israeli–Turkish relations. A Turkish "periphery strategy"?', in H.J. Barkey 1996a, pp. 147–70.
—— (1999a) 'The new activism in Turkish foreign policy', SAIS Review, (19), 92–113.
—— (1999b) 'Marching in step, mostly!', Private View, Spring, http://www.tusiad.org/tr/yayin/private.
Malik, H. (ed.) (1994) Central Asia: Its Strategic Importance and Future Prospects, New York: St. Martin's Press.

Mallet, L. (1995) 'Nell'ex Asia sovietica Sionismo fa rima con capitalismo', LiMes, (5), 249–65.

Mango, A. (1993) 'The Turkish model', Middle Eastern Studies, 29 (4), 726–57.

—— (1994a) Turkey. The Challenge of a New Role, The Washington Papers 163, Westport: Praeger, for the Center for Strategic and International Studies.

—— (1994b) 'Turks and Kurds', Middle Eastern Studies, 30 (4), 975–97.

—— (1999) 'Atatürk and the Kurds', Middle Eastern Studies, 35 (4), 1–25.

Manisali, E. (1996) 'Water and Turkish–Middle East relations', in Karpat (ed.), pp. 166–70.

Mardin, S. (1962a) The Genesis of Young Ottoman Thought. A Study in the Modernization of Turkish Political Ideas, Princeton: Princeton University Press.

—— (1962b) 'Libertarian movements in the Ottoman Empire 1878–1895', The Middle East Journal, 16 (2), 169–82.

—— (1969) 'Power, civil society and culture in the Ottoman Empire', Comparative Studies in Society and History, 11 (1), 258–81.

—— (1971) 'Ideology and religion in the Turkish revolution', International Journal of Middle East Studies, (2), 197–211.

—— (1973) 'Center–periphery relations: a key to Turkish politics?' Daedalus, 102 (1), 168–90.

—— (1974) 'Super-westernization in urban life in the Ottoman Empire in the last quarter of the nineteenth century', in Benedict et al. (eds.), pp. 403–46.

—— (1978) 'Youth and violence in Turkey', Archives Européennes de Sociologie, 19 (2), 229–54.

—— (1981) 'Religion and secularism in Turkey', in Kazancigil and Özbudun (eds.), pp. 191–220.

—— (1988) 'Freedom in an Ottoman Perspective', in Evin and Heper (eds.), pp. 23–35.

—— (1991) 'The Naksibendi order in Turkish history', in Tapper (ed.), pp. 121–42.

—— (1997) 'The Ottoman Empire', in K. Barkey and Hagen (eds.), pp. 115–28.

—— (1999) Religion, Society and Modernity in Turkey, Syracuse: Syracuse University Press.

Marr, P. (1996) 'Turkey and Iraq', in H.J. Barkey (ed.) 1996a, pp. 45–69.

Matuz, J. (1985) Das Osmanische Reich. Grundlinien seiner Geschichte, Darmstadt: Wissenschaftliche Buchgesellschaft.

Mayall, S. V. (1997) Turkey: Thwarted Ambition, McNair Paper 56, Washington, D.C.: Institute for National Strategic Studies.

McDowall, D. (1996) A Modern History of the Kurds, London: I.B.Tauris.

McFadden, J.H. (1985) 'Civil–Military Relations in the Third Turkish Republic', Middle East Journal, 39 (1), 69–85.

Meeker, M.E. (1972) 'The great family aghas of Turkey: a study of a changing political culture', in Antoun and Harik (eds.), pp. 237–66.

—— (1991) 'The new Muslim intellectuals in the Republic of Turkey', in Tapper (ed.), pp. 189–219.

Menashri, D. (ed.) (1998) Central Asia Meets the Middle East, London: Frank Cass.

Meyer, J.H. (1999) 'Politics as usual: Ciller, Refah and Susurluk: Turkey's troubled democracy', East European Quarterly, 23 (4), 489–502.

Moltke, H. von (1981) Unter dem Halbmond. Erlebnisse in der alten Türkei 1835–1839, (reprint), Tübingen: Erdmann.

Mosley, P., J. Harrigan and J. Toye (eds.) (1991) Aid and Power. The World Bank and Policy-based Lending, Vol. 2, Case Studies, London and New York: Routledge.

Müller, H.-P. (1986) 'Kultur, Geschmack und Distinktion, Gurndzüge der Kultursoziologie Pierre Bourdieus', Kultur und Gesellschaft, Sonderband der Kölner Zeitschrift für Soziologie und Sozialpsychologie, 162–90.

Mufti, M. (1998) 'Daring and caution in Turkish foreign policy', Middle East Journal, 52 (1), 32–50.

Muller, M. (1996) 'Nationalism and the rule of law in Turkey: the elimination of Kurdish representation during the 1990s', in Olson (ed.) 1996a, pp. 173–99.

Murakami, M. (1995) Managing Water for Peace in the Middle East, Alternative Strategies, Tokyo: United Nations University Press.

Mutlu, S. (1996) 'The Southeastern Anatolia Project (GAP) of Turkey: its context, objectives and prospects', Orient, 37 (1), 59–86.

Nachmani, A. (1987) Israel, Turkey and Greece: Uneasy Relations in the East Mediterranean, London: Frank Cass.

—— (1998) 'The remarkable Turkish–Israeli tie', Middle East Quarterly, 5 (2), 19–29.

Naff, T. and R. Owen (eds.) (1977) Studies in Eighteenth Century Islamic History, Carbondale and Edwardsville: Southern Illinois University Press.

Naumkin V.V. (ed.) (1994) Central Asia and Transcaucasia, Westport: Greenwood Press.

Neumark, F. (1980) Zuflucht am Bosporus. Deutsche Gelehrte, Politiker und Künstler in der Emigration 1933–1953, Frankfurt am Main.

Nye, R.P. (1977) 'Civil–military confrontation in Turkey: the 1973 presidential election', International Journal of Middle East Studies, (8), 209–28.

Oestreich, G. (ed.) (1970) Feudalismus – Kapitalismus, Göttingen: Vandenhoeck & Ruprecht.

—— (1980) Strukturprobleme der frühen Neuzeit. Ausgewählte Aufsätze, Berlin: Duncker & Humbolt.

Öner, M. (1998) 'Notes on the joint Turkish alphabet', Eurasia Studies, (13), 70–79.

Önis, Z. (1991) 'The evolution of privatization in Turkey: the institutional context of public-enterprise reform', International Journal of Middle East Studies, (23), 163–76.

—— (1995) 'Turkey in the post-Cold War era: in search of identity', Middle East Journal, 49 (1), 48–68.

—— (1997) 'The political economy of Islamic resurgence in Turkey: the rise of the Welfare Party in perspective', Third World Quarterly, 18 (4), 743–66.

Özbudun, E. (1966) The Role of the Military in Recent Turkish Politics, Occasional papers in international affairs 14, Harvard: Center for International Affairs.

—— (1981) 'Turkey: the politics of political clientelism', in Eisenstadt and Lemarchand (eds.), pp. 249–68.

Özelli, M.T. (1974) 'The evolution of the formal educational system and its relation to economic growth policies in the First Turkish Republic', International Journal of Middle East Studies, (5), 77–92.

Öztürk, B. (1999) 'Die rechtsstaatlichen Strukturen der Türkei', Politische Studien, 50, September–October, 78–104.

Ohlsson, L. (ed.) (1992) Regional Case Studies of Water Conflicts, Padrigu Papers, Göteborg: Department of Peace and Development Research, Göteborg University.

Olson, R. (1973) 'Al-Fatah in Turkey: its influence on the March 12 Coup', Middle Eastern Studies, 9 (2), 197–205.

—— (1989) The Emergence of Kurdish Nationalism and the Sheikh Said Rebellion, 1880–1925, Austin: University of Texas Press.

—— (ed.) (1996a) Kurdish Nationalist Movement in the 1990s. It's Impact on Turkey and the Middle East, Lexington: University Press of Kentucky.

—— (1996b) 'Kurdish question and Turkey's foreign policy toward Syria, Iran, Russia and Iraq since the Gulf War', in Olson (ed.) 1996a, pp. 84–113.

—— (1997) 'Turkey–Syria relations since the Gulf War: Kurds and water', Middle East Policy, 5 (2), 168–93.

Ortayli, I. (1994) 'Ottomanism and Zionism during the second constitutional period, 1908–1915', in Levy (ed.), pp. 527–37.

Pahlavan, T.H. (1996) 'Turkish–Iranian relations. An Iranian view', in H.J. Barkey (ed.) 1996a, pp. 71–91.

Parla, T. (1998) 'Mercantile militarism in Turkey 1998: 1960–1998', New Perspectives on Turkey, (19), 29–52.

Payaslioglu, A.T. (1964) 'Political leadership and political parties', in Ward and Rustow (eds.), pp. 411–33.

Pipes, D. (1997/98) 'A new axis: the emerging Turkish–Israeli entente', The National Interest, (50), 31–38.

Polanyi, K. (1957) The Great Transformation. The Political and Economic Origins of Our Time, Boston: Beacon Press.

Polk, W.R. and R.L. Chambers (eds.) (1968) Beginning of Modernization in the Middle East. The Nineteenth Century, Chicago: University of Chicago Press.

Pope, H. (1992) 'Treading softly in Armenia', Middle East International, 426, 29 May.

Pope, N. and H. Pope (1997) Turkey Unveiled, Atatürk and After, London: John Murray.

Poulton, H. (1997) Top Hat, Grey Wolf and Crescent – Turkish Nationalism and the Turkish Republic, London: Hurst.

—— and S. Taji–Farouki (eds.) (1997) *Muslim Identity and the Balkan State*, London: Hurst.

Rashid, A. (1994) *The Resurgence of Central Asia*, London and New York: Zed Books.

Reed, H.A. (1954) 'The revival of Islam in secular Turkey', *Middle East Journal*, 8 (3), 267–82.

Rittenberg, L. (ed.) (1998) *The Political Economy of Turkey in the Post-Soviet Era: Going West and Looking East?*, Westport: Praeger.

Robins, P. (1991) *Turkey and the Middle East*, London: Royal Institute of International Affairs (Chatham House Papers).

—— (1993) 'Between sentiment and self interest: Turkey's policy toward Azerbaijan and the Central Asian States', *Middle East Journal*, 47 (4), 593–610.

—— (1996) 'More apparent than real? The impact of the Kurdish issue on Euro–Turkish relations', in Olson (ed.) 1996a, pp. 114–32.

—— (1997) 'Turkish foreign policy under Erbakan', *Survival*, 39 (2), Summer, 82–100.

—— (1998) 'Turkey's Ostpolitik. Relations with the Central Asian States' in Menashri (ed.), pp. 129–49.

Robinson, R.D. (1963) *The First Turkish Republic. A Case Study in Political Development*, Cambridge, Mass.: Harvard University Press.

Rodinson, M. (1966) *Islam et capitalisme*, Paris: Éditions du Seuil.

Rogers, P. and P. Lydon (eds.) (1994) *Water in the Arab World. Perspectives and Prognoses*, Cambridge, Mass.: Harvard University Press.

Rosecrance, R. (1996) 'The rise of the virtual state' *Foreign Affairs*, 75 (4), 45–61.

Rosenberg, J. (1994) *The Empire of Civil Society. A Critique of the Realist Theory of International Relations*, London: Verso.

Rubinstein, A.Z. and O.M. Smolansky (eds.) (1995) *Regional Power Rivalries in the New Eurasia – Russia, Turkey and Iran*, New York: M.E. Sharpe.

Ruggie, J.G. (1993) 'Territoriality and beyond: problematizing modernity in international relations', *International Organization*, 47 (1), 139–74.

Rustow, D.A. (1959) 'The army and the founding of the Turkish Republic', *World Politics*, 11 (4), 513–52.

—— (1964) 'The Military, Turkey', in Ward and Rustow (eds.), pp. 352–88.

—— (1979) 'Turkey's Travails', *Foreign Affairs*, 58 (1), 82–102.

Sadlowski, M. (ed.) (1998) *Nato's Sixteen Nations & Partners for Peace – Defence and Economics in Turkey; Pillar of Regional Stability*, Bonn. München.

Sahin, M. (1999) *Türkei–Kurdistan: Eine Reise durch die jüngste Vergangenheit*, Cologne: Pro Humanitate.

Salih, K. (1999) *Kurdfrågan i Turkiet*, Världspolitikens Dagsfrågor (9), Stockholm: Utrikespolitiska Institutet.

Salt, J. (1990) 'Britain, the Armenian question and the cause of Ottoman reform', *Middle Eastern Studies*, 26 (2), 308–28.

—— (1993) *Imperialism, Evangelism and the Ottoman Armenians 1878–1896*, London: Frank Cass.

—— (1999) 'Turkey's military "democracy"', *Current History*, February, 72–8.

Salzmann, A. (1993) 'An ancien régime revisited: "privatization" and political economy in the eighteenth-century Ottoman Empire', *Politics & Society*, 21 (4), 393–424.

Saran, N. (1974) 'Squatter settlement (*gecekondu*) problems in Istanbul', in Benedict et al. (eds.), pp. 327–61.

Sayari, S. (1977) 'Political patronage in Turkey', in Gellner and Waterbury (eds.), pp. 103–14.

—— (1992) 'Turkey: the changing European security environment and the Gulf Crisis', *Middle East Journal*, 46 (1), 9–21.

—— (1994) 'Turkey, the Caucasus and Central Asia', in Banuazizi and Weiner (eds.), pp. 175–96.

—— (1997) 'Turkey and the Middle East in the 1990s', *Journal of Palestine Studies*, 26 (3), 44–55.

—— and B. Hoffman (1994) 'Urbanisation and insurgency: the Turkish case, 1976–1980', *Small Wars and Insurgencies*, 5 (2), 162–79.

Schick, I. and A.T. Ertugrul (eds.) (1987) 'Turkey in Transition', New York and London: Oxford University Press.

Schilling, H. (1992) *Religion, Political Culture and the Emergence of Early Modern Society. Essays in German and Dutch History*, Leiden: Brill.

Schivelbusch, W. (1986) *Lichtblicke: Zur Geschichte der künstlichen Helligkeit im 19. Jahrhundert*, Frankfurt. am Main: Fischer.

—— (1989) Geschichte der Eisenbahnreise: zur Industrialisierung von Raum und Zeit im 19. Jahrhundert, Frankfurt am Main: Fischer Taschenbuch Verlag.

Schölch, A. (1987) 'Der arabische Osten im neunzehnten Jahrhundert 1800–1914', in Haarmann (ed.), pp. 365–431.

Schüler, H. (1996) 'Parlamentswahlen in der Türkei. Wohlstandspartei gewinnt Stimmen im Hinterland', Orient, 37 (2), 241–63.

Schulz, M. (1992) 'Turkey, Syria and Iraq: a hydropolitical security complex – the case of Euphrates and Tigris', in Ohlsson (ed.), pp. 84–117.

Scott, R. (2000) 'Kurdish peace: hanging in the balance', The Middle East, January, 5–7.

Seufert, G. (1997) Politischer Islam in der Türkei. Islamismus als symbolische Repräsentation einer sich modernisierenden muslimischen Gesellschaft, Stuttgart: Steiner.

—— (1998) 'Das Gewaltpotential im türkischen Kulturkampf', in Bielefeldt and Heitmeyer (eds.), pp. 360–92.

—— (1999) Café Istanbul. Alltag, Religion und Politik in der modernen Türkei, Munich: C.H. Beck.

Sever, A. (1998) 'The compliant ally? Turkey and the West in the Middle East 1954–1958', Middle Eastern Studies, 34 (2), 73–90.

Sezer, D. (1992) 'Turkey's grand strategy facing a dilemma', International Spectator, 27 (1), 17–32.

—— (1997) 'From hegemony to pluralism: the changing politics of the Black Sea', SAIS Review, 17 (1), 1–30.

—— (2000) 'Turkish–Russian relations: geopolitical competition and economic partnership', Turkish Studies, 1 (1), 59–82.

Shaw, S.J. (1968) 'Some aspects of the aims and achievements of the nineteenth-century Ottoman reformers', in Polk and Chambers (eds.), pp. 93–108.

—— (1971a) Between Old and New: The Ottoman Empire under Sultan Selim III, Cambridge, Mass.: Harvard University Press.

—— (1971b) 'Das Osmanische Reich und die Moderne Türkei', in Grunebaum (ed.), pp. 24–159.

—— (1993) Turkey and the Holocaust. Turkey's Role in Rescuing Turkish and European Jewry from Nazi Persecution, 1933–1945, London: Macmillan.

Simmel, G. (1989) Die Philosophie des Geldes, (reprint), Frankfurt am Main: Suhrkamp.

Simpson, D.J. (1965) 'Development as a process. The Menderes phase in Turkey', Middle East Journal, 19 (2), 141–52.

Slutsky, Y. (1971) History of the Hagana, Vol. III: From Resistance to War, Tel Aviv.

Smolansky, O. M. (1994) 'Turkish and Iranian policies in Central Asia' in Malik (ed.), pp. 283–310.

Sonyel, S.R. (1989) 'Mustafa Kemal and Enver in conflict 1919–1922', Middle Eastern Studies, 25 (4), 506–15.

—— (1990) 'Enver Pasha and the Basmaji movement in Central Asia', Middle Eastern Studies, 26 (1), 52–64.

Spain, J.W. (1954) 'Middle East defense: a new approach', Middle East Journal, 8 (3), 251–66.

Steinbach, U. (1996) Die Türkei im 20. Jahrhundert. Schwieriger Partner Europas, Bergisch Gladbach: Lübbe.

Stirling, A.P. (1958) 'Religious change in republican Turkey', Middle East Journal, 12 (4), 395–408.

Strange, S. (1996) The Retreat of the State: The Diffusion of Power in the World Economy, Cambridge: Cambridge University Press.

Stuart, D. (ed.) (1988) Politics and Security in the Southern Region of the Atlantic Alliance, London: Macmillan.

Sweet, L.E. (ed.) (1970) Peoples and Cultures of the Middle East. An Anthropological Reader, Vol. II: Life in the Cities, Towns and Countryside, Garden City, N.Y.: Natural History Press.

Szyliowicz, J.S. (1962) 'The political dynamics of rural Turkey', Middle East Journal, 16 (4), 430–42.

Tapper, R.L. (ed.) (1991) Islam in Modern Turkey. Religion, Politics and Literature in a Seculare State, London: I.B. Tauris.

Tauber, E. (1994) 'Syrian and Iraqi nationalist attitudes to the Kemalist and Bolshevik movements', Middle Eastern Studies, 30 (4), 896–915.

Tilly, C. (1990) Coercion, Capital and European States, AD 990–1990, Cambridge Mass.: Basil Blackwell.

Toprak, B. (1984) 'Politicisation of Islam in a secular state: the National Salvation Party in Turkey', in Arjomand (ed.), pp. 119–33.

Trimberger, E.K. (1978) Revolution from Above. Military Bureaucrats and Development in Japan, Turkey and Peru,

New Brunswick: Transaction Books.

Tryjarski, E. (1998) 'Towards better mutual understanding among Turkic–speakers' in Atabaki and O'Kane (eds.), pp. 109–17.

Türkes, M. (1994) 'The Balkan Pact and its immediate implications for the Balkan states, 1930–34', Middle Eastern Studies, 30 (1), 123–44.

Türsan, H. (1996) 'Ersatz democracy: Turkey in the 1990s', in Gillespie (ed.), pp. 215–30.

TUSIAD (1997) 'Perspectives on Democratisation in Turkey', http://www.tusiad.org/tr/english/main/frame/rapor.html.

Tufan, H. and S. Vaner (1984) 'L'armée, la société et le nouvel ordre (a)politique (1980–1983)', Les Temps Modernes, 41 (456–7), 175–94.

Turan, G. and I. Turan (1998) 'Turkey's emerging relationship with other Turkic republics' in Rittenberg (ed.), pp. 177–203.

Turan, I. (1994) 'Leadership change in Turkey', in Gillespie (ed.), pp. 232–45.

—— (1998) 'Mediterranean security in the light of Turkish concerns', Perceptions, June–August, 16–31.

Ülman, H.A. and F. Tachau (1965) 'Turkish politics: the attempt to reconcile rapid modernization with democracy', Middle East Journal, 19 (2), 153–68.

Unbehaun, H. (1996) 'Türkische Arbeitsmigration in den Nahen Osten, nach Osteuropa und Mittelasien', Orient, 37 (1), 87–109.

US State Department (1999) Turkey Country Report on Human Rights Practices for 1998, Bureau of Democracy, Human Rights, and Labor.

Volkan, V.D. and N. Itzkowitz (1984) The Immortal Atatürk: A Psychobiography, Chicago and London: University of Chicago Press.

Vorhoff, K. (1998) ' "Let's reclaim our history and culture!" – Imagining Alevi community in contemporary Turkey', Die Welt des Islams, 38 (2), 220–52.

Ward, R.E. and D.A. Rustow (eds.) (1964) Political Modernization in Japan and Turkey, Princeton: Princeton Uuniversity Press.

Watts, N.F. (1999) 'Allies and enemies: pro-Kurdish parties in Turkish politics, 1990–94', International Journal of Middle East Studies, (31), 631–56.

Weber, M. (1968a) Economy and Society. An Outline of Interpretive Sociology, edited by Guenther Roth and Claus Wittich, Volume I, New York: Bedminster Press.

—— (1968b) Economy and Society. An Outline of Interpretive Sociology, edited by Guenther Roth and Claus Wittich, Volume II, New York: Bedminster Press.

—— (1968c) Economy and Society. An Outline of Interpretive Sociology, edited by Guenther Roth and Claus Wittich, Volume III, New York: Bedminster Press.

—— (1991) From Max Weber: Essays in Sociology, edited with an introduction by H.H. Gerth and C.Wright Mills, with a new preface by Bryan S. Turner, London: Routledge.

Wedel, H. (1996) 'Binnenmigration und ethnische Identität – Kurdinnen in türkischen Metropolen', Orient, 37 (3), 437–52.

Wehler, H.-U. (1989) Deutsche Gesellschaftsgeschichte, Bd. 1: Vom Feudalismus des Alten Reiches bis zur defensiven Modernisierung der Reformära 1700–1815, Munich: C.H. Beck.

Weiker, W.F. (1962) 'Academic freedom and problems of higher education in Turkey', Middle East Journal, 16 (3), 279–94.

—— (1963) The Turkish Revolution 1960–1961. Aspects of Military Politics, Washington D.C.: Brookings Institution.

—— (1981) The Modernization of Turkey. From Atatürk to the Present Day, New York: Holmes and Meier.

—— (1988) 'The Unseen Israelis. The Jews from Turkey in Israel' Lanham: University Press of America.

White, J.B. (1997) 'Pragmatists or ideologues? Turkey's Welfare Party in power', Current History, January, 25–30.

White, P.J. (1998) 'Economic marginalization of Turkey's Kurds: the failed promise of modernization and reform', Journal of Muslim Minority Affairs, 18 (1), 139–57.

Wießner, G. (1997) 'Grundfragen aktueller poltischer und militärischer Entwicklungen in den kurdischen Provinzen der Türkei', Orient, 38 (2), 289–310.

Winrow, G.M. (1992) 'Turkey and former Soviet Central Asia: national and ethnic identity', Central Asia Survey, 11 (3), 101–11.

—— (1995) Turkey in Post-Soviet Central Asia, London: Royal Institute of International Affairs.

—— (1996) 'Turkey's relations with the Transcaucasus and the Central Asian Republics', *Perceptions*, 1 (1), 128–46.

—— (1998) 'Turkish policy in Central Asia', in Atabaki and O'Kane (eds.), pp. 91–108.

Winter, M. (1984) 'The modernization of education in Kemalist Turkey', in Landau (ed.), pp. 183–94.

Yavuz, H. M. (1991) 'Turkey's relations with Israel', *Foreign Policy* (Ankara), 5 (3–4), 41–59.

—— (1997) 'Turkish–Israeli Relations through the Lens of the Turkish Identity Debate', *Journal of Palestine Studies*, 27 (1), 22–37.

—— (1998) 'Turkish identity and foreign policy in flux: the rise of neo–Ottomanism', *Critique*, 1998 (12), 19–41.

—— (1999a) 'Search for a new social contract in Turkey: Fetullah Gülen, the Virtue Party and the Kurds', *SAIS Review*, 19 (1), 114–43.

—— (1999b) 'Towards an Islamic liberalism?: the Nurcu movement and Fethullah Gülen', *Middle East Journal*, 53 (4), 584–605.

Yegen, M. (1996) 'The Turkish state discourse and the exclusion of Kurdish identity', *Middle Eastern Studies*, 32 (2), 216–29.

Yesilbursa, B.K. (1999) 'Turkey's participation in the Middle East Command and its admission to NATO, 1950–52', *Middle Eastern Studies*, 35 (4), 70–102.

Yilmaz, S. (1999) 'An Ottoman warrior abroad: Enver Pasa as an expatriate', *Middle Eastern Studies*, 35 (4), 40–69.

Zeidner, R.F. (1976) 'Britain and the launching of the Armenian question', *International Journal of Middle East Studies*, 1976 (7), 465–85.

Zviagelskaya, I. D. (1994), 'Central Asia and Transcaucasia: new geopolitics' in Naumkin (ed.).

Zürcher, E.J. (1984) '*The Unionist Factor: The Role of the Committee of Union and Progress in the Turkish National Movement, 1905–1926*', Leiden: Brill.

—— (1991) *Political Opposition in the Early Turkish Republic. The Progressive Republican Party 1924–1925*, Leiden: Brill.

—— (1993) *Turkey: A Modern History*, (reprint 1998), London: I.B.Tauris.

—— (1999) 'The Rise and Fall of "Modern" Turkey', TULP working paper, www.let.leidenuniv.nl/tcimo/tulp/research/htm.

Index

Abdücelmid I, Sultan, 40-41
Abdülhamid II, Sultan, 30-1, 47-8, 50-3, 55,
    76, 79, 200, 203
absolutism, Hamidian, 52
Afghani, Jamal al-Din al, 177
Afghanistan, 135, 137
Agar, Mehmet, 112
Ahmad Bey, Tunisia, 39
Ahmad, Feroz, 6, 11-12
Akayev, Askar, 179-80
Akcura, Yusuf, 177
Albania, 63, 74; revolts, 62
Alemdaroglu, Kemal, 198, 204
Alevi community, 3, 129
Algeria, 138
Ali Pasha, 30, 41
Almaty, 186
alphabets, 60, 189
Ankara, 60, 68-9; General Staff HQ, 97;
    mayorality, 118; Parliament, 70;
    University, 124
Arab: League, 137; -Turkish relations, 139-
    41, 150; pan-ideology, 44
Arafat, Yasir, 166
Ardahan province, 51, 136
Armenia, 64, 146, 155, 182; -US lobby,
    169; massacre, 51-2, 76, 102, 183;
    nascent state, 65; nationalism, 52;
    question, 106
Army Mutual Assistance Association (OYAK),
    95-6, 102
Ashgabat, 186
Asi Dam, 144
Association for the Defence of the Rights of
    Eastern
Anatolia, 68
'Atatürkist Society', Istanbul, 89

Ates, Atilla, 202, 204
austerity policy 1994, 188
Austria, 63
Austria-Hungary, 51
authoritarianism, 204; Kemalist, 72, 75, 79;
    Ottoman traditions, 85
authority: traditional, 17, 23; types, 15-16
ayan/agas, 35-8, 44
Ayatollah Khomeini, 147
Azerbaijan, 112, 146-7, 176, 179, 181-3,
    185-6, 189, 193

Badie, Bertrand, 206
Baghdad Pact, 135, 138, 148; disintegration,
    158
Bahrain, Bank of, 141
Baku, 178, 183; -Ceyhan pipeline, 186
Balkans, 120, 184; Pact, 134-5; War (1912-
    13), 63, 67
Balta Limani, Commercial Convention, 42
Bandung Conference, 138
Barak, Ehud, 165
Barkey, Henri, 167
Barzani, Massoud, 146, 149
Bashir Shihab II, Emir, 39
Bashkotostan, 190
Batum province, 51
Bayar, Celal, 86
Bayraktar Mustafa Pasha, 37
Bayzeid, Sultan, 153, 155
Begin-Sadat research centre, 163
Bektasi order, 38
Ben-Gurion, David, 154
Berlin, 29, 125; Treaty/Congress (1878),
    51, 61
Bir, Cevik, 162
Birand, Mehmet Ali, 93

225

Bishkek, 186
Bitlis province, 74
Black Sea, 32
Bloch, Ernst, 26, 45
Bosnia, 39, 62, 168
Bosphorus, 64-5, 136
Bourdieu, Pierre, 4, 25
Britain, 32, 39, 42, 63-5, 134, 137-8, 148,
    158
Brown, Carl, 32, 39
Brussels, 125-6
Bucak, Sedat, 111, 114
Buda, Peace of, 34
Bulgaria, 62-4, 67, 135, 157; revolts, 51;
    uprising, 39
bureaucracy, Ottoman, 21
Burke, Peter, 12
Bush, George, 179-80

Candar, Cengiz, 96
capitalist mode of production, 17
'capitulations', 50; abolition, 65
Carlowitz, Treaty of, 32
Catli, Abdullah, 111-12, 128
Caucasus, 63, 120, 146, 181, 184; corridor,
    186
Cemal Pasha, 67
Central Asia, 7, 165, 179, 183-4
Central Treaty Organisation (CENTO), 138
Cetin, Hikmet, 116, 162, 165-6
Christians, 156; minorities, 75; Orthodox,
    155
Cilicia, 38, 65
Ciller, Tansu, 112, 118, 126
Cizre-Sakallioglu, Ümot, 94
clientelism, 99-100, 120, 127
Cold War, 2, 4-5, 56, 104, 137, 154-5, 167,
    193, 205
COMECON, 185
Commercial Convention, 42
Committee of Union and Progress, 73
Comte, Auguste, 73
Conference for Security and Co-operation in
    Europe, 181, 187
'confessionalisation', 78, 202
Constitution, 1961, 95
Copenhagen Summit 1993, 168
corruption, 99, 112-13
Council of Europe, 2, 137, 180
counter-elite, Sunni Turkish, 128
Crete, 62
crime (see organised crime)
Crimea: Khanate, 32; War 1853-56, 42
Cuba, missile crisis, 139
Cyprus, 66, 140, 148, 159; British
    annexation, 64; crises, 139; Greek

Cypriots, 140; Northern, 190

Damascus, 74
Dardanelles, the, 63-5, 136
defence industry, Turkish, 163
Demirel, Süleyman, 92, 97-8, 115, 117,
    119-21, 145, 160, 164-5, 175-6, 182-3,
    193-4
Democratic Left Party, 98
Democratic Party, 83, 86-9, 91-2, 97-9, 119,
    138-9, 159
Denmark, 168
derebeys, 36, 38, 44, 51
Deringil, Selim, 48
Directorate of Post, Telegraph and
    Telephone, 189
Directorate of Religious Affairs (Diyanet), 78
Diyarbakir, 71, 74, 123
Dogan, media company, 102

earthquake, 1999, 128
East Jerusalem, Israeli occupation, 147
Eastern Question, 52, 54, 66, 104; system,
    200
Ecevit, Bulent, 98, 117, 119
Economic Cooperation Organization (ECO),
    181
economy, statist, 76
Edib, Halide, 70, 127
Edirne, 67
education, 120, 122, 128, 177, 191-2;
    Kemalist, 124-5; religious, 148
Ege University, 191
Egypt, 64, 148, 154; Muhammad Ali, 38
Elchibey, Aboulfez Aliyev, 146, 182-3
Elekdag, Sükrü, 167, 169-70, 209
elema, 38
Elias, Norbert, 4, 13-14, 16-17, 20, 22, 24,
    25, 35, 54-5, 96, 100, 104, 109
elites/elitism: attitude, 46; authoritarian, 86;
    bureaucratic, 101; continuity, 205;
    counter-, 128; economic, 102; German
    state, 25; Kemalist, 3, 62, 119, 129, 150,
    154, 199, 204; military-bureaucratic, 73,
    96, 105; modern, 91; new Ottoman, 55;
    Ottoman, 31, 33, 56, 79, 100, 103-4,
    200; republican, 66; social habitus, 26;
    state, 5, 49, 88, 116, 203;
    transformation, 77
embassies: Ottoman, 29; Turkish, 89
Enver Pasha, 63, 67, 80, 175-6, 178, 192-3
Erbakan, Necmettin, 97-8, 102-3, 118-21,
    132-3, 140
Ergüvenc, Sadi, 116-17
Erim, Nihat, 92
Erzerum, 68

Eskisehir, 65
Euphrates river, 144, 170
Eurasia television network system (TRT
    Avrasaya), 189
Europe: Kurdish diaspora, 125-6;
    manufacturers, 37; Middle Ages, 23; state
    system, 21, 34, 42; Western, 87, 188
European Union (EU), 2, 126, 132, 137,
    167-8, 207, 210; Helsinki decision, 209;
    Transport Corridor programme, 186;
    Turkish application, 101
Evren, Kenan, 93, 113, 148
Eximbank, 185
exports: -oriented policy, 112; strategy, 141

'February 28th Process', 96, 118
feudalisation, 2-23, 31-2, 35-6, 38, 41-2,
    49, 54, 56
First World War, 63, 80
foreign policy, Arab, 116; Turkish, 132-3
Foundation for Strengthening the Turkish
    Armed Forces, 95
France, 32, 50, 64-5, 148, 183
Free Republican Party, 72
Free Trade Agreement (Israel-Turkey), 164
Free Trade association, 165
Fuad Pasha, 30, 41
Fuller, G.E., 187

Galicia, 63
gas, Russian, 186
Gasprinsky, Ismail, 177 8, 192 3
gecekondu (squatter settlements), 91
generative grammar, 25
Georgia, 186
German Institute for Technical Assistance,
    191
Germany, 63, 76, 112, 168; aristocracy, 25;
    state, 24
Giddens, Anthony, 4
globalisation, 206
Gökalp, Ziya, 61, 178, 193
Golan Heights, 162, 170
Grand National Assembly 1923, 59
Greater Middle East, 2, 5-7, 20, 56, 78, 105-
    6, 150, 155, 176, 192-3, 199, 205-6,
    208-9
Greece, 63-4, 134, 139; Anatolia offensive,
    68; invasion of Turkey, 80; Muslims
    from, 71; nationalism, 52; resettled, 76;
    Turco-Greek War, 65; -US lobby, 169;
    War of Independence, 32, 39, 42
Gregorian Calendar, 60
Grey Wolves, 93, 111
Gruen, George, 160
Gülen, Fethullah, 120-1, 191-2

Gürsel, Cemal, 83
guerrilla war, urban, 93
Gulf States, 141
Gulf War, 145-6, 148, 167

Habsburg Empire, 32
Hamas, 147
Hamidian period, 47-8, 52, 72, 78, 178,
    203; 'Islamism', 79
Harish, Micha, 165
Hatay province/republic, 135-6, 143, 144
hatt-i-humayun, 41
hatt-i-sherif, of Gülhane, 40-1
Hedjaz province, 64
Helsinki summit, 1999, 2
Heper, Matin, 101
Herzegovina, 62; revolts, 39, 51
Hittites, 61
Hizbullah, 147
Holland, 168
Hourani, Albert, 35
'hydro-paranoia', 149
human rights, 168
Hurd, Douglas, 180

Idiz, Semih, 170
import substitution policy, 93, 102
Imrali, prison island, 122
Inbat, Efraim, 163
Incirlik military base, 140
Independent Industrialists' and
    Businessmen's Association, 103
industrialisation, 91
inflation, 2, 87, 112
Inönü, Ismet, 59, 65, 71, 73, 86, 92, 98,
    136, 139
intelligensia: conservative, 121; urban, 87;
    Ottoman, 40, 193; Tatar, 177
International Monetary Fund, 181; austerity
    package, 93
Iran, 116-17, 134, 137-8, 141-3, 146-7,
    154, 157, 159, 161, 179, 186; -Turkish
    relations, 135; Islamic revolution, 118
Iraq, 63-4, 117, 134-5, 138, 140-2, 144,
    146, 157-8; northern, 2, 132, 145, 149,
    162
Islam, 69, 78, 123-5; culture, 105;
    internationalism, 106; law, 41; pan-
    Islamic ideology, 44, 48, 66; political, 5,
    103, 112, 114-16, 121, 129, 149, 172,
    202-3, 206; resurgence, 119, 127;
    universalist terms, 52
Islamist Virtue Party, 98, 115
Islamist Welfare Party, 97-8, 103, 118-19,
    122, 132, 147

Israel, 132, 140; arms sales, 163-4;
CINADCO, 165; Golan annexation, 160;
Negev desert, 162; state recognition,
157; -Turkish relations, 133, 141-2, 147,
153-5, 159, 161, 166-7, 171, 207; US
lobby/ties, 158, 169; water, 170
Istanbul, 53, 60, 69; Hippodrome, 28;
manufacturing, 49; mayoralty, 118;
School of Law, 83; university, 191, 198-
9
Italy, 65, 135; colonialism, 63
Izmir, Plot, 71-2

Jadidism, 177, 192
Janissaries, 28-9, 31, 33, 35, 38, 46, 96,
198; 'new', 86
Japan, 188
Jerusalem, 147, 160; 'Jerusalem incident',
Sincan, 147
Jews: American, 159; Ottoman tolerance,
154-6, 172; Turkish defence of, 157
Johnson, Lyndon B., 139
Jordan, 144, 154
Jupiter missile crisis, 139
Justice Party, 84, 119

Karadyi, Ismail, 162
Karaosmanoglu, Ali, 116
Karimov, Islam, 179-80
Karpat, Kemal, 44
Kars province, 51, 136, 186
Kavacki, Merve 'affair', 115-16
Kazakhstan, 176, 179, 181, 185-6, 189-90,
193
Kelbejar offensive, 182
Kemal, Mustafa (Atatürk), 3, 5, 11, 59-62,
65-6, 68, 70-4, 78-9, 81, 89, 99, 104-5,
125, 134-6, 156, 175, 178, 203, 205,
209; cult of, 102; era, 122;
historiography, 176; ideology, 96, 202;
myth around, 85; project, 80; six
principles/arrows, 75
Kennedy, John F., 139
Kenya, 122
Keyder, Caglar, 32
Köni, Hasan, 168
Köprülü, Fazil Mustafa, 35, 86
Koc, industrial holding, 102
Koran, the, 41, 122
Korean War, 87, 137
Kosovo, 168; revolts, 62
Küçük Kaynarca, Treaty of, 32
Kurdish Democratic Party (KDP), 126, 146-
7, 149
Kurdish Parliament in Exile, Holland, 126
Kurdish people, 64, 92, 113, 119, 128; 1925

insurgency, 70; culture, 126;
communications use, 207; conflict, 169;
hamidieh regiments, 52; identity, 102;
insurgency, 2, 116, 127, 141, 143; issue,
144, 147, 164, 168, 172; language
rights, 117; nationalism, 3, 5, 106, 112,
114-15, 122-3, 125, 129, 132, 149,
206; separatism, 145; society, 124; tribal
leaders, 51; Turkish citizens, 121, 208
Kurdistan Workers Party (PKK), 113-14,
116-17, 122, 124-6, 128, 145-7, 149,
162-3, 172, 209
Kuwait: Bank of, 141; Iraqi invasion, 142
Kyrgyzstan, 176, 179-80 185, 189

Laicism, Kemalist principle, 22
Lalumière, Catherine, 180
land mines, Iraq, 162
Landau, J.M., 190, 192
language, 188, 192; Turkic, 189
Lausanne, 135; Treaty of, 65-6, 69
League of Nations, 135; Council of, 64
Lebanon, 39, 64, 162
legitimacy, 15-17, 20, 55, 77; crisis, 48
Levy, A., 156
Lewis, Bernard, 6, 11-12, 32
Libya, 140
London, 29, 126

Maastricht Treaty 1991, 168
Macedonia, 63, 73, 74; Russo-British
intervention, 53
Mahmud II, 28-9, 37-8, 40, 42, 48, 198;
bureaucratic structure, 30
Malta, 60, 68
manufacturing: Marmara, 49; Ottoman, 50
Mardin, Serif, 6, 11, 26, 124
Marmara University, 191
Marmara, Sea of, 64-5
Marxism, 25; Marxism-Leninism, 124
Mayall, S.V., 188
Mecca, 38, 60, 64, 121
MED TV, 125-6
media, growth, 101
Medina, 38, 64
Mehmet II, 68
Mehmet VI, 60, 63, 67
Menderes, Adnan, 83, 86-9, 119-20, 138,
140, 142, 148, 159, 208; execution, 92
Middle Eastern policy, Turkish, 149
Midhat Pasha, 45
military, the, 1-2, 5, 85 202; autonomy, 95-
6, 105; bureaucracy, 88; 1960 coup, 83-
4, 86, 89-90; 1971 coup, 92-3; 1980
coup, 93-4, 112-13; 'democracy', 84;
image, 100; Israeli, 157, 161, 171; US

bases, 132
millet system, 33, 50, 52, 75
Miss Turkey contest, 61
modernisation, 3, 5-6, 13, 19-20, 23-4, 31,
37, 81, 84, 91, 98; concept, 11;
'defensive', 39; elitist, 61, 204;
military-bureaucratic, 105; Ottoman, 44-5,
54-5, 78, 103; top-down, 100-101, 200
modernism, Islamic, 120
modernity, 4; concept, 12; Kemalist, 209
Montenegro, 51, 63; revolts, 62
Montesquieu, Henri 73
Montreux Conference, 136
Mordechai, Yitzhak, 163, 169
Mosul, 134; province, 146; 1926 decision, 145
Motherland Party, 97-8, 113, 118, 120
Mudanya, truce, 65
Mudros, armistice, 63, 134
Muhammad Ali, 42
Mujaheddin-e Khalq, 147
Multilateral Training Centre on Taxation,
Ankara, 191
'Murad', operation, 145
Mus province, 74, 123
Muslims, 75; brotherhoods, 203; Ottoman,
50
Mutlu, Servet, 144

Nagorno-Karabakh, 182-3
Naksibendi order, 123
Nasi, Joseph, 155
Nasser, 'Abd al-, 138, 158
National Action Party, 93, 98, 116, 121, 128
National Movement, 59, 67-9, 97, 115, 209
National Salvation Party, 119-20
National Security Council, Turkey, 90, 95,
97, 105, 150
National Unity Committee, 84, 89, 90
Navy, Turkish, 162
Nehru, Jawaharlal, 138
neo-Ottomanism, 3, 120, 193
Netanyahu Binyamin, 163
Netas company, 185
non-alignment, 138
North Atlantic Coordination Council, 181
North Atlantic Treaty Organisation (NATO),
2, 132, 137, 139, 167; enlargement, 168
Norway, 168
novels, Ottoman, 44
Nurcu movement/sect, 120, 191
Nursi, Said, 120

Öcalan, Abdullah, 117, 122, 124, 145
Oestrich, G., 22
officer corps, 85
oil: Caspian, 186-7; imports, 160; Iran-

Turkey pipeline, 159; price shock (1973-
74), 93, 140
'Operation Flag', 93
'Operation Provide Comfort', 132, 145
Organisation of Economic Co-operation and
Development (OECD), 137, 191
organised crime, 111-12, 114, 127-8
Ortalyi, Ilter, 46
Orun, Sitki, 164
Ottoman Constitutional Movement, 72
Ottoman Russian War, 32
Ozal, Türgut, 94, 112-13, 120, 141-6, 148,
161, 176, 179-80, 193

Pakistan, 137-8, 148
Palestine, 64; Liberation Organisation (PLO),
140; Turkish ambiguity, 158
pan-Turkism, 44, 66, 106, 134, 147, 175-8,
183, 188, 192-4, 208
Paris, 29; Peace Conference/Treaty 1856, 42-
3, 63
parliamentary phase, Ottoman, 30, 46
Paros, 125
patrimonialism, 23
Patriotic Union of Kurdistan (PUK), 146-7
patronage, urban, 100
Peace Pipeline proposal, 145
Peoples Democratic Party (HADEP), 126
Peres, Shimon, 163, 165
physical force, state monopolisation, 14, 17,
20-2, 35, 37, 69, 93, 96, 114, 199
population growth, high rates, 91
'pragmatic escapism', 172, 207
press, Turkish, 102
PRP, 70
Public Debt Administration, Ottoman, 48

Qaddafi, Muammar al, 132-3

Rabin, Yitzhak, 163, 166
realism, international relations theory, 12
referendum (1982), 94
reforms, Kemalist, 101, 119; Ottoman, 3-4,
20, 24, 31, 85
'Reliant Mermaid', 162
religion: 'fundamentalism', 97; liberty, 41
minorities in Ottoman Empire, 102
Republican People's Party (RPP), 69-70, 84-
8, 98-9, 201
Research of the Culture of the Turks, 190
Reshid Pasha, 40
Reza Shah, 135
Robins, P., 157
Romania, 51, 63-4, 134
Rosenberg, Justin, 12, 16
Rousseau, Jean-Jacques, 73

Rumelia, 36
Russia, 39, 63-5, 181, 186, 193; -Ottoman War, 51; -Turkey relations, 187
Rustow, Dankwart, 11, 73, 85

Saadabad Pact, 135
Sabah, media company, 102
Sabanci, industrial holding, 102
Sakarya river, 65
Salonika, 53, 72-3
Samsun town, 65
San Stefano, Treaty of (1848), 51
Sanders, Liman von, 74
Sarraut, Albert, 81
Saudi Arabia, 38, 116, 140-1, 154; financial power, 160; Islamist financing, 147-8
Savas, Vural, 115
science, Ottoman period, 198
Sèvres, Treaty of, 63-8, 101, 117, 138; syndrome, 105, 115-16, 129, 139, 172, 204-5
Second Turkish Republic, 84, 92, 94
Second World War, 74, 136
secularisation, 22, 76-78; law code (1926), 60
security, Kemalist concept, 149-50
Selim II, 155
Selim III, 4, 28, 30, 35-8, 40, 66; reform attempts, 29
Senate, the, 90
'separatist terrorism', 97
Serbia, 51, 63; revolts, 39, 42
Sexer, Duygu, 167
Sezer, Ahmet Necdet, 193, 210
Shaposhnikov, Marshall, 183
Sheik Said, 122-3; rebellion, 71, 127
siyaset, 26
Smyrna (Izmir), 64
social habitus, concept, 25-6, 79, 115
Sofia, 74
South Korea, 188
South-eastern Anatolia Development Project (GAP), 144-5, 165
Stalin, Josef, 136
state: bureaucratic, 24; modern, 18, 60; nation, 20, 206
Straits Commission, 136
students, unrest, 93
Sublime Porte, 63, 67-8, 72, 156, 192, 201
Suez Canal, 63
'suitcase trade', 187
Sumerians, 61
'survival units', 13
Susurluk, 112; 'Investigation Committee', 111
Syria, 2, 38, 64, 117, 135-6, 138, 142, 144-5, 147-9, 154, 157, 162-3, 169-70;

1958 crisis, 158; Golan Heights, 160; military front, 74

Tajikistan, 175
Talabani, Jalal, 146-7
Talat Pasha, 67
Tanzimat period, 30-1, 38-40, 43-7, 49, 52, 62, 67, 72, 74-75, 77, 79, 101, 201; industrialisation, 76; intellectuals, 104; reforms, 50, 200; second, 41-2
Tashkent, 186
Tatarstan, 190
taxation, 33, 45, 55; administration, 29; state monopolisation, 21, 35, 37, 49, 199
Tayan, Tirjhan, 153
Tbilisi, 186
telecommunications, 185-6
textiles, 165
Third Turkish Republic, 94, 127
Thrace, 63, 73, 135, 156
Tigris river, 144
Tilly, Charles, 54
Tito, Josip Broz, 138
Torimtay, Necip, 142-3
tourism, industry, 164
trade unions, suppression, 94
traditional societies, 13, 18, 24
Trans-Caspian pipeline, 186
Transcaucasus, 165, 176, 178, 181-2, 184, 187-8, 193-4
'transformative capacity', 14
Treaty of Amity and Commerce, 50
Treaty of Westphalia, 21
Trimberger, E.K., 11
Tripoli, 74
True Path party, 98, 111-12, 118, 120
Truman Doctrine, 89
Tsarist-Ottoman rivalry, 184
Türkcell company, 185
Türkeri, Fezvi, 116
Türkes, Alparslan, 83, 89, 93, 98, 121
Tunisia, 39
Turkey: language, 53; political left, 124, 125; strategic position, 87
Turkic Cultures and Arts Joint Administration, 190
Turkic republics, 6, 181, 184, 186-9, 190-1, 194, 208; summit meetings, 176, 179-80, 182
Turkish Airlines (THY), 186
Turkish Armed Force Foundation, 164
Turkish Co-operation and Development Agency (TIKA), 184-5
Turkish Foreign Economic Board (DEIK), 185, 187

Turkish Historical Society, 61, 179, 190
Turkish Industrialists' and Businessmen's
    Association, 102-3
Turkish Intelligence Service (MIT), 112
Turkish International Co-operation Agency,
    165
Turkish International Contractors Union, 187
Turkish Linguistic Society, 61, 1891
'Turkish model', 188
Turkish National Movement, 64-5
Turkish Republic, 19, 84, 89, 200;
    establishment, 3, 40, 62, 79, 203, 207;
    image, 80; political structures, 5;
    proclamation, 60
Turkish-Soviet friendship pact, 136
Turkistan, 193
Turkmenistan, 166, 176, 179-80, 185, 189-
    90

Ültel, Netas subsidiary, 185
ulema, 28-9, 44, 47, 120
Unionists, 201
'Union of the World of Islam', 148
United Nations Development Programme,
    191
Union of Soviet Socialist Republics (USSR),
    6, 76, 158, 182, 184; Bolsheviks, 134,
    175; containment, 137; demise, 2, 5, 74,
    105, 179
United States of America (USA), 64, 87, 117-
    18, 136-9, 142, 146, 148, 153, 157-9,
    161-2, 164-5, 167-8, 170, 179, 183,
    186, 188; aid, 88; Congress, 169;
    hegemony, 4; Jewish lobby, 171
urbanisation, 91

Uzbekistan, 165, 176, 179-80, 185, 189-90

Vesnet, Nertas subsidary, 185
Vienna, 29
Voltaire, 73

Ward, Robert, 11
War of Independence, 69, 80, 134, 156
Warsaw Pact, 168
water, politics, 143, 146, 149, 165, 170-2
wealth inequality, 112
Weber, Max, 4, 13-20, 23, 77
Weiker, W.F., 11
Weizman, Ezer, 153
Western European Union (WEU), 168
women: political equality, 61; public role,
    60
World Bank, 112, 181
World Depression, 76
World Health Organisation, 191

Yakutia, 193
Yalcin, Aydin, 194
Yemen, 63
Yerevan, 183
Yilmaz, Mesut, 97, 118, 164
Young Ottomans, 43-6, 52, 77, 177, 201
Young Turks, 46, 66-7, 201; movement, 31;
    regime, 31; revolution, 30, 47, 53, 72-3,
    156
Yugoslavia, 134

Zionism, 156, 160
Zohab, Treaty of, 146
Zurcher, Erik Jan, 6, 11-12

Books Titles on the Middle East

Zed Books publishes on international and Third World issues. In addition to our general lists on economics, development, the environment, gender and politics, we also publish area studies titles in the fields of African Studies, Asian and Pacific Studies, Latin American and Caribbean Studies, and Middle East Studies. Our Middle East titles include:

Al-Omar and Abdel-Haq, Islamic Banking: Theory, Practice and Challenges

Augustin, E, Palestinian Women: Identity and Experience

Boulares, H., Islam: The Fear and the Hope

CARDRI, Iraq since the Gulf War

Chaliand, G., The Kurdish Tragedy

Chorbajian, Donabedian and Mutafian, The Caucasian Knot: The History and Politics of Nagorno-Karabagh

Goldenberg, S., Pride of Small Nations: The Caucasus and Post-Soviet Disorder

Guyatt, N., The Absence of Peace: Understanding the Israeli-Palestinian Conflict

Halvei, I., A History of the Jews

Hoodbhoy, P., Islam and Science

Khoury and Moghadam (eds.), Gender and Development in the Arab World

Kocturk, T., A Matter of Honour: Experiences of Turkish Women Immigrants

Kreyenbroek and Allison (eds.), Kurdish Culture and Identity

Laizer, S., Martyrs, Traitors and Patriots: Kurdistan after the Gulf War

Laizer, S., Into Kurdistan: Fronters under Fire

Mansour, Fawzi, The Arab World: Nation, State and Democracy

Marcus, J., A World of Difference: Islam and Gender Hierarcy in Turkey

Mernissi, Fatima, Women's Rebellion and Islamic Memory

Moghadam, Val (ed.), Gender and National Identity: Women and Politics in Muslim Societies

Moghissi, H., Feminism and Islamic Fundamentalism: Limits of Postmodern Analysis

Nimni, E. (ed.), The Challenge of Post-Zionism

Nomani and Rahnema, Islamic Economic Systems

Poya, M., Women, Work and Islamism: Ideology and Resistance in Iran

Rahnema, Ali (ed.), Pioneers of Islamic Revival

Rahnema, Ali and Nomani, The Secular Miracle: Religion, Politics and Economic Policy in Iran

Rashid, Ahmed, The Resurgence of Central Asia: Islam or Nationalism?

Saadawi, Nawal el, The Hidden Face of Eve: Women in the Arab World

Saadawi, Nawal el, The Nawal El Saadawi Reader

Sayigh, Rosemary, Too Many Enemies: The Palestinian Experience in Lebanon

Sayyid, B., A Fundamental Fear: Eurocentrism and the Emergence of Islamism

Van Bruinessen, M., Agha, Shaikh and State: The Social and Political Structures of Kurdistan

White, Paul J., Primitive Rebels or Revolutionary Modernisers? The Kurdish Nationalist Movement in Turkey

For full details of this list and Zed's other subject and general catalogues, please write to:
The Marketing Department, Zed Books, 7 Cynthia Street, London N1 9JF, UK
or email Sales@zedbooks.demon.co.uk
Visit our website at: http://www.zedbooks.demon.co.uk